CANADA'S UNIVERSITIES
GO GLOBAL

CANADA'S UNIVERSITIES
GO GLOBAL

Editors
Roopa Desai Trilokekar
Glen A. Jones
Adrian Shubert

A CAUT Series Title
James Lorimer & Company Ltd., Publishers
Toronto

James Lorimer & Company Ltd., Publishers acknowledge the support of the Ontario
Arts Council. We acknowledge the support of the Government of Canada through the
Book Publishing Industry Development Program (BPIDP) for our publishing activities.
We acknowledge the support of the Canada Council for the Arts for our publishing pro-
gram. We acknowledge the support of the Government of Ontario through the Ontario
Media Development Corporation's Ontario Book Initiative.

The Canada Council | Le Conseil des Arts
for the Arts | du Canada

ONTARIO ARTS COUNCIL
CONSEIL DES ARTS DE L'ONTARIO

Mixed Sources
Cert no. SW-COC-001271
© 1996 FSC
FSC

Library and Archives Canada Cataloguing in Publication

Canada's universities go global / editors, Roopa Desai Trilokekar,
    Glen A. Jones, Adrian Shubert.

Includes bibliographical references and index.

ISBN 978-1-55277-041-2

    1. International education — Canada.   2. Universities and

colleges — Canada — International cooperation.   3. Education and

globalization — Canada.   4. Higher education and state — Canada.

5. Education, Higher — Canada.   I. Trilokekar, Roopa Desai

II. Jones, Glen Alan, 1961–   III. Shubert, Adrian, 1953–

    LA417.5.I68 2009   378'.0160971   C2008-906333-3

Cover design by Meghan Collins

A CAUT Series Title
James Lorimer & Company Ltd., Publishers
317 Adelaide Street West, Suite 1002
Toronto, Ontario
M5V 1P9
www.lorimer.ca

Printed and bound in Canada

Table of Contents

Faculty & Students

III. Conflicting Agendas & Ethical Practices

IV. Conclusion

Introduction

Adrian Shubert, York University
Glen A. Jones, Ontario Institute for Studies in Education/
University of Toronto
Roopa Desai Trilokekar, Ontario Institute for Studies
in Education/University of Toronto

Internationalization has come to be seen as an innate good in the discussion of higher education. While the meaning of the term itself is contested, there is an increasing expectation that universities will take steps to incorporate internationalization into institutional missions. The "practice" of internationalization, however, varies considerably by institution and jurisdiction, as does the range of activities subsumed by the term. Internationalization includes various forms of student mobility; the recruitment of international students; the incorporation of international dimensions into the curriculum; the development of intercultural skills, competencies and global citizenship; the hiring of international faculty; and many other initiatives and approaches.

The pressures driving the internationalization agenda are also multiple and varied. Globalization, manifested in the increasing mobility of human capital and the quest to develop a knowledge workforce matched to a global knowledge economy, is demanding university graduates who are comfortable and capable of working in these emerging contexts. For this reason, business schools are frequently at the forefront of internationalization. Globalization has also been a factor underscoring significant changes in higher education policy, including reduced public subsidies for universities and parallel increases in tuition — a context in which high-tuition-paying international students are viewed as important sources of revenue. In many American states, what were once regarded as public universities are now more accurately termed "state-supported" universities, and in a number of European jurisdictions tuition fees have been introduced in what had formerly been regarded as wholly state-funded systems. Globally, higher education is increasingly viewed as predominantly a private good.

The shift in education from being a public to being a private good is directly connected to a second development which sees the status of universities increasingly measured in international terms through competitive mechanisms. Where once universities were primarily viewed as local or national institutions, they are now subject to an international competitive environment manifested by a number of widely cited worldwide institutional ranking systems. Academic programs closest to the international marketplace, with business schools again as an early example, have been subjected to these competitive forces for some time; but, in recent years, these forces have expanded to include a range of professional and international programs and, in the last decade, whole-university rankings by Shanghai Jiao Tong University and the *Times Higher Education Supplement*. Formerly common only in the United States, this phenomenon has now become more global.

Canadian governments and universities are subject to these same global pressures, but while some initial attention was paid to internationalization by the scholarly and policy communities — evidenced in a number of reports and studies that emerged at the end of the 1990s — there has been no national discussion of this topic in the new millennium. Canadian universities have made independent decisions related to their internationalization agenda, with surprisingly little involvement or interest from the federal government. At the provincial level, a number of provinces have developed strategies and established offices, but with the exception of a few provinces, such as Québec and, more recently, Ontario, these strategies have focused exclusively on the international marketing of Canadian higher education. Pan-Canadian organizations engaged with international education, such as the Association of Universities and Colleges of Canada (AUCC), the Canadian Bureau for International Education (CBIE) and the Canadian Education Centres Network (CECN), have succeeded in providing an alternate forum for a nationwide discussion of these issues; however, these discussions have been limited within local contexts and without adequate public debate. We are left with a phenomenon that everyone agrees is important but one that no one is studying and, outside a few annual meetings of relevant organizations and a small group of government officials, no one is talking about.

In an attempt to catalyze an institutional conversation on this topic, York University has sponsored a series of local conferences on aspects of internationalization since 2003. Early themes included languages, science and engineering, and experiential education. In the spring of 2005, York decided to sponsor a major national discussion of policies, practices, challenges and opportunities designed to facilitate conversation among stakeholders, including federal and provincial governments, universities, non-profit organizations, and the private sector. The program emerged out of a national call for papers, as well as a decision to invite selected national and international figures who could contribute new perspectives on the Canadian experience. This conference took place on March 2 and 3, 2006, and involved more than two hundred participants, including representatives of all levels of government and thirty-three universities from nine provinces.

This book includes a selection of papers chosen to represent the diverse issues, themes and perspectives that emerged during this important national discussion. A central objective of the volume is to review significant changes in government policy and institutional practices in recent years and to fill the enormous gap in the research literature. Contributors to this volume focus on issues that have received almost no previous attention in the literature, including the implications of internationalization for teaching and learning, conflicting agendas for internationalization and ethical concerns, reviewing the Canadian experiences from an international/comparative frame and looking at internationalization in the context of Canadian higher education policy.

The national discussion gave rise to four major themes. The first is that Canada is unlike many other nations in that no predominant impetus has driven the country's internationalization agenda. Australian initiatives have largely been led by dramatic changes in government policy regarding the funding of universities to encourage foreign student recruitment and the export of Australian education abroad. European initiatives have focused on the broader desire to create a European Higher Education Area, facilitating regional student mobility and harmonizing degree structures and even curricula as part of a reconstruction of higher education systems and structures. And in the United States recent federal initiatives have largely been a response to national security concerns provoked by the events of September 11, 2001. There is no Canadian national parallel to these strategic political and/or economic initiatives. In Canada, the closest analogue would be a limited number of activities at the provincial level, but there is no pan-provincial coordination or policy direction. Canadian internationalization is characterized by multiple and uncoordinated processes that have primarily emerged at the local institutional level.

Given the absence of national directives or strategy, the particular nature of the Canadian higher education system becomes an important part of the story. Canada has the most decentralized policy approach to higher education in the Western world, with high levels of institutional autonomy, a federal government role limited to a patchwork quilt of policy areas excluding anything that might be directly defined as education, and increasingly different provincial government educational policy approaches.

However, unlike our neighbours to the south, the Canadian university sector is relatively homogeneous, at least in the sense that there is no formal hierarchy of institutions but rather a general assumption that only modest variations in educational quality exist throughout the system. Most Canadian students attend local institutions, and most universities therefore serve local undergraduate populations. Historically, provincial governments have generally treated all universities as equals in terms of funding and public mandate: there are no Canadian flagship universities. Given this context, some observers may be surprised that a number of Canadian universities have been ranked quite highly on international ranking systems, contradicting the assumption that world-class universities require world-class funding and focused, strategic government support. Canadian universities have been amazingly successful in providing a high-quality education and generating important research in spite of a highly decentralized public policy context.

Jane Knight defines internationalization as a process "of integrating an international/intercultural dimension into the teaching, research and service elements of an institution." The second theme, therefore, is that the Canadian approach to internationalization, like higher education more broadly, has been highly decentralized and essentially defined by individual institutions. With universities left on their own, the approaches that have emerged have been multifaceted, with a strong emphasis on teaching and learning and the student experience. In many cases, internationalization began with involvement in international development projects, and at a number of institutions this remains at the heart of the approach. In this way, the Canadian experience is distinct from the Australian experience, which focuses on international student recruitment and overseas program delivery models, or from the European experience, which focuses on international student mobility within the European Union.

The third theme also relates to this uniquely Canadian context. As higher education in Canada is still generally valued or perceived as a public good, and given that internationalization is largely a product of institutional discussion and decision-making, there has been considerable debate within individual universities over the motivations, objectives and directions of institutional strategies. The economic imperative attached to globalization and the innate inequities in resource distribution have raised concerns about the broader role of internationalization. So, too, has the question of what internationalization might mean for relations between Canadian universities and those in the Global South. The view of international students as revenue generators challenges strongly held views about access and the social role of universities. The Canadian university community is far from seeing internationalization as an innate good. Internationalization has been taken up in different ways by different parts of the institution and there has been a healthy debate about the pros and cons of internationalization, with a limited consensus on a common set of goals and an understanding of the measurement of its success. This book is an attempt to share the various perspectives about the meaning and value of internationalization within the context of Canadian higher education.

The fourth theme speaks to the complex link between internationalization and Canadian multiculturalism. Since the 1980s, there has been an increasing interest in developing a more inclusive curriculum within Canadian educational institutions to address the needs of an increasingly diverse student body. While the success of these initiatives is frequently contested, Canadian university faculty are keenly aware of issues of race, ethnicity and diversity and of the link between immigration and issues of diaspora, culture and identity. There is a tremendous parallel between this kind of sensitivity and the goals of internationalization. This experience is one reason why Canadian universities have approached internationalization in the manner they have. The challenge, however, is that it becomes extremely difficult to distinguish between the goals of inclusivity for a local population and the goals and objectives of internationalization. The problem is further exacerbated by the difference between larger urban centres in Toronto, Vancouver and Montreal, with their tremendously diverse populations, and universities located in smaller centres where the local population is more homogeneous. While approaches to internationalization will always be influenced by the home nation, the Canadian experience has been unique because it is largely framed by a national conversation on issues of culture, identity and the nature of citizenship.

The York conference made clear that internationalization continues to be an important topic within Canadian higher education and its importance will only increase over the next decade. It also became clear that much can be gained through a sustained national conversation on internationalization for individual institutional success, challenges and critical analysis. It is our hope that some of the thoughtful issues that arose through the York conference will receive further attention as a result of this volume. At the same time, there are a number of key issues that should become the basis for future conversations. The first issue is whether Canada really needs a national strategy for internationalization. While there has been considerable consensus that an absence of a national strategy has made the Canadian approach unique, there is also an assumption that the creation of such a strategy would significantly enhance internationalization initiatives. Given that the Canadian approach has been successful along certain dimensions in terms of allowing for experimentation at the institutional level, is there a danger that a national strategy might lead to a more homogeneous approach that constrains individual institutions? Below the level of strategy is the second key issue, the question of public funding for specific internationalization initiatives. On the one hand, there have been laudatory programs such as the Canadian Studies Program initiatives of the Department of Foreign Affairs and International Trade, the Tier I and II program initiatives of the Canadian International Development Agency (CIDA), the international mobility programs of Human Resources and Skills Development Canada, and Students for Development, a CIDA-funded program administered by AUCC, to name only a few. On the other hand, national funding for international scholarships and student mobility programs analogous, for example, to the Fulbright Program, has been embarrassingly poor. We need to understand more about the implications of these particular initiatives and how they relate to broader institutional goals and objectives. We need a more thoughtful conversation about both our failures and our successes at the program level and about their relation, if any, to broader public policy objectives.

A third set of questions revolves around the ways in which both students and faculty experience and understand internationalization. Much of the literature on internationalization is based on a series of assumptions about the benefits of introducing particular student and curriculum initiatives, but there has been surprisingly little research on whether these initiatives actually are successful. Finally, there is a need to explore and understand the specific meaning of internationalization in a country in which national identity, indeed self-definition, is founded on multiculturalism. In Canada, multiculturalism is often included as a component of discussions of both Canadianization and internationalization and is at the core of both national and international identity. Internationalization needs to be researched and understood within this broader national Canadian context to strengthen policy and practice and overcome the persisting challenges

We wish to thank each of the individuals who have contributed to making this publication comprehensive in providing a diversity of voices and perspectives on a wide range of issues related to the internationalization of Canadian universities, their policies, practices and challenges. We would also like to thank Human Resources and Skills Development Canada for their financial contribution to this process and recognize the department for their efforts and leadership in promoting the importance of international education in Canada.

Notes on Globalization and Higher Education: With Some Reference to the Case of Australia

Simon Marginson, University of Melbourne

Introduction

This chapter discusses the phenomenon of globalization in higher education in the light of recent literature on the topic and explores something of what globalization means in and to the national domain in higher education through discussion of one national case, Australia. The first part of the chapter reviews the notions of *internationalization*, *globalization* and *Europeanization*. The second part maps the emerging global market in universities, with special reference to the American hegemony in worldwide higher education. The third part provides a brief overview of the global market in cross-border degrees and then reviews the Australian case, with particular reference to the national and global logics of the expansionary entrepreneurial sector in cross-border education.

The focus is on research and doctoral universities whereon most of the literature on global aspects of higher education is concentrated and where global practices are at their most extensive. No doubt this focus imparts a "globalist" bias to the argument.

I. Globalization, Europeanization, Internationalization
The Distinction Between *Internationalization* and *Globalization*

In higher education studies, the terms *internationalization* and *globalization* are variously contrasted with each other. To take one example, Luijten-Lub et al.[1] suggest that internationalization refers to cross-border interconnectedness that leaves the nation-state unquestioned and is policy-controlled as in recent European initiatives, while globalization is external to nations and to higher education, is almost beyond policy control and is more transformative. This suggests that splits between politics/economy and Europe/world are at the root of the distinction.[2] Smeby and Trondal[3] take a similar approach. Welch[4] creates a dualism in the form of Weberian ideal types. His globalization is a pro-capitalist ideology supporting the extension of worldwide markets, whereas educational internationalization is about cultural exchange and cooperative relationships based on equality of respect. Welch wants more internationalization and less globalization. Knight[5] takes a more modest normative approach, defining internationalization as "the process of integrating an international, intercultural or global dimension into the purpose, functions or delivery of post-secondary education," in the national system or in individual institutions. Knight also sees the distinction as geo-spatial. Her *international* refers to relations between nations while *global* is at the world level. Globalization is "the flow of technology, economy, knowledge, people, values [and] ideas ... across borders." Unlike Welch, Knight does not see globalization as being opposed to internationalization in zero-sum terms but as part of the environment in which internationalization takes place and one reason why the international dimension of higher education is becoming more important.

The approach taken in this chapter draws on some but not all of the above elements. It is generally consistent with that of Teichler[6] and some theorists of globalization from outside higher education studies such as Held et al.[7] and Castells.[8] Normative elements have been avoided. Internationalization and globalization are not understood here as contrasting ideologies (cultural cosmopolitanism versus economic neo-liberalism) or as different calls to action or reaction by university agents. Rather, internationalization and globalization refer to *two different dimensions of cross-border human action,* dimensions that have differing geo-spatial dynamics and differing implications for transformation.

Internationalization means the thickening of relationships conducted between nations (*inter-national* relations) where national institutions and practices are affected at the margins but essentially remain intact.

Globalization means the enhancement of the worldwide or pan-European spheres of action. It has potentially transformative effects within nations as well as remaking the common environment in which they are situated and they relate to each other.

Thus in part the distinction is geo-spatial. Both internationalization and globalization encompass the nation-state but in a contrasting manner. In the international realm, national politics and culture might still be dominant. In the global realm, the nation-state is decisively relativized by global relations and no longer the ultimate horizon of possibility. This does not necessarily imply the negation of the nation-state as such; in fact, nation-states are often primary instruments of global transformation in higher education and in other sectors. The one globally dominant nation-state, the United States, generates continuous global effects while remaining self-referenced and, in that respect, nation-bound. Thus the distinction between internationalization and globalization does not correspond to a national/global distinction. Arguably, those who imagine the global higher education environment simply in terms of a global/national or global/local dialectic, as if there is only one kind of cross-border relationship, have seriously misunderstood that environment. Nor does the distinction between international-ization and globalization correspond to a European/global distinction. Rather than Europeanization being opposed to global-ization, some aspects of Europeanization constitute globalization.[9] Nor does the distinction between internationalization and global-ization rest on free will/determinism. It is true that educational institutions or political movements exercise a more ready influence over national governments than over the global order. Politics and government remain largely nation-bound. Nevertheless, all agents whose compass is not entirely localized have the potential to con-tribute to global relations, given that global relations have reciprocal elements, even though the capacity to affect global relations is unevenly distributed (for example, agents located in the US or at metanational regional levels potentially have more influence than others). Finally, the distinction between internationalization and globalization does not correspond to the distinction between poli-tics and economics. We have not just national politics and national public goods but global politics and global public goods, as recent changes in Europe demonstrate. This enables us to imagine the potential for global governance[10] at the worldwide or regional lev-els, in higher education and other sectors, rather than leaving the reordering of the world to the spontaneous workings of global economy and culture.[11]

Internationalization and globalization are understood here as dis-tinct from each other but interpenetrating, each creating conditions of possibility for the other. In other words, the relationship between them is dialectical but not dualistic. It should also be noted that the dialectic is not carved in stone. It varies historically. International processes and global processes sometimes substitute for each other and sometimes feed into each other; and at different times one or another set of practices grows in importance relative to the other.

Despite the conceptual spadework needed to establish the contrast between globalization and internationalization, it is an important distinction for higher education studies to make. Arguably, the dialectic between these two different kinds of cross-border action, international and global, is foundational to the contemporary university as an institution. The university was originally grounded in pan-European mobility and scholarly Latin; that is, global relations. Worldwide disciplinary networks today often constitute stronger academic identities than do domestic locations.[12] But each university was also locally idiosyncratic and partly open to other powers and, in the nineteenth and twentieth centuries, the institution became a primary instrument of nation-building and population management.[13] Enders and de Weert[14] remark on "the prominent historical role of science and universities in the process of nation building and their dependence on the nation-state." Today higher education is subject to national culture and government while imagined by national policy-makers as a primary instrument of the competition state in the global setting.[15] Here all governments have some room to move strategically, even those in poorer developing nations,[16] though the global strategic options before governments and institutions are limited by the economic strength and demographic size of the nation, the languages of use, the robustness of state agencies and the inherited resources and reputation of higher education. In sum, global and international practices have become layered onto and mixed with each other; and this plays out in different ways in different nations, different disciplines, different kinds of institutions and different parts of a single institution. For example, research-related activities in science and the disciplines, the first set of institutions noted by Kaulisch and Enders,[17] including doctoral and postdoctoral work, tend to be more globally universal in character than are more nation-bound and locally idiosyncratic processes of appointment, promotion, performance management and remuneration.

Globalization and Higher Education

In reviewing internationalization in Europe prior to the Bologna Declaration, Van der Wende notes that:

> Internationalization was mainly shaped as an add-on, marginal and short-term policy based on temporary funding mechanisms (project-based or pump-priming). It was usually not integrated in regular planning and evaluation, and there was hardly any regulation or legislation … there was a disconnection between internationalization and mainstream higher education in conceptual, political and practical terms. Conceptually, internationalization was for a long time mainly seen as concentrating on the cross-border mobility of individual students and scholars and not as a strategy that affected higher education institutions or systems.[18]

The practice of cross-border relationships as disposable "add-ons" at the margins of the heartland was typical of a world with robust separation between nation-states — the world prior to the Internet and the integration of world financial markets. International contact took place at the borders, cross-over points and zones of exchange rather than passing through central national institutions. That world has gone. Contemporary globalization transforms the heartlands. David Held and collaborators define it as "the widening, deepening and speeding up of world wide interconnectedness."[19] Globalization is vectored by cross-border flows of people, money, communications, messages, knowledge, ideas, policies and organizational cultures.[20] In higher education, global transformations play out in nations and localities in varying ways. Some cross-border effects are felt directly in institutions on a daily basis through global dealings. Others are mediated by national policy or academic cultures. These patterns of direct/indirect global effect vary by nation, by discipline and over time.[21]

What distinguishes the globalization of the last thirty years from that of earlier times, such as the spread of world religions from 800 BCE to 1000 CE, the navigation empires of the sixteenth century and the gunboat imperialism of the nineteenth century? And how does contemporary globalization play out in higher education? Much discussion of globalization suggests that it is essentially an economic process, world capitalism writ large, but this confuses the political and cultural legitimizations of world markets with globalization itself. The essence of today's globalization lies in *the combination of global transformations in political economy with global transformations in communications and culture.* On one hand, globalization involves the formation of integrated worldwide markets with instantaneous transactions in real time underpinned by a single financial system. On the other hand, it is constituted by a worldwide communications and cultural environment based on telecommunications, media and Internet and on the exchange of information, research and knowledge. Neave's description of globalization as "quickening exchange" is suggestive of both elements.[22] It is striking how economic and cultural globalization sustain each other. Communications, computing and information provide conditions of possibility for global markets. The drive for capitalist accumulation powers the ever-extending networks of communications and knowledge. The other identifiable aspects of globalization, the extended and intensified movement of people and the spread of common policy ideologies and notions of business practice, are important but secondary effects. These are quantitative expansions of global traffic that express the essential qualitative evolution at the global level: the symbiosis of worldwide markets with worldwide communicative identity.[23] In fact, it is possible for economic and cultural globalization to advance (though at a slower rate) even while some forms of global people mobility are inhibited, as in the US after September 11, 2001.

In this unity of economic and cultural globalization, the old relationship between public and private goods in national political economy is reworked in a novel manner on the global plane.[24] In economic markets, the expanding global production of private goods is sustained in the cross-border relations of firms. The national regulation of international trade follows in their wake, so the global environment is imagined as a trading environment, as at the World Trade Organization/General Agreement on Trade in Services (WTO/GATS). At the same time, global communications, information and knowledge are largely constituted as public goods resting on collective government financing. Even in the neo-liberal era, much transport and communication infrastructure, and more of education and research, are sustained by national governments and public financing. This is inherent in the very nature of information and knowledge, which constitute *public goods* in the technical sense whether produced in public sector institutions or not. An immense array of information, including basic research, is openly accessible and subject to nominal charges well below its use value. Knowledge is an almost pure public good that is underproduced in capitalist markets.[25] At the same time, information and knowledge are highly mobile, readily slipping across any border. The public goods-producing cultural sphere is more globalized than the economic sphere, where only about one-fifth of production enters cross-border trade. But it is not hard to see why the notion has taken hold that globalization is largely about the capitalist economy and private goods, as if the economy is more global than are communications or research. In the symbiosis between global economy and global culture, much of the content of public information and knowledge goods is saturated in the products, policy ideologies and legitimizations of global markets. Between private goods in the trading economy and public cultural goods, the real distinction lies not in degrees of *globalness* but in the different processes at work in global construction. Cross-border cultural relations are shaped by a denser set of policy regulations, public financing and public and quasi-public institutions. There are fewer obstacles to intervening in higher education than in industry and business; and national governments understand that a nation's infrastructure of public goods, including its institutions of higher education and research, is a key factor determining the capacity of its people to engage proactively in the global setting.

Globalization has not meant that national and local contexts have lost their importance in higher education or that national governments have abandoned their system-ordering power. It *has* expanded their horizons beyond themselves. Another change is that institutions have developed intensified direct dealings with foreign institutions and governments, partly bypassing their own national governments. This is facilitated by the process of corporatization whereby individual institutions gain greater scope for autonomous action as organizations without becoming detached from national regulation.[26] Policy-makers in many nations see corporate autonomy as essential to global effectiveness and corporatization and globalization together as the drivers of reflexive modernization:

> The internationalization process takes place
> concurrently with a certain degree of de-govern-
> mentalization in the daily life of higher education
> in terms of administrative control and determining
> the position of the individual higher education
> institutions on a national map. This de-govern-
> mentalization affected the international arena even

> more strongly because governments also only had
> limited control of international cooperation
> between institutions in the past. But nations and
> strategic policies of national governments continue
> to play a major role in setting the frames for inter-
> national communication, cooperation and
> mobility as well as for international competition.[27]

In this manner, higher education is transformed on both sides of the economy/culture symbiosis. It is swept up in global marketization: it trains the executives and technicians of global businesses and provides them with resources; its main areas of student growth are in business and computing, the most globally mobile degrees; it is shaped by economic policies undergoing global convergence; and in higher education itself the first global market has emerged. But arguably the larger changes are happening on the cultural side.[28] Teichler[29] remarks that "it is surprising to note how much the debate on global phenomena in higher education suddenly focuses on marketization, competition and management in higher education. Other terms, such as knowledge society, global village, global understanding or global learning, are hardly taken into consideration."[30] This is ironic given that, while higher education is only a second-level player in the circuits of capital and the creation of economic wealth, it is pivotal to research and knowledge systems and essential also in language, communications and information systems. Higher education is central in global cultural transformation and is transformed itself in turn. It is scarcely possible to exaggerate the potential of networked communications technologies in higher education. Cross-border e-learning conflates the functions of communications and learning, but this is just one small part of the e-potential: "The size, speed and complexity of information increasingly penetrate the daily life of scientists."[31] In a networked higher education world, intellectual communities multiply continually. Here the notion of borderless education is most salient.[32] The expanding Internet[33] facilitates worldwide databases and all kinds of faculty collaboration, stimulating more face-to-face meetings as well.[34]

Global communications in themselves do not generate mobility of ideas and people, but they encourage and facilitate it. Once-closed nations and institutions are opened up. Teferra[35] associates the Internet with "virtual brain drain." Without moving from home, faculty personnel in developing nations are seduced by foreign institutions and networks; later, "virtual brain drain" becomes real. The Internet also facilitates a flattening of difference. It is both cause and effect of the spread of English as the global language of research and scholarship.[36] Communication via e-mail messages and Web pages encourages cultural convergence between and within national systems; demystifies foreign institutions, environments, rewards and career structures; and provides ready data on advertised faculty positions in each nation so that all can be seen simultaneously. This establishes the technical preconditions for global labour markets, though to this point faculty labour markets remain largely nationally bounded.[37]

Americanization and Europeanization

Contemporary globalization is also associated with Americanization in higher education and other sectors.[38] This is code for the Anglo-American imperial hegemony in which the United States is supreme in the military, technological, economic and political spheres, while the UK plays a secondary role alongside the US in the spheres of language, culture, education and governmental ideologies (neo-liberalism is a British invention). The benefits of globalization in higher education are distributed asymmetrically, disadvantaging not just the developing nations where capacity is weaker[39] but also the non-English-speaking developed nations. As we shall see, more than two-thirds of the top one hundred research universities are in English-speaking nations. Global convergence *in itself* does not have to be Anglo-American or imperialist; it could be associated with many different configurations of power and cultural content. Nevertheless, in this era it is Anglo-American.

For the most part, global Americanization is not managed by the US government but pursued directly in the cross-border relations of American individuals and institutions, including the sale of degrees in foreign nations by American for-profit institutions.[40] In multilateral negotiations, the United States argues for trade liberalization outside the US while protecting American institutions within. This contrasts with Europeanization which is an explicitly political project.[41] Concretized in a common currency and intergovernmental agencies, Europeanization has led to a closer economic integration,[42] growing cross-border mobility in higher education, and the common European Higher Education Area and European Research Area. If part of the European project consists of negotiating closer collaboration between sovereign states that remain unchanged (internationalization), another involves creating pan-European systems and spaces with the potential to modify the role of nation-states (globalization). European initiatives in higher education mix these approaches.[43] Enders and de Weert[44] remark that the early resistance of national governments to conceding their sovereign authority over higher education encouraged a bottom-up internationalization through intensified staff and student mobility.

Potential Global Transformations

Have universities become subject to internationalization, or globalization, or a mix of the two? Enhanced internationalization would imply that mobility and exchange among them across national borders is more intensive and extensive, but national higher education systems, including elements such as faculty labour markets and career dynamics, are largely unchanged. Globalization would here imply that core national elements are converging, marginalized by or even dissolving into the global.

Arguably there are three kinds of potential global transformation of higher education institutions:

1. Global (distinct from national) processes which, once established, are difficult for national agents to block or modify, particularly the formation of a global market in universities or, say, a global market in academic labour potentially capable of swallowing or crowding out national markets/systems.

2. Global systems, relationships and flows that directly engender common changes in different national higher education systems leading to convergence. Examples within higher education include cross-border disciplinary networking, the use of English as the principal language of academic exchange, and Internet publishing. Examples in policy include the creation of the European Higher Education Area, with its potential for common structures and habits, and also the increasing similarity of approaches to Ph.D. training. The question here is not just the existence and the salience of global flows, which are unquestionable, but whether these flows actually flow so far into national higher education systems as to create greater homogenization in national labour markets and career norms.

3. Parallel reforms by the different autonomous national governments, following globally common ideas and templates, which lead to some convergence (though rarely to complete identity) among different national higher education systems. For example, almost everywhere policy and management are affected by global models from the US and the UK, in which national systems are understood

as quasi-markets and institutions as quasi-firms. Cross-border parallelization is facilitated by homogeneity in a national system and retarded by intrasystem diversity.[45]

We can note here also that changes made under national auspices — type 3 transformations — may lead to a tipping point that facilitates global transformations of the first and second type. Likewise, Enders and de Weert suggest that Europeanization — combining transformations of type 2 and 3 — opens European higher education to a larger transformation than envisaged:

> European countries are creating a process towards
> an open higher education system and research area
> which means that a return to a "closed" public
> higher education system based on the nation-state
> — given there are adherents for such a move — is
> an illusion. Sooner or later, developments beyond
> the current pan-European approach and landscape
> will gain in importance and challenge European
> policies in this area.[46]

This is particularly the case with national system reforms or single institution reforms focused on opening up higher education to the global: "The notions of 'internationalization' and 'international competitiveness' can ... function as ice-breakers to stimulate policies and reforms on the national level."[47] Once the global genie has been released inside familiar territory, changing sensibilities and daily practices and perhaps bringing in new players, the consequences cannot be wholly forecast or controlled.

Whether or not these changes are occurring, and, if so, to what extent and with what transformative implications, are questions that can only be settled by detailed empirical research, both in relation to particular national cases and institutions and in relation to the relational dynamics of the cross-border environment.

II. The Global University Market and the Role of the United States
Emergence of the Global "Super-League"

The era of the Internet has also seen the emergence of the first genuinely global provider market in university education. This is not coincidental. While the Harvards and Oxfords have always commanded worldwide status, the world's research universities can appear as an integrated group for the first time thanks to the Internet and interuniversity electronic networking plus worldwide research publication in English and enhanced global people mobility. The development of credible global rankings on the basis of common criteria of comparison completes the process. The most globally influential rankings are prepared by the Shanghai Jiao Tong Institute of Higher Education (SJTIHE) based on research performance.

In its upper echelons, higher education is not a conventional economic market in which firms/institutions compete on the basis of market share, equity price and profitability. It is a competition for status. The principal differentiating factor and the motor of competition is university reputation, as numerous studies attest, for example Avveduto; [48] and the main driver of global reputation is research. In the shaping of cross-border movement, the reputation of the nation, as well as the institution, is important. Strong university nations with well-financed research and well-known research universities attract mobile faculty and doctoral students. The *Economist*[49] refers to a "super-league" of research universities centred on the US and the UK and led by the household names: Harvard, Stanford, Yale, Berkeley, MIT, Cambridge and Oxford. All are demand magnets for academic personnel from around the world.

Work and study in those universities enhances one's career opportunities everywhere. Table 1 lists the top thirty universities on the basis of 2005 research performance, incorporating measures of publications, citations, and the incidences of high-citation researchers and winners of Nobel Prizes and Fields Medals in Mathematics.

Global research competition also reinforces a hierarchy of nations in higher education, with implications for the positioning of national labour markets in relation to each other. In terms of nations, research competition as calculated by Jiao Tong is dominated by the US. That nation has 53 of the top 100 research universities and an awesome 17 of the leading 20. The UK has 11 of the top 100. When Canada's 4 and Australia's 2 are added, the English-speaking nations have 70 percent of the top 100 universities between them.[50] English-language nations have an advantage in research-based comparison given that English is the only global language of research. Nevertheless, several Western European nations are strong in research, especially relative to their economic capacity, including Switzerland, Sweden, the Netherlands and Finland. Israeli higher education is small but research-strong. Japan has several outstanding research universities. Germany and France are also important research nations with a broad spread of high-quality institutions, though none have concentrated performance at the level of the leading American universities.[51]

Table 1

Towards a Description of the Global Super-League: Leading Research Universities, 2005

	University	Nation	Points
1	Harvard U	US	100.0
2	U Cambridge	UK	73.6
3	Stanford U	US	73.4
4	U California, Berkeley	US	72.8
5	Massachusetts IT	US	70.1
6	California IT	US	67.1
7	Columbia U	US	62.3
8	Princeton U	US	60.9
9	U Chicago	US	60.1
10	U Oxford	UK	59.7
11	Yale U	US	56.9
12	Cornell U	US	54.6
13	U California, San Diego	US	51.0
14	U California, Los Angeles	US	50.6
15	U Pennsylvania	US	50.2
16	U Wisconsin-Madison	US	49.2
17	U Washington (Seattle)	US	48.4
18	U California, San Francisco	US	47.8
19	Johns Hopkins U	US	46.9
20	Tokyo U	Japan	46.7
21	U Michigan, Ann Arbor	US	44.9
22	Kyoto U	Japan	43.8
23	Imperial College London	UK	43.7
24	U Toronto	Canada	43.1
25	U Illinois, Urbana-Champaign	US	42.8
26	U College London	UK	42.6
27	Swiss Federated IT, Zurich	Switzerland	41.7
28	Washington U, St Louis	US	40.7
29	New York U	US	38.8
30	Rockefeller U	US	38.2

U = University; IT = Institute of Technology.

Source: Shanghai Jiao Tong University Institute of Higher Education, Academic Ranking of World Universities (2005). Retrieved February 1, 2006 from http://ed.sjtu.edu.cn/ranking.htm.

The Pool of Globally Mobile Researchers

The emerging global provider market in turn is associated with a global pool of highly mobile faculty labour ranging from highly-paid élite researchers and scholars to those at a more junior point in their faculty careers. This global pool constitutes its own global labour market that is recognizably distinct from national labour markets — that is, apart from the US faculty labour market, which coincides with the global pool. Global comparison of research performance encourages convergence in research standards and cultures. It focuses research-intensive universities across the world on the common criteria needed to secure success. The Jiao Tong data are highly sensitive to each university's number of high-citation researchers, especially in the science-based disciplines. Universities striving with each other to lift their positions in the rankings find themselves competing for researchers, intensifying global mobility. It is not yet clear exactly how global competition for élite researchers will shape global and national labour markets, but it will continue to expand the global pool of high flyers and enhance bifurcation between globally mobile researchers and faculty bound to national labour markets and careers.

The Second-tier Global Providers

The second tier of the global provider market consists of the higher education institutions outside the super-league providing places for foreign students, ranging from comprehensive research-intensive universities to for-profit colleges specializing in business studies. Approximately 2.1 million students now cross borders for education each year, either by travelling to the exporting nation or by accessing its institutions via a campus in the student's own country or through distance education.[52] Some enter the super-league universities, but most enrol in the second tier. The largest export nations are the US, the UK and Australia, plus Germany and France. The English-language nations tend to dominate foreign student education, and English is increasingly used as the language of instruction in Western European and Asian programs. The worldwide market in doctoral students is partly scholarship-based and so less commercialized than for first degrees and business education, but is highly competitive. As noted, the doctoral market is shaped by research reputation. This global market is discussed further below.

America the Magnet

Higher education in the United States is central in all three ways in which academic personnel use the global dimension: it is the main site of élite research activity; it provides early career platforms; and it is the main zone of "second-chance" opportunities. Quantitatively, most of the élite global labour market is centred on the US. The foreign doctoral enrolment in the US of 102,084 (2004-05) dwarfs the *national* doctoral population in most parts of the world. Equally significant are the growth of the foreign proportion within American doctoral cohorts and the increasing stay rates of doctoral graduates. The indicators vary by field of study and nation of origin. Stay rates are high for graduates in engineering, computing and technologies and low for English and political science.[53] In 1985, 50.0 percent of foreign science and engineering doctoral degree-holders had plans to stay; in 1995, 70.6 percent had such plans. Most of the increase took place after 1992.[54]

Of the 1996 doctoral recipients in science and engineering, 56 percent were still in the US in 2001. Stay rates by discipline ranged from computing/electrical engineering (70 percent), physical sciences (64 percent), computer science (63 percent) and life sciences (63 percent) down to 26 percent in economics.[55] Students who self-finance their doctoral studies in the US are much more likely to stay compared to those receiving scholarship support from home.[56] Potential migration is particularly high for students from China, Israel, Argentina, Peru, Eastern Europe and Iran; and from some developed countries including the UK, Canada, New Zealand and Germany. All have stay rates of more than 50 percent five years after completion. Between 1992 and 2001, the stay rate for Chinese graduates in science and engineering jumped from 65 to 96 percent and for Indian graduates from 72 to 86 percent.[57] In 2003, three-quarters of European Union citizens who obtained a US doctorate said they had no plans to return to Europe.[58] On the other hand, stay rates are very low for Korea, Japan and Indonesia and relatively low for Mexico.[59]

"Pull" Factors That Favour the US

One "pull" factor encouraging mobility into the US is financial support. In 1996, more than three-quarters of foreign doctoral recipients in the US reported that their universities were the primary source of support for their graduate training.[60] A second "pull" factor is the level of American faculty salaries compared to those paid in most other nations, especially for leading researchers. In 2003-04, the average salary at American doctoral universities for full professors for nine to ten months of the year was US$100,682 and average total compensation was US$125,644, rising to US$152,540 in the independent private universities. Faculty have further earning opportunities during the summer break. There are greater rewards at the peak of the American system: 6 percent of full professors earned more than $200,000 in salary alone in 2003-04.[61] This compares with standard salary levels of 55,000-60,000 Euros in the Netherlands and Germany, though some Netherlands professors earn above that range.[62] However, a number of Asian nations are approaching or exceed European salaries; for example, in relation to Singapore, Lee remarks that "the recently revised salary scales are internationally competitive and rank among the highest in the region." In Singapore, salaries are on a par with all but the top end of American levels. Singapore has set out to create a cosmo-politan and globally competitive higher education system: 20 percent of the faculty are expatriates.[63] Taking into account differ-ences in the cost of living, Korea is on par with Europe, though still short of American levels.[64] Some faculty salaries in China are also becoming more competitive. For China to build a world-class uni-versity system, it must be able to attract back expatriates and doctoral graduates in the US, UK and Europe.

In Argentina in 2001, the annual salary of the small minority of full professors paid full-time varied from US$12,492 to US$27,084, depending on seniority.[65] In most developing nations faculty salaries are lower. Altbach[66] remarks that in many cases a full-time academic salary cannot support a middle-class standard of living. Working in two jobs is common, reducing the potential time for original research.

It should be noted that salary differentials do not prompt a uni-versal movement to higher-paying jurisdictions. Salaries are not the sum of faculty incentives. Non-salary aspects of career structures and working conditions must also be taken into account: "The per-spective of obtaining a tenured position early, may be decisive for a young foreign academic to apply in a foreign country"[67] or persuade internationally employable faculty to stay home.[68] The US tenure track is slower than those of France and the UK.[69] Cultural incen-tives are also important. In Poland between 1997 and 2001, average faculty salaries fell from 109.2 to 95.5 percent of the average national wage, yet brain drain is minor; those going abroad for short periods such as one year almost always return.[70]

A third "pull" factor is the relative openness of the national labour markets to foreigners. In the American markets in high-skilled labour, foreign entrants often outperform locals. In 1996, at eleven to fifteen years after earning the degree, the median salary of foreign-born Ph.D.s in science and engineering was US$64,000 compared to US$56,000 for the native-born.[71] Unlike universities in many other nations, American universities are often open to the merit-based appointment of foreigners despite visa and work permit obstacles and the post-September 11, 2001 climate. At the peak of the profession(s), foreigners have a major presence: "The foreign born and foreign educated are disproportionately represented among individuals making an exceptional contribution to science and engineering in the United States ... 18.1 per cent of recipients of highly cited patents (the top 3.5 per cent over the period 1980-91) are foreign born" compared to the expected figure of 11.8 percent.[72] But that does not mean that any nation opening itself to foreigners will attract and hold them. It is openness *combined with* superior opportunities resting ultimately on the economic strength and global cultural hegemony of the US that makes it the global magnet. Strength and success shape the liberal global ideology of a nation that is open in its political economy yet monocultural at heart. Just as imperial Britain advocated the free global exchange of people and capital in the nineteenth century, so does the US today. It is the main beneficiary.

Brain Drain/Brain Circulation

The growing hegemony of US higher education poses difficulties for other national systems with traditionally strong global roles such as Germany and France and even the UK. Net brain drain is a potential problem for all nations other than the US, though more for some than for others; for example, as well as losing many doctoral graduates to the US and UK, Germany is losing its own standing as an attractor of foreign faculty and doctoral students. Berning[73] remarks that, while German research universities are seen as uniformly good, there is a lack of the highest-prestige "centres of excellence" found in the US, and:

> German study courses and degrees have lost part
> of their former international reputation. This is

mainly due to the worldwide expansion and adoption of the Anglo-American HE [higher education] system, its courses and degrees, but not to a lack of scientific quality in Germany. The consequence is a loss of foreign students from countries close to Germany but now following the Anglo-American mainstream (e.g. East Asia, Turkey). The loss of foreign students may cause a loss of young scientists from abroad too. Within the frame of the Bologna process HE institutions in Germany try to gain back that intellectual power by introducing new study courses and degrees, sometimes by using English as a teaching language, and by internationalizing all academic activities.[74]

In developing nations that lack established higher education systems, the seductions of academic mobility are more strongly felt and the consequences of brain drain are potentially more severe: "The professoriate in developing countries is a profession on the periphery. Research is, with few exceptions, undertaken at the major universities in industrialized countries." Faculty in the developing world seldom operate at the frontiers of world science or "share in the control over the main levers of academic power worldwide" unless they move to another country.[75] Though the Internet enables worldwide access to knowledge, it has also "increased the peripherality of developing country academics ... developing countries use information from the north, but contribute relatively little to the total flow of knowledge."[76] Even a small number of defections each year may prevent a developing country system from gaining the critical mass needed to reproduce specific disciplines[77] and establish a viable national labour market and career system. These effects are reinforced in the long shadow of the global super-league. Even leading national universities in the developing world are locked out of the top tier of the world market and tend to lose standing at home as well as abroad. This exacerbates faculty flight to the global centre. The other side of this coin is that cross-border mobility improves academic capacity in some emerging systems.[78] Much faculty migration is temporary and there are complex two-way movements of people and ideas between the national systems and other nations. Nations such as Korea and Taiwan have been highly successful in strengthening the national faculty labour market and reversing or modifying net brain drain.[79] The sum of mobility is more negative in poorer developing nations in Africa[80] and tends to be negative also in small nations proximate to large receiving countries.[81]

Here we need to be careful to avoid falling into a binary analysis based simply on the constructs of developed/developing worlds or North/South. The salience of those tensions is undeniable, but the global higher education environment is also more complex and more differentiating than this. There are many different kinds of developing/emerging system, and the role of the developed nations looks very different whether one is in, say, Finland, or Singapore, compared with the United States. Above all, binary analyses miss much of the special significance of US higher education; for example, Altbach argues that "the most visible impact of globalization is the emergence of a worldwide market for academic talent, stimulated in part by the large numbers of students who study abroad." He also remarks that the global faculty labour market and doctoral student flows "are overwhelmingly a South-to-North phenomenon."[82] While these statements are largely correct, they are incomplete. By themselves they paint a misleading picture of the global element in academic labour markets. While we can identify a global element in the faculty labour markets, it has not subsumed national labour markets into a single worldwide set of regulations, salaries and conditions. Nor is there a global pool of labour that is common across the whole "North," as Altbach implies. Rather, a relatively small-sized global tier has been imposed on top of the national labour markets where the great majority of faculty continue to be employed. The global labour market also takes in the rest of the American doctoral sector, as well as some British institutions. It also includes a sprinkling of other research universities in Europe, Asia and the Americas (Japan, Singapore, Hong Kong, Australia, Canada), though only a minority of their faculty are potentially mobile on the global scale. The effect of Americanization is to sustain and enhance the US-dominated global market in high-priced, high-quality researchers while also establishing US higher education for doctoral students and faculty in each other nation as the primary site of extranational opportunity. Americanization does not abolish other national labour markets and career systems. Rather, it tends to make them residual on the global scale and weaken the reproduction of their national traditions at home.

The position of the US in higher education is qualitatively different to that of the other nations of the North, all of which face potential net brain drain to the US themselves unless they invest heavily in global recruitment as Singapore has done. The scale of foreign doctoral education and the recruitment of foreign faculty in the US, combined with the US-led and dominated global competition for high-quality academic labour, has long-term transformative implications in every other national labour market. The full implications are yet to become apparent, but arguably this is a global transformation of type 1 in which the tipping point has already been reached.[83] One suspects that, in the medium term, all nations will be faced with the question of whether to move closer to American faculty salaries and career norms, at least for the élite layer of researchers. If so, one option will be to differentiate the national system along American lines between research-intensive universities and the others, facilitating the differentiation of status and rewards within systems, without creating an across-the-board increase in the fiscal cost of higher education. Another option will be to deregulate or regulate faculty salaries and conditions of work sufficiently so as to enable a more pronounced differentiation within individual universities. If so, both moves would tend to undermine national egalitarianism and professional traditions and will be resisted.

Through all this, American higher education remains *American*. Its global leadership is exercised not as global leadership (that responsibility is not acknowledged) but as national practice: not in terms of worldwide norms but in terms of American policies, institutional traditions and professional norms. The dynamic of hegemony is nonreciprocal; for example, the academic profession(s) in the US are undergoing such changes of their own as the partial replacement of tenured labour by part-time teaching.[84] Such changes are scarcely affected by the labour markets in other nations; they are indigenous to the US yet they move into other national systems as norms for imitation. Likewise, US universities admit foreign persons freely without risking their own identity. These robust nation-centred institutions borrow from time to time but only on their own terms. They are readily closed to the potential of foreign practices to transform US faculty norms.

A Note on WTO/GATS

The WTO/GATS negotiations focus on the national regulatory conditions governing trade in services, including higher education, in each nation. WTO/GATS[85] has been talked up as a driver of change by national governments wanting to facilitate trade and/or the corporate reinvention of institutions and talked up as a danger by others with a protectionist stance. But the transformative potential in national systems has been exaggerated. The negotiations focus on commercial cross-border activity, but most cross-border relations in higher education are noncommercial in nature, including research cooperation, faculty exchange and doctoral mobility. Second, under the terms of WTO/GATS, governments choose the degree to which they open up their systems to foreign competitors; for example, by creating equality in the funding and regulatory structure among providers. Most nations have opted for little change to the status quo except to open up their borders to foreign e-learning (which in any case none can effectively exclude). Some developing nations have adopted more liberal trade régimes to facilitate the entry of foreign providers as a means of expanding higher education capacity. Even so, the entry of foreign providers is proceeding in many nations and does not rest on WTO/GATS. In Europe, GATS has been "discussed in only a few countries" and "any conclusive statements on this topic are difficult to make."[86]

More specifically, the GATS Mode 4, "Presence of natural persons," refers to people travelling to another country on a temporary basis to provide an educational service, including teachers and researchers working abroad.[87] Under Article 1.2(d) of the GATS, it is defined as "the supply of a service … by a service supplier of one Member, through presence of natural persons of a Member in the territory of another Member."[88] This does not include locals employed by a foreign firm, or foreigners employed by local partner organizations; it covers foreigners working for a foreign firm. The intention is to facilitate the freedom of movement of such "natural persons," which could facilitate the presence of both foreign institutions and foreign personnel, with potential for flow-on effects in the faculty norms and career structures of the nation. The transformative potential is limited by three factors. First, signing the GATS commitment does not mean that the national system is obliged to admit such professionals or providers; for example, they must still meet the domestic regulatory requirements as to qualifications.[89] Second, the GATS protocols apply only to commercial activities. Third, there have been fewer national government commitments under Mode 4 than under any other aspect of GATS.[90]

III. The Global Market in Degrees and the Role of Australia

Between 1998 and 2003, the number of cross-border students entering member nations of the Organisation for Economic Co-operation and Development (OECD) rose by 48.9 percent. In 2003, there were 2.117 million such students in the main exporting nations,91 just over 1 percent of all people living outside their country of origin. Of these cross-border students, 46 percent travel from China, India and other Asian nations to the OECD nations. Most of this group enter English-language education systems, mostly to study for globally-portable qualifications in business, computing and intensive English. Later many will migrate to the nation of education. The second largest group of cross-border students (29 percent) is moving within Europe.92

In 2004, the OECD estimated the total global market in post-secondary education at US$30 billion. As noted, most of it is located in the mass education tier of the global market, below the super-league. This tier takes in three types of provision. One is the for-profit sector, specializing in vocational programs with no research, led by institutions such as the University of Phoenix, the largest private university in the US and now spread to Mexico, India and Western Europe. The for-profit sector is underpinned by American equity trading, a fast-growing source of investment funds. Second is the commercial provision of foreign education by non-profit institutions, designed in order to generate surplus revenues. This includes public research universities in the UK, Australia and New Zealand, private colleges and universities in Malaysia, institutions in Singapore and China, and some first-degree and sub-degree programs in four-year and two-year US institutions. The liberalization of cross-border trade in services such as education is currently being negotiated within the World Trade Organization framework.93 Third are those institutions and nations where foreign education is subsidized by governments, foundations and/or universities and an expansionary capitalist dynamic is absent. This type is found in Japan — where cross-border enrolments are publicly subsidized to assist the internationalization of domestic students — and Germany, where many foreign students pay no fees.

Unlike the super-league, universities in the second tier are not household names. Here reputation is formed more in terms of nations rather than individual institutions:

> In considering where to study, mobile students'
> key choice factors are, in order, country (54%),
> course (18%), institution (17%) and city (10%)
> … While awareness of quality (or even reputation)
> of institutions is mostly local (and difficult to
> compare across countries), international students
> clearly tend to assimilate institutions with their
> country and to build their perceptions on the
> assumption that quality depends on perceived
> quality of post-secondary education in a given
> country rather than in a specific institution. This
> is evident in a study of Chinese students who tend
> to separate countries (rather than institutions) into
> reputation "tiers"… Countries and institutions
> that wish to attract international students (rather
> than just let them in) have to make sure that the
> reputation of their higher education system is not
> damaged by the misbehavior of certain institu-
> tions.[94]

In 2003, the leading exporters were the US (28 percent of cross-border tertiary students), the UK (12 percent), Germany (11 percent),[95] France (10 percent), Australia (9 percent) and Japan (4 percent)[96] (Figure 1). In the 1990s and early 2000s, the mass market grew particularly rapidly in English-language nations. The map of providers is now becoming more diverse, largely through the growth of income-generating English-language programs in non-English-speaking nations such as Malaysia, Singapore, the Netherlands, Germany, Finland and Sweden. There has been a slowing in the growth of movement into the English-language nations, particularly the US, whose share of the world market is falling and where the proportion of foreign students who enrol in globalized disciplines such as business, computing and intensive English is down. There has been a sharp decline in Muslim student entry into the US[97] due to both supply and demand factors, while there is growing student mobility from the Middle East to Europe.[98] Australian patterns are discussed below.

Figure 1.
Proportion of World's Foreign Students, by Export Nation, 2003

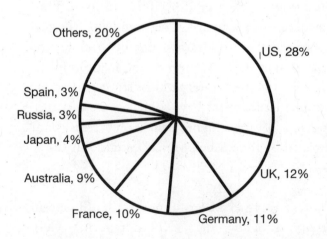

Source: Organisation for Economic Cooperation and Development, *Education at a Glance* (Paris: OECD, 2005).

Australia's Share of the Global Market in Degrees

Figure 1 illustrates national carve-up of the global market in degrees. These market shares have varied meanings according to national system size. The 9 percent of the world market located in Australia has a major impact. It has a much greater domestic impact than the US's share of the global market, though the latter is three times as large. This is because Australia, with 20 million people, is the smallest of the major export nations: in 2003, its 9 percent share of the global market in cross-border tertiary study constituted 18.7 percent of its tertiary enrolments, the highest level recorded for any country.[99] This compares with 11.3 percent of students in the UK and only 3.5 percent in the US, which helps explain the marginal role of foreign education in most American universities, except in doctoral education. Australian government data for 2004 list 228,555 foreign students in the doctoral universities and there are approximately 200,000 more in sub-degree tertiary education, specialist English language colleges and schools.[100] The number of foreign students in the doctoral universities is at 40 percent of the level of the US.

Three-quarters of the foreign higher education students attend institutions in Australia. The remainder are in distance education or at campuses in importing nations — including Malaysia, Singapore, Hong Kong, Vietnam and South Africa — operated either by the Australian institution itself or by a local partner. A December 2003 survey found that Australian institutions offered 1,600 programs abroad, 57 percent solely through offshore programs and 16 percent in mixed mode including offshore centres.[101]

All foreign students are classified as full-fee-paying students except for the 0.9 percent with foreign aid scholarships.[102] Scholarship support is low compared to that offered by other major exporters. In the US, more than four graduate students in ten receive university or government scholarships.[103]

There is a substantial foreign enrolment in all Australian universities

Table 2

Largest Australian Higher Education Providers of International Education, 2004

University and State	Number of international students 2004	Proportion of all university students 2004	International student fee revenues 2003	Proportion of all university revenues 2003
		%	$s million	%
Monash U (Victoria)	17,077	30.6	138.3	17.9
RMIT UT (Victoria)*	15,132	39.0	111.9	21.7
Curtin UT (WA)*	14,319	39.7	95.0	24.2
Central Queensland U	10,460	46.8	78.2	38.2
U South Australia *	10,257	31.5	49.1	16.0
U Sydney (NSW)	9,806	21.2	102.2	11.7
U New South Wales	9,481	23.5	118.6	16.0
U Melbourne (Victoria)	9,215	22.0	137.3	14.9
Macquarie U (NSW)	8,725	29.2	69.8	22.8
Charles Sturt U (NSW)*	8,429	23.5	12.3	6.0
U Southern Queensland	8,333	32.8	18.2	15.1
U Wollongong (NSW)	7,940	37.6	49.1	20.7
U Technology, Sydney	7,369	23.7	63.0	20.3
Griffith U (Queensland)	7,261	21.9	58.9	16.4
Total Australia	228,555	24.2	1,700.9	13.8

*more than 40 percent of international enrolments offshore.

U = University. UT = University of Technology. RMIT = Royal Melbourne Institute of Technology.

Source: Department of Employment, Education and Training, DEST (2005). Selected higher education statistics (2005). Accessed August 20, 2005 at http://www.dest.gov.au/sectors/higher_education/publications_resources/statistics/default.htm.

and, in 2004, nineteen of them enrolled more than 5,000 foreign students. The largest complement was 17,077 at Monash University.[104] To place this in comparative context, in 2003-04, the largest foreign enrolment in any American doctoral university was 6,647 students at the University of Southern California.[105] Several Australian universities derive more than 20 percent of their income from the market, a high level of dependence (Table 2). Much as in other English-speaking nations, almost two-thirds of the foreign students are enrolled in business studies and computing. Foreign students are concentrated in first-degree and master's degrees by programs of courses; as noted, doctoral education plays a lesser role than in the US, the UK and Western Europe. Approximately 80 percent of all foreign students are from East and Southeast Asia. Australia is the world leader in providing foreign education to its proximate region, Southeast Asia; it educates more students from Singapore, Malaysia and Indonesia than does the US with fifteen times Australia's population, and also has a role of global significance in China. In 2004, Australia took in 65,000 students from mainland China and Hong Kong combined, compared to the 67,000 enrolled in the US in 2003-04. The US has a much stronger drawing power than does Australia in Japan and Korea. Australia has a quarter the US's number of students from India.[106] Australia's standing within Asia varies. Market research indicates that it is often the nation of first choice in Indonesia and has very good credibility in Malaysia. It has lesser status in Singapore, Korea and India.

Early returns for Australian higher education in 2005 indicated that commencing foreign students grew by just 4 percent, with declines in some institutions. As in the US enrolment, trends were uneven by nation of origin. In 2004, the numbers of higher education students entering Australia from each of Indonesia, Singapore and Hong Kong were down 4-5 percent from the 2003 levels. The number of students from Malaysia rose by 6 percent, and there was a 47 percent increase from India and 37 percent from China.[107] Australia was faring better than the US in maintaining enrolments from Muslim nations, though the decline in students from Indonesia was significant. Some nationals faced greater difficulties in obtaining visas to enter Australia, and there were heightened concerns about security.[108] Whereas Australia was perceived by foreign students as being safer than the US and UK prior to 9/11 and the War in Iraq,[109] it was unclear this was still the case afterwards. Market research also indicated there were some concerns about the quality of Australian universities in relation to research capacity and performance, concerns that appeared to have increased following the publication of the Jiao Tong university rankings.[110]

Dynamics of Expansion

In 1985, the national government reinvented international education in Australia as a market of institutions in competition for full-fee-paying foreign students. It began to phase out the existing subsidized places scheme, installed full-cost pricing with no ceiling and lifted all quotas on the number of full-fee-paying foreign students. It provided early assistance with marketing in Southeast Asia, and, for the first decade, visa policy consistently facilitated market growth. Subsequent visa policies have been more contradictory in their effects, but the provision of fast-track migration opportunities for graduates in demand in the skilled labour markets has been an important element in the continued growth of student numbers.[111] In establishing a commercial international education industry, the government had several objectives. First, it wanted to improve foreign trade balances following a downturn in the prices of Australia's commodity exports. It saw services as a growing part of world trade where Australia could exercise a comparative advantage, including educational services, where Australian universities enjoyed a sound reputation as an established doctoral system organized and funded on British lines. By creating a larger university sector incorporating the former colleges of education in 1987-90,[112] the government sought to extend this reputation across all higher education institutions. Second, it was hoped that the marketing of foreign education would generate income to supplement public university funding and encourage a more outward-looking and entrepreneurial spirit.[113] Third, there was global positioning itself. Higher education was expected to facilitate national responses to globalization and was seen as one key to a deeper engagement in the Asia-Pacific, where much of Australia's future lay. Opening up the universities to foreign trade was part of the twin process of opening up Australia itself to global competition while fashioning its competitiveness.[114]

By comparison with other nations, the development of international education in Australia had three distinctive and related features. First, the settings were unambiguously commercial. Subsidy was minimized and the regulatory conditions facilitated the open-ended expansion of numbers and hence of university revenues. Second, there was a marked growth in business functions and non-academic student servicing, more so than in academic capacity. Increasingly marketing, recruitment and non-academic student servicing became managed by commercial companies associated with the university. In offshore operations involving local partners, the commercial companies often came to shape teaching programs and employ teaching staff. Third, there was an astonishing rate of growth. Between 1990 and 2004, the number of foreign students grew from 25,000 to 228,555. The target of US$200 million a year in revenue was soon exceeded. In 2002, in all sectors of education, the export industry earned almost US$4 billion in fees and other spending by students.[115] In 2003, foreign students provided the universities alone with US$1.3 billion in fee revenues.[116] What powered this growth was the need for revenues.

The keys to the rise of foreign education in Australia are the following: (1) there was growing demand for cross-border education in the Asia-Pacific, and, of the developed English-language higher education systems, Australia was closer and cheaper than the US and UK; (2) deregulation and business techniques provided necessary conditions for growth; (3) the government used reductions in its own funding to install dependence on market revenues and to position university leaders as the drivers of the business model and export objective. By 2002, public funding per student was at half the level of the mid-1980s.[117] Foreign student fees became the solution to all problems and needs, whether for new staff, buildings or communications systems. Turning necessity into virtue, universities incorporated internationalization and cultural diversity into missions and strategic objectives. In changing behaviour, spending cuts can be as potent a policy weapon as new funded programs.

The government share of total income tumbled from 91 percent in 1983 to 58 percent in 1996 and 44 percent in 2003. All forms of tuition fees and other charges reached 34 percent of university income in 2003.[118] The OECD notes that, between 1995 and 2002, Australia was unique in that an increase in private spending on tertiary education of 78 percent was joined to a reduction in public spending of 8 percent, not an increase in the latter as in other nations:[119]

> Public investment in [tertiary] education has
> increased in most of the OECD countries for which
> 1995 to 2002 data are available, regardless of
> changes in private spending. In fact many countries
> with the highest growth in private spending have
> also shown the highest increase in public funding of
> education ... increasing private spending on tertiary
> education tends to complement, rather than replace,
> public investment. The main exception to this is
> Australia, where the shift towards private expendi-
> ture at tertiary level has been accompanied by a fall
> in the level of public expenditure in real terms.[120]

Over 1995-2002, the number of tertiary students increased by 31 percent, public funding per tertiary student dropped by 30 percent, and total spending on education institutions per tertiary student fell by 7 percent.[121] The fall in total resources per student coupled with expanding business functions and nonacademic services triggered a decline in the resourcing of teaching and research functions. In the two decades after 1984, the average student-staff ratio in Australian institutions rose from thirteen to twenty; and the growth of nonacademic staff outstripped that of academic staff, especially in the new universities.[122] Remarkably, in their position-taking strategies, Australian universities became more dependent on their business acumen than their academic capacity. This generalization is less true of the old and strong research universities and more true of the newer universities, often more aggressive in recruiting foreign students, but all institutions have become dependent on the foreign market to fill the revenue gap. There has been less innovation on the curriculum side of international education than might be expected, and it is doubtful if Australian universities have proven much better than UK or US universities in mixing international and domestic students.[123]

In the outcome, Australian higher education has successfully fulfilled the business objectives of institutions and the policy objectives of government. Base-level quality is ensured by a national system of quality assurance and periodic audit.[124] The downside is the negative implications of this resource configuration, and these policy and institutional cultures, for the infrastructure enabling teaching and research and hence for Australia's long-term academic capacity and global competitiveness.

Australia's Comparative Research Performance
Australia's global position in research is not as strong as in commercial

teaching. According to the Jiao Tong University data, Australia has 14 (2.8 percent) of the top 500 research universities, exceeding its share of worldwide economic capacity (1.7 percent). There are established areas of research strength such as astrophysics, philosophy and parts of agriculture and the life sciences. Two Australians, Barry Marshall and Robin Warren, won the 2005 Nobel Prize for Medicine. The Australian National University (ANU), which specializes in research, is ranked by Jiao Tong at 56, down from 49 in 2003. The ANU has extensive cross-border networks and probably houses more experts on China and Indonesia than any North American university. The University of Melbourne is at 82, the Universities of Sydney and Queensland are in the top 150, and the Universities of New South Wales, Western Australia, Monash, Adelaide and Macquarie are in the top 300. Tasmania, Newcastle, La Trobe, Flinders and Murdoch are in the top 500.[125] No university founded in 1987-90 has built research to the point of entering the world's top 500; and three established as research universities prior to 1987 are outside the top 500.

Australia's problem here is that, among the top 100, it is weaker than the other English-speaking nations and parts of Western Europe and its comparative performance may have declined.[126] The most obvious comparators are the UK and Canada. In Canada, the University of Toronto with a Jiao Tong ranking of 24 and the University of British Colombia at 37 are well ahead of ANU. Australia made a major commitment to basic research infrastructure between the 1960s and 1980s but has since focused one-sidedly on commercialization. Canada continued to invest in basic research infrastructure, including 2,000 publicly-funded professorships. Australia doubled its allocation to research project funding in 2001, but not to research infrastructure, which continued to be weakened by the decline in public funding. The UK has three times Australia's gross domestic product (GDP) but five times its funding for research performance, and allocates those funds on the basis of research quality. Australian performance measures are primarily quantitative: grant dollars, research student numbers and volume of publications. This creates quantity/quality trade-offs such as more publishing but in lower-status journals.[127]

Policy and Funding Changes in the Australian System

In the merged Australian university system established in 1987-90, universities shared a common mission but were differentiated in status, resources and capacities. The polarization between selective research-intensive institutions and volume-building teaching institutions was modified but not eliminated by policy. The standard template was a large, often multi-site, university, comprehensive in disciplines and professional programs, entrepreneurial, globally engaged and aspiring to research outputs and reputation.[128] Undergraduate tuition took the form of standardized Higher Education Contribution Scheme (HECS) charges paid to government rather than variable market fees fixed by the universities. All institutions apart from the ANU, regardless of their prestige or role in research, were locked into a volume-building trajectory in the global market to supplement declining public funding. Everywhere, business functions and non-academic servicing became principal avenues for development while academic resources were under severe pressure.[129] But the new universities were never provided with the "blue sky" research funding of their predecessors and the pre-1987 stratification of research outputs survived. Under the Institutional Grants Scheme (IGS), institutions received extra funding for research performance. In 2004, 64 percent of the IGS money went to the universities in the Group of Eight or G8 (ANU, Melbourne, Sydney, Queensland, New South Wales, Western Australia, Monash, Adelaide); 21 percent to eleven other universities created before 1975 (Tasmania, Macquarie, New England, Newcastle, Wollongong, La Trobe, Deakin, James Cook, Griffith, Flinders,

Murdoch); and only 15 percent to the twenty universities designated after 1985.[130]

The Minister for Education, Science and Training, Brendan Nelson, reset the system in late 2003.[131] First, universities can now charge undergraduate fees at any level for up to 35 percent of students in each program. Second, HECS charges are set by the universities themselves within standard maxima, bringing the HECS closer to a variable market fee. Third, students paying tuition fees in both public and private institutions can access low-cost loans (FEE-HELP), repaid on an income-contingent basis. As with the HECS, the threshold for income-contingent repayment is set at average weekly full-time earnings, minimizing the impact of fees on participation. FEE-HELP makes private institutions economically competitive with HECS-charging public universities for the first time. Fourth, emphasizing the virtues of mission diversity,[132] the minister foreshadowed a loosening of the boundaries of the sector to permit teaching-only universities, including private and foreign institutions. Finally, he began the creation of an Australian equivalent of the UK Research Assessment Exercise, the Research Quality Framework (RQF), to distribute research funding on the basis of research quality and impact. It is expected that these policies will be continued under Nelson's successor, Julie Bishop.

Stratification Effects

These changes will lead to the deconstruction of the standard template, based on indigenous norms, and a steeper stratification of the Australian institutions, which are now being pulled between the two Americanized global norms of selective research university (though without the philanthropic, alumni and corporate dollars that support the Ivy League) and expansionary "customer-focused" teaching provider. In the first instance, the two models are being installed in the public sector, but the private sector is also coming into play. Mission specialization is now officially valued, rather than comprehensive provision. This change provides more opportunities for private-sector than public-sector institutions; public universities positioned as teaching-only would lose status. Across both sectors, price variation has created conditions for a hierarchy of product value and for the vertical segmentation of markets and resources. The G8 universities are clear winners, able to mobilize their research rankings and student selectivity so as to draw a surplus from full-fee places. They will use part of this surplus to compete globally for academic labour, build research infrastructure and push up the Jiao Tong rankings. The G8 universities will also receive most of the RQF funding, benefiting from two mutually-reinforcing processes of stratification: an American high tuition market and a British policy-driven differentiation of research funding based on measured performance. This might allow the G8 to eschew volume-building, become more student-selective in both the global and domestic student markets and substitute some domestic fee-paying students in place of foreign. However, without more public funding it is not possible for research-intensive Australian universities other than the ANU to follow the full logic of size reduction, selectivity and research concentration. A fall in student numbers does not generate a proportional fall in infrastructure costs. The number of domestic HECS places is fixed by government, and they are underfunded. It is impossible to become a demand magnet for foreign research students without extensive scholarship funding. And part of the extra private revenues will be lost to prestige-building infrastructure, marketing, enrolment management and other costs of competition as in the US.[133]

Middle-ranking institutions will have little scope for upward mobility. With public funding in decline and minor prospects of surplus from domestic fees, they will be hard pressed to accumulate resources for building research and institutional status. It will be hard to dispense with volume-building as the source of additional revenues, but universities that try to combine research intensity with continuous expansion will tend to lose out: low student entry levels will be punished in local and global student markets; dividing scarce resources between heterogeneous strategies is a recipe for failure at both; and the Jiao Tong indicators have made research performance transparent. There is always scope for imaginative position-taking, at any level of status and resources, but universities at the bottom of the hierarchy will have a narrower range of options. Many institutions will be more dependent on global market revenues than before, but some prospective students will respond to the more overt stratification of the Australian system, in conjunction with the data from Jiao Tong, by distinguishing research universities from largely teaching institutions. If total foreign student entry levels off, then times will be tough. Some such universities may become locked into a low price bracket servicing low-quality student intakes and/or those on immigration tracks. Certain institutions may create new niche roles for themselves, at the price of a painful reduction of infrastructure and personnel.

The Nelson reforms entrench the global research indicators at the centre of system stratification and in the shaping of mission in the top half of the system. This brings Australian higher education closer to the international mainstream, modifying its distinctive reliance on business acumen, though no doubt Australian universities will still be entrepreneurial in temper and the business model more potent than ever in lower status universities repositioned outside the main research game. The remaking of the Australian system underlines the lure of the super-league and the symbolic power of credible research rankings. The government has found a quick and economical route to stronger research universities — but is its re-engineering sufficient? That is doubtful. Without ANU-style public research funding, no other Australian university is likely to enter the Jiao Tong top fifty, let alone super-league status. Additional private revenues will create more scope for position-taking. However, the concentration of research capacity, status and freedoms is achieved by reducing the status of the other institutions and locking them into volume-building. In most cases, if not all, this will create firm barriers to a qualitative lift in research capacity. Arguably, the Nelson system buys research depth at the expense of breadth. While in the context of scarcity there will always be a trade-off between research depth and breadth, a shift from public funding to market funding sharpens that trade-off, as the US shows. Australia might place more universities in the Jiao Tong top one hundred but fewer in the top five hundred. This poses questions about what spread of research universities is optimal for local and national needs and also what configuration of research universities enables optimum global positioning for Australia. Is its position in the cross-border degree market enhanced overall by the strengthening of a small number of research-intensive universities, or is it weakened overall by the narrowing of research capacity and the mixing of national "brands" in the global marketplace?

Summary: Australia's Global Position and Position-taking

Like all national systems, Australian higher education has been positioned globally by its inherited history and geography. The nation has a strong economy, though stronger in commodities and services than manufacturing, and a stable polity. Its 2004, GDP at US$605.9 billion was sixteenth in size and Gross National Income per capita at US$29,200 was in twenty-first place.[134] The higher education system is mature with above-OECD average participation rates and doctoral programs in all fields. The British inheritance is both a strength and a weakness. On one hand, the similarity between Australian universities and modern British universities has ensured the former a sound global reputation. There is some variation of opinion on how good they are, and Australian research has now been positioned in an upper middle position, below the UK, by the Jiao Tong survey. On the other hand, Aus-

tralia is a settler state located on the cultural periphery of two larger English-speaking powers, the UK and the global hegemon, the
US. Australia has always been partly dependent on the economic
and cultural resources of the UK and the US; and Australian imaginings are too readily colonized by British and American
mentalities, inhibiting the range of global position-taking strategies. Yet Australia is also geographically located at the southeastern
tip of the Asian continent, close to the emerging university systems
of three of the four most populous nations on earth: China, India
and Indonesia. Almost 10 percent of the citizens in the two largest
cities, Sydney and Melbourne, are Asian-born. This opens a broader prospect.

Australian higher education institutions have made good but not
great position-taking use of their location in Asia. In addition to
building student markets, they have become more engaged with
Southeast Asian and Chinese universities than have British, American and European institutions. The journey to a more regionally
grounded identity has a way to go. Australia's curriculum is little different from those of the US and the UK, especially in the business
and technology programs in which most foreign students are
enrolled, programs that reflect Anglo-American notions of "global
knowledge." No doubt an industry model of foreign education, in
the context of income-driven growth, scarce academic resources and
economies of scale, privileges standard products and inhibits deeper curriculum innovation and cultural encounters. But the problem
is also general to Australian society. Despite the fact that one in five
citizens is overseas-born, Australia remains a monoculture that neg-
lects the potential resources provided by its cultural and linguistic
diversity.[135] Australia has sought to differentiate itself from the US
and the UK not through the educational and cultural contents of its
programs but on the basis of cheaper price due to a depreciated Australian dollar; proximity, safety, tolerance and non-academic
services; climate and other tourist benefits; and generic claims about

excellence. Essentially, Australia has promised to supply American education but in a friendlier setting. As a position-taking strategy it is vulnerable to shifts in price and to changes in perceptions about qualities such as safety and academic standards. Climate and proximity to Asia constitute a firmer comparative advantage. But these factors are of second-order importance if foreign students believe the better product is elsewhere.

In sum, though the Australian export industry has been brilliantly successful in economic terms, its outstanding growth has been exhibited along relatively narrow lines and has yet to be consolidated in a distinctive comparative advantage based on product. Australia has specialized in high-volume, medium-quality, standard-cost degrees, in generic Anglo-American applied vocational programs rather than foundational knowledge. The UK has also adopted a commercial approach to foreign education but its public/private development is more balanced. Compared with Australia, the UK seems to be less stymied by trade-offs between research capacity and commercial development and between quantity- and quality-driven globalization. Compared with Australia, American universities sustain stronger basic disciplines. Doctoral programs in the US and the UK are more generous and more attractive.

If national identity and material resources are central to the global reputation of individual institutions, then it is unsurprising that government policy and funding play a direct part in shaping global potential. Australia's policy settings have constrained the potential position-taking strategies. Research-intensive universities such as Melbourne, Sydney, New South Wales and Queensland have been forced to exhibit a Jekyll and Hyde personality in the global environment. At home they are selective and focused on research and they engage in global benchmarking and cross-border research collaborations. But they also have another international agenda, identical to that of the thirty-two lesser Australia universities, which is to build a massive fee-paying enrolment to fill the revenue gap. Compared to academic activities, business methods provide a more limited set of position-taking options. Unfortunately it has been difficult to synergize the academic capacities of Australian universities with their business strengths. There is limited scope to bring research insights and cultures to bear on improving standardized high-volume course work programs for middle-level students. ANU is the strongest research university but a minor player in fee-based markets. Several universities with very large foreign enrolments have little research infrastructure. Most Australian research collaborations are in North America, the UK and Europe, while the fee-paying students come mostly from Asia. Australia is weak in international doctoral education where the potential nexus between global research and teaching is maximized. There are few interfaces between scholars of Asian languages and area studies and those teaching large cross-cultural classes.

What are the implications of Australian position-taking for the shaping of the global field of higher education? Australia provides a regional alternative for Asian students wanting to enter Anglo-American programs and, to the extent that supply fosters demand, it has fed cross-border movement out of Asia. Further, along with the UK, it has normed a business model of cross-border education driven by revenues and market share. This is a truly momentous development with pros and cons that will not be exhausted here. Briefly, commercial programs have a remarkable capacity to identify and respond to demand and can generate organizational innovations; for example, Australian and UK universities are active in "program and institutional mobility"[136] in the form of campuses, partnerships and distance education in importer nations. This enables a closer engagement in local systems that can expand capacity and participation rates in the importing nations, and may lead to bilingual and hybrid curricula and other initiatives. Further, in the commercial model, quality assurance should be able to protect students against bad provision, though it has yet to be applied consistently to offshore programs. The other side of the coin is that when education is produced as a commodity, autonomous professional input is reduced; there is less scope for adapting programs to different sites; harder contents are emptied out;[137] and competition generates costly functions decoupled from product improvement. Commercial provision also stratifies educational opportunities in importing nations.[138]

How does global stratification affect the hierarchy in Australia and vice versa? As noted, the Jiao Tong rankings have catalyzed desires for an Australian presence in the super-league, strengthened research as the differentiating element in Australia and robbed Australian universities of some authority at home and abroad. The exception is the ANU. Long given lesser status in Australia than Melbourne or Sydney because of its regional location in Canberra and its minor role in competition for school leavers, its academic reputation as leading research university is now a public fact. This brings its national standing into line with its global standing. The global implications of Australian stratification are harder to read. While a mid-status American doctoral university can readily accumulate global power, sharks in Australia are merely salmon abroad, regardless of the recent policy changes in Australia. Some G8 universities may be en route to a more elevated future, but at this stage there is not enough in the Nelson reforms to decisively change the global weight of research in any one Australian university or over all. The open declaration of teaching-only institutions, and heterogeneity of mission and status, will not change the fact that reputation is nationally rather than institutionally defined, but it will stratify demand within that national reputation and will probably affect Australia's standing vis-à-vis other nations. Because all Australian universities apart from ANU engage in high-volume commercial programs and only some are intensive research institutions, there is a clear and present danger that, in the longer run,

Australian universities will become differentiated from other nations, especially the US and the UK, not on the basis of Australia's research or its strategically advantageous geo-cultural location in Asia, but on the basis of a distinctive commercial orientation to high-volume, middle-level degree programs.

Universities are rarely credited for good teaching on a comparative basis, and in building a positive global reputation it is research outcomes that count. For Australia, the worst-case scenario is that it becomes locked into the role of global polytechnic by its fiscal settings and business culture, its position-taking strategy becomes a downward spiral, its strong quantity position in the cross-border market is eroded, and the material resource base of Australian higher education is further eroded with it. The way out for Australia is public reinvestment at scale and especially in research infrastructure. This would broaden its range of options at the global level. Australia's policy-makers want Australian universities to be globally competitive: whether they want them to be globally competitive across the full range of functions (coursework teaching, doctoral education, research) remains to be seen.

2

The Internationalization of Higher Education: Study-related Policies and Trends in Germany

Ulrich Teichler, University of Kassel

Introduction

Higher education all over the world is shaped by the universal character of knowledge in many areas, by international links and by national settings, as far as the structures of institutions and curricula, the study program and degrees, the regulatory system, the careers of academic staff and the conditions for study are concerned. But national systems handle their relationships to other parts of the world in quite different ways. In a study of the academic profession undertaken in the early 1990s, we argued that, for the higher education systems of small economically advanced countries, it is almost a matter of life and death to be deeply embedded internationally. In contrast, we called the dominant approach in the United States and the United Kingdom an "internationalization by import" approach: one tends to be interested in inward mobility of foreign students and in the academic knowledge deriving from other parts of the world, if the scholars from other parts of the world carry this information to the US and the UK. In between these models, we positioned countries such as France, Germany and Japan as "two-arena countries" in which scholars are free to opt for a dominant national or international role.[1] Many factors come into play other than differences in the quality of teaching and research in the respective countries, such as the international spread of knowledge about the home country and the readiness to learn other languages, the size of the country, the regional neighbourhood and the international politics of the country, among them prominently the tuition fee policies regarding internationally mobile students.

Germany is traditionally a country with internationally minded universities — one which has returned, after the exceptional situation of the Nazi regime — to being quite open to international relationships in higher education. The proportions of both foreign students and German students studying abroad are among the highest of the large, economically advanced countries. International staff mobility and international cooperation among scholars are also sizeable.

In recent years, we have observed two waves of increasing internationalization of higher education. First, there was the establishment of the ERASMUS program in 1987 to promote temporary student mobility within Europe in an environment of increasing organizational and curricular cooperation; this had the effect of moving international cooperation from a marginal position towards the centre of attention in higher education institutions. Thereafter, not only did study abroad become one normal option for students but also each general policy option was examined in terms of how it affects international links and each international higher education option was examined in terms of how it affects all the core activities.[2] Second, since about the mid-1990s, international policies have been mainstreamed further. On the one hand, study programs and degrees as well as research policies are increasingly being developed in cooperation with other

European countries, in order to promote convergent systems and close cooperation. On the other hand, the increasing use of the term *globalization*[3] has become linked to the notion that German universities should become more similar to universities in the US and in the UK in terms of underscoring competitive elements in the relationships to other institutions, strengthening the power of the management and stratifying the higher education system in order to be "fit" for global competition.

The aim of this chapter is to shed some light on recent developments in the internationalization of higher education in Germany. Emphasis will be placed on study-related policies and actual developments as well as on mobility and cooperation as the still-dominant elements of explicitly international policies and activities. Research-related policies and joint European policies, as well as changes to the regulatory system and funding in the name of globalization, will be referred to only briefly.

The German Policy Setting

Most institutions of higher education in Germany are publicly funded, and higher education is supervised by the sixteen *Länder* (states) of the country. Most national coordination of higher education takes place through joint activities by the *Länder*. They cooperate within the framework of the Permanent Conference of the Ministers of Education of the *Länder* of the Federal Republic of Germany, called the KMK. With regard to higher education, the KMK coordinates modes of handling admission and of curricula (including the coordination of the accreditation system established in 1998). However, national coordination powers are stronger in Germany than, for example, in the federal systems of the United States and of Canada. In Germany, the national government (called the federal government) cooperates with the *Länder* in establishing framework legislation on higher education, undertaking mid-term planning, and partially funding both programs and capital projects:

construction in higher education; public research institutes outside higher education and research promotion schemes for higher education; a public need-based scholarship system for students; a system for student services (dining halls, dormitories, etc.).

Finally, the national government is solely in charge of international higher education policy. This includes coordination and support of activities of exchange and cooperation across borders. In contrast, international offices of higher education institutions or internationally oriented study programs are an integral part of the funding und supervisory arrangements of the *Länder*. Cooperation with international and European organizations is coordinated by the federal government, but the *Länder* participate.

Funds for international student and academic staff mobility are in part provided by the Ministry of Foreign Affairs, which is in charge of international cultural cooperation and exchange, in part by the Ministry of Education and Research and finally in part by the Ministry of Economic Cooperation, which is in charge of support for developing countries.

In Germany, intermediary bodies play a strong role. The Hochschulrektorenkonferenz (HRK), i.e., the conference of rectors of higher education institutions, recommends joint policies for higher education institutions. The Deutsche Akademischer Austauschdienst (DAAD), called the German Academic Exchange Service in English, is funded by the three above-named national ministries. Some of its funds are closely earmarked for the specific purposes of exchange and cooperation, but it is owned and supervised by the German higher education institutions. They vote for the members of the board and thereby determine the policy of the DAAD which, as noted above, is the German institution in charge of financial support for student mobility and, to some extent as well, for academic staff mobility and other cooperation activities. There are other public agencies in Germany primarily in charge of academic staff mobility, particularly as related to research activities.

Some of these other agencies as well as some other foundations also fund the mobility of doctoral candidates.

Past Internationalization Policies

For a long time, Germany has been a country open to international cooperation and mobility. The DAAD, established more than eighty years ago, often points out that more than half of the mobile students prior to World War I went to Germany. After World War II, again, strong efforts were made by the Federal Republic of Germany for international cooperation and mobility, although conditions had dramatically changed. Germany was no longer viewed as the leading country of research, English had become the lingua franca of international communication in higher education, and political concerns had a strong impact on the flow of students between countries.

As in other countries, policy documents expressed a mix of educational, cultural, socio-political and economic rationales for promoting international cooperation and mobility in higher education. The Federal Republic of Germany was actively involved in many international activities relevant to student mobility; for example, in treaties and conventions for the recognition of study in other countries (bilateral treaties with single other countries or multilateral conventions coordinated by UNESCO and the Council of Europe). For many years, the Federal Republic of Germany provided more money for mobility scholarships for students and doctoral candidates both from Germany and abroad than many other leading economically advanced countries. The German governments provided the institutions of higher education as much funding per individual foreign student as they provided for German students. Thus, foreign students could study in Germany and pay no, or at most nominal, tuition fees. In other words, unlike the numerous foreign students in some other countries, those in Germany faced no financial discrimination compared with students holding citizenship there.

It would be fair, however, to state that international cooperation and exchange was not a priority area in public debates on higher education and in higher education policies in Germany until the 1990s. Also, Germany was not a front-running country in the framework of supranational organizations with regard to international higher education policies.

Available statistics show that, since the 1960s, Germany has been:

- among the top five countries in terms of absolute numbers of foreign students (higher numbers only in the US, the UK and, for some years, the Soviet Union and France);
- in second or third place among the large economically advanced countries in the proportion of foreign among all students (lower than the UK, for some years lower than France and recently than Australia, but substantially higher than the US and Japan);
- leading among the large economically advanced countries in the ratio of study-abroad students to students enrolled at home.

Also, we notice more or less continuous increases. For example, the ratio of foreign students to total students in the Federal Republic of Germany increased from about 5 percent in 1970 to about 10 percent soon after 2000. Similarly, the proportion of students from countries all over the world studying abroad who actually studied in Germany has increased from about 5 percent to more than 10 percent during the same period.

These statistics, however, were not received in Germany with satisfaction or pride.[4] On the contrary, there was constant criticism. For example, it was often pointed out that mobility from other European countries was as high as these statistics suggest because a substantial proportion of foreign students were children of foreign "guest workers" and had earned their secondary education credentials in Germany. That there was a high concentration of students from just a few countries outside Europe (changing over time; for example, from Turkey, Indonesia, Korea, Iran) rather than from a wide variety of countries was viewed with mixed feelings. Some observers questioned whether German higher education succeeded in attracting the best foreign students. The declining role of the German language internationally was often deplored as a hindrance to attracting good foreign students. Finally, the fact that large numbers of doctoral candidates and young postdoctoral scholars from science and engineering went to the US for doctoral study, short-term postdoctoral work or long-term employment was often deplored as "brain drain." Correspondingly, study in Germany by students from developing countries was often criticized as not sufficiently contributing to the development of these countries, because a substantial number of these persons did not want to return to their country of origin.

Recent Debates and Policies

Around 1990, student mobility became a popular issue in Germany and many other European countries. The predecessor organization of the European Union (EU), having gotten involved in higher education policy in the mid-1970s and having introduced a pilot program for student mobility in 1976, established the large-scale student mobility program ERASMUS in 1987. In recent years, the European Commission has provided funds for more than 100,000 students annually to spend a temporary study period in another European country. The program, which in 1995 became a sub-program of the large educational program SOCRATES, is very popular, even though the supplementary funds are not sufficient to cover all the additional costs of studying for one semester or one academic year in another European country and even though the administrative burden is often criticized by universities.[5] ERASMUS made temporary study abroad a normal option for all students, and many experts argue that the Bologna Process would not have been possible without the pre-existing success story of ERASMUS. The German government and other European countries supported these European cooperation and exchange activities, but somewhat cautiously, because some activities, such as the promotion of a European credit system, were viewed as interfering with the rights of the individual countries to preserve the characteristics of their higher education in the process of growing European cooperation.

Germany has become a front-runner in stimulating new internationalization activities in Europe since about 1995. At that time, concern grew in Germany and various other European countries that one might fall further behind English-speaking countries in being an attractive destination for student mobility and higher education cooperation — notably with regard to students and universities from economically emerging countries in Asia.[6]

In 1996, the German ministries for foreign affairs and for education and science, research and technology called jointly for action to strengthen the attractiveness and competitiveness of the "German site for higher education and science." The German Academic Exchange, with the support of the national government, launched major action schemes for internationalization in 1996, 2000 and 2004.[7]

In the 1996 action scheme, the main targets were:

- the development of attractive study programs for foreign students;
- the improvement of academic recognition for mobile students;
- the improvement of procedures regarding admission and entry and also regarding residence and work permits for foreign students and scholars;
- the enhancement of conditions regarding the learn-

ing, teaching and examinations of the German and
English languages;
- the development of an international marketing
  strategy for German higher education.

In the 2000 action scheme of the DAAD, various activities were
added. Notably, the international marketing of German universities
was to be strengthened, and efforts were advocated to create more
hospitable and service-oriented conditions and provisions for foreign students and scholars at German institutions of higher
education.

In the 2004 DAAD action scheme,[8] four major policy areas "on
the way towards an international higher education institution" were
specified:

- to provide internationally attractive study and research
  opportunities in Germany (more international study
  programs, more doctoral students in Germany, extension of German study programs in other countries,
  extension of cooperation in specific fields with developing countries and newly emerging economies);
- to qualify German students and junior academics
  internationally (making temporary study abroad a regular activity), internationalization of curricula,
  extension of fellowships and other support (countermeasures to brain-drain);
- to establish professional structures and efficient framework conditions (quality-oriented admission, fostering
  a service culture, professionalization of the international management, modernizing immigration
  legislation);
- to overcome the language barrier (German as a foreign
  language, foreign languages for Germans).

It might be added here that European study-related activities are viewed in the DAAD action programs as part of international activities. This corresponds to the prevailing view at German institutions of higher education that study in other European countries is study abroad, albeit certainly less contrasting than study, for example, in Africa.

Beginning in 1996, various key actors in German higher education began to advocate the introduction of a staged system of study programs and degrees. The introduction of three-year bachelor programs and two-year master programs was viewed as the most desirable solution, i.e., a solution somewhat between the dominant models in England and the United States. Germany was among the four countries signing the 1998 Sorbonne Declaration advocating such a new system of study programs and a substantial extension of temporary study abroad in Europe so that finally European students spent some amount of time studying in another European country. By the summer of 1998, the Framework Act for Higher Education had been revised — on the initiative of the federal government, by the national parliament and representatives of the German *Länder* — in order to provide individual universities and faculties the opportunity to introduce new bachelor and master programs. The new staged system of study programs and degrees was to be established either beside or instead of the old long initial study programs at universities which led to a master's-level degree and the old initial study programs at universities of applied sciences (*Fachhochschulen*) which led to a level between a bachelor and a master. Thus, the implementation of this reform was already underway when the Bologna Declaration was signed in 1999 by a large number of European countries agreeing to establish a convergent structure of study programs and degrees, notably with the aims of increasing the worldwide attractiveness of higher education in Europe and of facilitating intra-European student mobility.[9]

Since the late 1990s, internationalization in German higher education has tended to focus on three activities that are only partly interrelated:

- trends and policies towards the *increase of mobility* of students and scholars and cooperation among scholars and institutions of higher education and research;
- *common activities in Europe*, notably towards establishing a converging system of study programs and degrees (the "Bologna Process") and towards strengthening the funding and the overall role of research in Europe (the "Lisbon Process");
- efforts to *change the steering, management and funding system of higher education to make German universities more competitive globally.*

The latter two activities certainly aim primarily to change the character of the national system of higher education, but they are expected as well both to facilitate and improve international cooperation and mobility and to increase the worldwide attractiveness of German higher education.

Internationalization Measures Supported and Advocated

The best available document on measures supported and advocated for the study-related internationalization of German higher education is the 2004 Action Program of the German Academic Exchange Service.[10] The measures suggested have been agreed upon by the sponsoring national ministries as well as by the German universities that are members of the DAAD. The action program aims to show both the status quo and intended activities up to about 2010:

1. *International study programs*: A new program was envisaged to provide funds for institutions of higher education

aiming to develop new internationally oriented study programs and study units. Altogether, the internationally oriented study programs (about three hundred at that time) ought to be at least doubled by 2010. Efforts should be made to ensure international recognition of the newly-established bachelor and master programs in Germany.[11]

2. *Doctoral awards at German universities*: According to the DAAD, the proportion of 7 percent foreigners among all doctoral award recipients in Germany is substantially lower than in France, the United Kingdom and the United States. Among various measures, for example, to provide fellowships or employment for foreign doctoral candidates at German universities and research institutes, the DAAD names a support scheme for the establishment of internationally oriented graduate schools or other organized doctoral programs for the period 2001-06.

3. *German study programs abroad*: The federal Ministry of Education and Research has provided the DAAD funds since 2001 for the export study programs of German institutions of higher education. Seed money as well as advice is provided to establish study programs abroad, often in conjunction with foreign institutions of higher education; for example, in Turkey, Bulgaria, Egypt and China. The 2004 action program sets as a target that altogether about seventy-five of these programs should exist by 2010, reaching at least 15,000 students.[12]

4. *Extension of cooperation with developing countries and newly emerging economies*: Among the broad range of activities in this area, the DAAD points out that training of experts and leaders in disciplinary areas as well as in higher education

management will be continued. In the framework of DIES
programs (Dialogue on Innovative Higher Education
Strategies), the DAAD and the Rectors Conference stimulate cooperation between individual foreign and German
university consortia to improve higher education management in the countries participating.

5. *Study period abroad as a regular feature*: The trend of a
   growing number of German students spending a period of
   study abroad should be encouraged further (the proportion of German students studying for at least one semester
   at a foreign institution of higher education increased from
   13 percent in 2000 to 15 percent in 2003; the proportion
   of those undertaking study-related activities abroad in
   general was 30 percent in 2003). The goal that by 2010 at
   least half of all German students should have spent a
   study-related period abroad should be helped by current
   promotion campaigns and improved information.

6. *Internationalization of curricula*: Efforts are encouraged to
   develop and improve curricula, notably within the process
   of establishing new bachelor and master programs,
   through an international emphasis in the substance of
   study programs and through optional or even mandatory
   study periods abroad.

7. *Extension of fellowships and other means of support*: Currently, ERASMUS fellowships as well as the need-based
   scholarships system for German students (BAFöG), which
   may be used for study periods in other countries, are the
   major funding sources for student mobility. The DAAD
   2004 action program suggests that more financial support
   should be provided for foreign students going to Germany

in the framework of joint study programs. The action program also suggests that the achievements of students using BAFöG abroad should be monitored similarly to those of students awarded other types of fellowships.

8. *Countermeasures to brain drain*: In order to ensure that not too many young academics (going notably to the US for doctoral study or subsequent research) leave Germany permanently, the DAAD and various German research bodies established GAIN (German Academic International Network) to foster contacts with young German scholars abroad. A mentoring program should be added in the future in order to facilitate their return.

9. *Quality-based admission*: Most universities examine foreign applicants' files in order to assess whether the applicants' qualifications are similar to those of German secondary school leavers. A national agency helps to assess the quality of secondary and higher education institutions in other countries. As a rule, foreign students are entitled to enrol according to the same standards as German students. *Studienkollegs* exist, providing one-year courses for foreign applicants who do not have thirteen years of prior education. The DAAD promotes a service system, *ASSIST*, shared by fifty German higher education institutions, in order to streamline the admission process. The DAAD suggests that individual universities should be free to establish individual ceilings for the number of foreign students they accept and should be free to establish, individually or in cooperation with other institutions, selection processes in order to increase the quality of foreign students.

10. *Fostering a service culture*: Select surveys suggest the suc-

cess rate of foreign students is only half as high as that of German students. By 2010, this ratio should be increased to at least 70 percent. Various efforts for improving services for foreign students should be undertaken, and institutions of higher education are encouraged to undertake longitudinal studies of foreign students in order to monitor their success.

11. *Professionalization of international management*: The DAAD aims to extend its training programs for staff of international offices and its funds for the enhancement of international offices at individual institutions of higher education (the so-called *PROFIS* program).

12. *Modernizing immigration legislation*: Efforts should be undertaken to find the best possible options for foreign students and scholars in the framework of new immigration legislation,[13] in order to ensure that hospitality towards foreign students and scholars is not lesser than in other countries competing for mobile students.

13. *German as a foreign language*: The action program calls for the extension of on-line study programs of the German language (in cooperation with the Goethe Institutes) and of German courses that foreign students might take along with their studies. The DAAD will reduce its funding for the established proficiency test, TestDaF, of the German language but will contribute funds for future improvements.

14. *Foreign languages for Germans*: The action program endorses the general policy that all German students and scholars should be versed in English and one other

foreign language. It advocates the extension of foreign language courses at individual higher education institutions and intends to provide higher education institutions with funds for the establishment of study units or programs and related written materials in English.

15. *Improving marketing for the most talented heads*: The proportion of foreign mobile students should increase further, and efforts should be made to attract and admit the most talented ones. The action program puts more emphasis on targeting certain countries (e.g., China, Brazil and Turkey). The DAAD supports a network of about fifty German institutions of higher education cooperating in marketing their study programs and research activities. It aims to encourage improved information as well as to counteract dubious methods of advertisement and the lowering of quality in order to attract more foreign students and scholars.

Conditions for Study in Germany

In Germany, foreign citizens from other EU countries, foreign students passing successfully through the German secondary school system, and family members of those employed in Germany are treated like Germans in the admission process. They can simply enrol in study programs open for all qualified applicants, or they have to undergo the typical admissions procedures as Germans, the so-called Numerus-clausus programs.

All other foreign students have to apply to the higher education institution of their choice a few months before the intended date of enrolment. The higher education institutions might select students according to the quality of the institution they come from, their German language proficiency or other achievement-oriented criteria. Only in a very few cases is access more restricted for foreign students than for German students.

Students admitted to German higher education institutions are entitled to receive a residence permit for the period of study. Students from EU countries, the US, Canada, Japan and a few other countries can obtain this during the first months of their study in Germany, whereas students from many other countries have to obtain a visa in advance. The procedures of German authorities both abroad and at home used to be criticized as lengthy and customer-unfriendly. Substantial improvements have been reported in recent years. Foreign students with a residence permit are entitled to work for income for a limited number of hours.

Until recently, residence permits ended at the time of study, and there was much complication and uncertainty around whether one could get a work permit. Under new legislation starting from February 2005, graduates can stay for a further year in Germany and seek employment.

As reported below, almost 10 percent of foreign students in Germany received German grants, almost the same proportion received financial support from their home country, and half as many (5 percent) received support from the European Union or other supranational agencies.

As noted earlier, foreign students are not treated differently from German students as far as tuition fees are concerned. Most German students do not pay any tuition fees in public universities, only fees for medical insurance and for the student union. Deutsches Studentenwerk, the agency in charge of scholarships, accommodation, dining halls, etc., offers a special service package for foreign students for about five hundred Euro. In some German *Länder*, students extending their period of study have to pay moderate fees, and students in continuing professional education have to pay substantial fees. Some German *Länder* are planning to introduce tuition fees of about 500 to 1,000 Euro per semester, but again, there are no differences intended for German and foreign students.

Table 1 Foreign Students in Germany and German Students Enrolled Abroad 2002/2003

All Students	All foreign students	% of foreign among all students	% of females among foreign students
2 242 397	240 619	10.7	49.3

Foreign students	ISCED levels	
	5A	**5B**
Absolute	226 931	13 688
%	94.3	5.7

Countries of nationality of foreign students			
Rank	Country	Absolute	%
1	Turkey	27 253	11.3
2	China (incl. HK)	20 141	8.4
3	Poland	13 629	5.7
4	Russian Federation	10 185	4.2
5	Bulgaria	9 960	4.1
6	Italy	8 003	3.3
7	Greece	7 798	3.2
8	Morocco	7 616	3.2
9	Austria	6 880	2.9
10	France	6 499	2.7
Top ten countries		**117 964**	**49.0**

Fields of study of foreign students			
Rank	Field of study	Absolute	%
1	Social & behavioural sciences, business & law	64 365	26.7
2	Humanities & arts	52 716	21.9
3	Engineering, manufacturing & construction	41 318	17.2
4	Science	37 783	15.7
5	Health & social services	14 372	6.0
6	Educational sciences	10 591	4.4
7	Agriculture	2 718	1.1
8	Services	2 585	1.1
9	Unknown or not specified	14 171	5.9
Total		**240 619**	**100.0**

Resident German students	German students enrolled abroad	Ratio of students enrolled abroad to resident German students	% of females among students enrolled abroad
2 001 778	62 821	0.031	no data

Rank	Country	Countries of study abroad of national students	
		Absolute	%
1	United Kingdom	13 149	20.9
2	United States	9 302	14.8
3	France	6 908	11.0
4	Switzerland	6 843	10.9
5	Austria	5 657	9.0
6	The Netherlands	5 252	8.4
7	Spain	5 154	8.2
8	Sweden	2 416	3.8
9	Australia	2 049	3.3
10	Italy	1 189	1.9
Top ten countries		**57 915**	**92.2**

Source: M. Kelo, U. Teichler & B. Wächter, EURODATA: Student Mobility in European Higher Education (Bonn: Lemmens, 2006), 28 (based on EUROSTAT and UNESCO statistics).

Foreign and Inward Mobile Students

According to statistics jointly collected by UNESCO, the Organisation for Economic Co-operation and Development (OECD) and EuroStat (UOE), the number of foreign students in Germany in 2003 (actual academic year 2002-03) was 240,619 (see Table 1). This was 10.7 percent of all tertiary education students in Germany. Of these, 225,931 (94.3 percent) were at the ISCED Va level (i.e., enrolled in bachelor and master-equivalent programs) and 13,688 (5.7 percent) were at the ISCED Vb level (tertiary education below the master). No complete statistics were available on foreign doctoral candidates.

According to German statistics, the number of foreign students at German higher education institutions (not including the ISCED Vb level) increased from 165,994 in 1998-99 to 246,136 in 2003-04.

Thus, the ratio of foreign students at German higher education institutions increased during that period from 9.2 percent to 12.2 percent in 2003-04.[14] It should be noted that the ratio presented in the German statistics is slightly higher than in UOE statistics, in particular because the German statistics do not include foreign and German students in other tertiary education below a bachelor level (i.e., ISCED Vb students).

The highest foreign student numbers in Germany in 2002-03, according to UOE statistics, came from Turkey, China and Poland. Many foreign students came as well from Russia, Bulgaria, Italy, Greece, Morocco, Austria and France. Altogether, about 60 percent of foreign students had the citizenship of other European countries.

According to a re-analysis of available data on nationality and mobility:[15]

- 163,178 of the foreign students on ISCED Va level can be viewed as mobile foreign students (see Table 2). These are called "*Bildungsausländer*" in the German statistics, i.e., foreigners with entry qualifications (as a

Table 2 Foreign Students ("*Bildungsausländer*") at German Institutions of Higher Education 2002/2003

Overview			
Total students	Number of Foreign Students		Number of female foreign students
	Absolute	**% of total**	**Absolute**	**% of foreign students**

Total students	Absolute	% of total	Absolute	% of foreign students
2 242 397	163 213	8.4	82 236	50.4

ISCED Levels

5A and 6		5B	
Absolute	% of female inwards mobile	Absolute	% of female inwards mobile
163 178	100.0	35	0.0

Most frequent countries of domicile

Rank	Country	Absolute	% of inwards mobile Students
1	China	19 374	11.9
2	Poland	10 284	6.3
3	Bulgaria	9 499	5.8
4	Russian Federation	8 113	5.0
5	Morocco	6 159	3.8
6	Turkey	5 728	3.5
7	France	5 495	3.4
8	Ukraine	4 975	3.0
9	Cameroon	4 709	2.9
10	Austria	4 231	2.6
Top 10 Countries		**78 567**	**48.1**

Fields of study

Rank	Field of Study	Absolute	% of inwards mobile Students
1	Law, economics/business administration, social sciences	42 099	25.8
2	Languages and cultural studies	41 887	25.7
3	Engineering	31 251	19.1
4	Mathematics, natural sciences	28 807	17.6
5	Art, art theory	7 787	4.8
6	Human medicine	6 622	4.1
7	Agricultural, forestry and nutritional sciences	2 928	1.8
8	Sport	977	0.6
9	Veterinary medicine	379	0.2
10	Others	476	0.3

Source: M. Kelo, U. Teichler & B. Wächter, EURODATA: Student Mobility in European Higher Education (Bonn: Lemmens, 2006), 119 (based on EUROSTAT and UNESCO statistics).

rule successful completion of secondary education) awarded abroad.

- 63,753 of the foreign students on ISCED Va level can be viewed as non-mobile foreign students (about 28 percent of all foreign students). These are called "*Bildungsinländer*" in the German statistics.

- In addition, there were 27,604 mobile German students, i.e., students with German citizenship who acquired their entry qualification abroad. This includes returners as well as persons who acquired their German citizenship after leaving secondary education.

- Less than 60 percent of the foreign and the mobile students in Germany are enrolled in fields of humanities and social sciences. More than 40 percent are enrolled in science and engineering fields. This corresponds by and large to the distribution of German students across fields of study.

Altogether, the number of foreign students in Germany is relatively equally distributed according to the academic reputation of the university. At most universities, the number of foreign mobile students ranges between 5 and 15 percent.

The relationship between student and doctoral fellowships awarded by the DAAD in 2000-01 and academic reputation of the university, measured by research grants awarded by the Deutsche Forschungsgemeinschaft, was analyzed in a study published by the Deutsche Forschungsgemeinschaft in 2003.[16] Accordingly, 10.6 student and doctoral grants per 100 academic staff were awarded to those enrolled at the top 20 universities, 9.6 grants to universities in ranks 21 to 40, 9.5 grants to universities in ranks 41 to 60, and 10.1 grants to universities in ranks 61 to 78.

These data suggest that the grant-awarding policy and the quality of foreign students and doctoral candidates does not differ substantially according to the academic reputation of German universities. One has to bear in mind that the hierarchy of German universities according to academic criteria is very flat in comparison with other large, economically advanced countries.

Study Abroad and Outward Mobility

In the same period, 57,915 students with German citizenship were enrolled abroad according to UOE statistics. This corresponds to 3.1 percent of German students enrolled in Germany. Among the large, economically advanced countries, a similar proportion of French students and a slightly lower proportion of Japanese students are enrolled abroad, while the proportion is less than half for British students and even substantially lower for US students.[17]

The countries most frequently chosen were the United Kingdom, the United States, France, Switzerland, Austria, the Netherlands and Spain. Other frequently chosen countries were Sweden, Australia and Italy. About 80 percent were enrolled in other European countries.

Only about one-third of German students studying abroad are enrolled in science and engineering fields. This proportion is clearly smaller than among German students studying at home and than among foreign students studying in Germany.

German higher education institutions register temporarily mobile (for example, ERASMUS) students from other countries as foreign students. In many other countries, however, temporarily mobile students are not registered in the general statistics. Therefore, the UOE statistics do not provide any complete picture of German students studying abroad. For example, we do not know what proportion of the 18,482 German ERASMUS students in 2002-03[18] are included in the UOE statistics.

The majority of German students study abroad for a temporary period rather than for a total degree program. A representative survey undertaken in 2003 of German students in advanced years of study and enrolled at German institutions of higher education showed that 30 percent of them had spent a study-related period abroad during their course of study. Actually, 15 percent had completed temporary study abroad and another 15 percent a practical training, internship or work placement. Six percent took language courses and 6 percent reported other activities abroad.

Views and Situation of Mobile Students According to Surveys

In Germany, every three years a large-scale survey is undertaken on the living and study situation of students. In 2003, emphasis was placed on achieving a high return rate by foreign students. In the end, more than 2,000 students (22 percent response rate) provided information. Some major responses of the survey include the following:

- Of the foreign respondents, 84 percent aimed for a German degree, 5 percent for a joint degree and 11 percent for a degree abroad.
- Foreign students were spending on average slightly more than thirty hours per week on study as compared to about 34 hours on the part of the German students.
- 23 percent of foreign students in Germany were studying on a full or partial scholarship (in comparison to 19 percent of the foreign students surveyed in 2000). This proportion — with 16 percent — was lowest for students from developing countries as compared to 22 percent for students from countries in transition and 41 percent for students from industrialized countries.
- Of the students receiving financial assistance, 35 percent received it from their home country, 40 percent from Germany, 13 percent from European sources, 3 percent from other international organizations and 9 percent from other sources.

- Among the educational motives for studying in Germany, good study conditions, gaining specialized knowledge and improving German language proficiency were most frequently named. Among other considerations, four stand out: "Studying in Germany improves career chances," "I want to meet the challenge of a foreign culture," "Germany is a technologically advanced country," and "No tuition [is] charged in Germany."
- Difficulties most frequently named were funding, contacts with German students (38 percent each), finding one's way around the study system (34 percent) and finding accommodation (33 percent).
- When the 2000 data are compared with the figures from 2003, the most striking areas in which difficulties declined were in getting work permits (from 43 percent to 29 percent) and in getting visa residence permits (from 37 percent to 27 percent).

It might be added that, of German students who had studied abroad for some time, 36 percent had received a European scholarship, 22 percent used the German need-based scholarship system and 18 percent received another German scholarship.[19] Also of note is the fact that 26 percent of the German students temporarily mobile were abroad in the framework of ERASMUS, 21 percent in the framework of other programs and 53 percent outside of any program.[20]

Other Study-related Activities of Cooperation and Mobility

Partnerships

The total number of formalized international cooperation agreements of German higher education institutions was about 1,400 in

1989, or less than 10 on average per institution of higher education. The figure was low because international cooperation and mobility were largely viewed at that time as initiatives by individual scholars and students or, at most, faculties which did not need any university-wide contractual support.

By 2003, the number of formal international cooperation agreements between German and foreign institutions of higher education had reached 15,368.[21] The number had increased more than tenfold in fourteen years, a period in which the number of mobile students had slightly more than doubled. The increase in the number of agreements is due partly to the fact that, since 1997, the European Commission has required the individual institutions of higher education to have a formal partnership with all institutions to which they send and from which they receive ERASMUS-supported students. Moreover, many German institutions of higher education agree more easily nowadays to embark on a formal partnership if a foreign institution requests it for either symbolic or practical reasons, even if such a partnership affects only a few people and units. Finally, as a consequence of managerial changes, German institutions of higher education are more inclined to emphasize the central level of the institution, even if the activities are highly decentralized.

International Study Programs

Various programs designed to meet the needs of foreign students have existed for a long period: for example, agricultural programs focusing on agriculture in developing countries or joint study programs with other European countries, notably those in the ERASMUS framework. Government support has been made available for joint German-French programs at German higher education institutions close to the French border and for German-Polish programs at the European University Viadrina in Frankfurt/Oder close to the Polish border. Other examples could also be mentioned.

In recent years, with the growing institutionalization of specific doctoral programs instead of the traditional individual supervision of doctoral candidates, and with the introduction of bachelor and master programs, the number of study programs specifically addressing mobile students has increased substantially. The German Academic Exchange Service published the brochure, "International Degree Programmes in Germany 2005/06" with funding from the Ministry of Foreign Affairs in order to provide an overview for foreign students: "The 400 or so courses presented in this catalogue are designed to attract foreign students and Germans looking to study with an international dimension."[22] The catalogue shows that many of these programs (somewhat more than 2 percent of all study programs at German institutions of higher education) are master programs and that in about half of them each, the language of instruction is either English or both German and English (some programs are in other languages as well). It is interesting to note that a substantial number of the German universities offering half a dozen or more international programs are neither conceived to be the most famous universities in terms of academic reputation nor specialized in international programs. Rather, the brochure suggests that many German institutions of higher education, depending on size and profile, offer about five to fifteen programs with an international emphasis.

A substantial number of new bachelor and master programs offer a few courses in English or, in some cases, in other languages in order to make temporary study for mobile students more attractive and in order to improve the international learning opportunities for German students. According to a survey undertaken in 2002, the study programs taught in English comprised about 3 percent of all study programs in Germany. This was a clearly smaller ratio than in the Netherlands (more than 10 percent), Belgium and the Nordic countries in Europe, similar to the ratio in Switzerland and clearly higher than in France and Southern European countries.[23]

Another survey of the newly established bachelor and master programs, however, suggests that the use of English might spread much more quickly in the near future: 2 percent of the new bachelor programs and 21 percent of the new master programs are taught in English.[24]

Offices, Transnational Education and Partner Institutions Abroad

The number of individual German universities establishing liaison offices abroad is marginal. Similarly, few German universities individually go to college fairs to recruit students. Rather, the German Academic Exchange Service (DAAD), a membership organization of the German institutions of higher education, as noted earlier, has increased its international presence in offices, fairs and other joint marketing activities substantially.[25]

Before 1990, the DAAD had offices abroad in the United States, the United Kingdom, France, Japan, Egypt, India, Brazil and Kenya. Since 1990, the DAAD has also established offices in Indonesia (1990), Russia (1993), China (1994), Poland (1997), Mexico (2000) and Vietnam (2003). In addition, the DAAD has forty-five information centres all over the world.

The German distance university, Fernuniversität Hagen, offers study programs in the German language. Study centres for students of the Fernuniversität Hagen exist not only in the German-speaking countries Austria and Switzerland but also in various Central and Eastern European countries.

In 2000, the German federal government provided the DAAD with funds to launch a program to foster German higher education export activities under the name, Future Initiative for Higher Education. Under this initiative, twenty-nine export activities were sponsored, e.g. summer schools abroad, off-shore campuses or centres, study modules and entire study programs, primarily in Asia,

Eastern Europe and Latin America. This program has provided seed money for the establishment of the German University in Cairo and the German Institute of Science and Technology (GIST) in Singapore. As has already been pointed out, the 2004 DAAD action program called for the realization of about twenty-five transnational programs by 2010, with a participation of at least 15,000 students.

For a long time, several US universities have maintained study centres in Germany to provide their own students with a study period abroad, for summer schools, etc. As a rule, they offer only short study terms. In recent years, one private English-speaking university has been established in Germany in cooperation with a US university: the International University Bremen, cooperating with Rice University.

Altogether, it is obvious that German institutions are highly interested in international cooperation and in supporting mobility. Also, many German students are interested in mobility. But as higher education is understood to be primarily in the public interest, it is predominantly publicly funded, and therefore foreign institutions of higher education have little interest in establishing universities or branch campuses in Germany. Similarly, German institutions of higher education are not moving to establish branch campuses or full universities in other countries. If no or low tuition fees were charged, the German universities would need resources to ensure the quality of teaching and research serving German and foreign students and scholars in Germany, and high cost-covering fees charged abroad would contradict the fundamental financial principles at home.

Internationalization Policies Beyond Students, Staff and Curricula

Internationalization policies in German higher education have not been confined to students, staff and curricula. On the contrary, we have noted in Germany — as in many other countries — inflationary use of the terms *internationalization* and *globalization* as well as, to a certain extent, *Europeanization*. Three areas might be named as the most visible ones.

First, all changes to the regulatory system of higher education currently advocated are legitimized with the argument that they will help make German higher education more fit for global competition. Strong efforts have been made in Germany since the mid-1990s to reduce detailed supervision by government, strengthen the strategic role of individual institutions of higher education, increase the power of university management, establish major mechanisms of systematic evaluation and put a stronger emphasis on the market and incentives mechanism. This follows, with some delay, the "Zeitgeist" of the prevailing reform mood in many countries of the world.

Second, Germany is involved in and affected by joint European research policies. In 2000, the European Council — i.e., the assembly of the governments of the member states of the European Union — agreed in the Lisbon Declaration to raise the level of public and private research expenditures from somewhat more than 2 percent to 3 percent of the gross domestic product (GDP) by 2010. This should contribute to making Europe "the most competitive economy" in the world. Until 2005, however, research expenditures hardly increased, and the so-called Lisbon Process obviously is in a deep crisis.

Third, there is intense debate on whether German higher education would be a stronger global player if the financial resources were more unevenly distributed among universities and there was a more visible élite sector. Again, the international argument is used to serve national reforms matching the "Zeitgeist."

Currently, the German higher education system is stratified vertically to a clearly lesser extent than higher education systems in all other larger economically advanced countries. In Germany, the acquisition of external research grants is the most popular indicator of the quality of a university. According to data available for 1999 and 2000, the top ten universities raised on average 61,000 Euros per scholar, the second ten universities 46,000 Euros and even the fifth group of ten universities 32,000 Euros per scholar.[26] Traditionally, German universities have been viewed as top quality in some disciplines and less than excellent in other fields. This low degree of stratification facilitated the mobility of students between different universities during their course of study as well as the mobility of professors, who did not care so much about the reputation of the individual universities, but rather about the resources offered to them by a specific institution.

Arguments in favour of strengthening top universities have gained momentum in Germany in recent years, given the popularity of ranking lists of top world universities and the underlying philosophy that only the élite can be "global players" in growing worldwide competition. There are also some in Europe who advocate that European countries should establish jointly a few world-class universities.

The German governmental agencies and other higher education policy actors eventually agreed in 2005 to reserve somewhat more than 1 percent of the total public higher education expenditure over a period of five years for thirty research "clusters" of excellence, mostly networks between various universities, for ten top universities and for a few dozen new graduate schools, in order to foster a sector of "excellence" within the German higher education system. In autumn 2006, three universities were selected, and others will follow in 2007.

Concluding Observations

In Germany, concurrent higher education reforms have been exceptional in magnitude. Only immediately around 1970 was there similar rapid change. Among the current reforms, innovation in governance — reduction of direct governmental supervision,

strengthening of management and increasing activities of evaluation — has been taking place at a similar speed and in a similar
direction as in many other countries. Internationalization and globalization are used as arguments for these reforms as they are in other
countries, but one cannot call these reforms internationalization or
globalization strategies, because the actions taken are not closely
intertwined with actions in favour of increasing mobility, transnational education, or the internationalization and globalization of
research and teaching activities.

Activities related to strengthening financial support for areas of
"excellence" and other policies in that direction are justified as contributions to strengthening the "global competitiveness" of the top
universities. "Internationalization" and "globalization" seem to be
popular jargon for justifying policies that would be pursued anyway
as part of national policies.

The reforms of the structure and content of study programs in
Germany within the framework of the so-called Bologna Processes
are embedded in parallel national reforms in other European countries. They are likely to have a substantial impact on the "national"
composition of the number and the kinds of competencies of the
university graduates and thus are likely to change the links between
higher education and the labour market. These reforms would not
have been undertaken if they were not expected to have a strong
international impact: namely, facilitating student mobility as well as
mobility of graduates between European countries and making universities in European countries more attractive for students and
scholars from other parts of the world. But they can be viewed as
primarily "national" policies undertaken at the same time and in
similar ways by a large number of European countries.

There is, however, a clear internationalization policy in Germany
on the part of national and regional policy-makers and also internationalization strategies of individual universities with the aims of
enhancing student mobility and academic staff mobility and

increasing international cooperation between universities for both research and teaching/learning. In this framework, German universities are strongly involved in encouraging and helping their students to study abroad. Altogether, it is interesting to note that strong international strategies and activities in Germany are not confined either to the top universities or to the universities with a specific international profile. Rather, every "provincial" university in Germany is similarly international in terms of foreign students, temporary and permanent foreign academics and academics cooperating internationally and travelling abroad.

Finally, globalization strategies of German universities in terms of establishing transnational study programs have grown. But altogether, they seem to remain an area of activity which is marginal for the strategic profile of German universities.

Thus, increased international activities are an integral part of reforms being undertaken in German higher education. Globalization, internationalization and Europeanization are not the dominant forces of reform, but in the current strong wave of higher education reforms, it is no longer possible to make clear distinctions that weigh national, European, international or global forces and indicate what role universal forces of knowledge play. Globalization occurs and is referred to in any debate on higher education reforms in Germany, and policies and strategies to increase international mobility and cooperation are visible and successful in German higher education. It would be wrong, however, to argue that German universities have really embarked on globalization strategies, because the various activities of changing governance, diversifying higher education, reforming curricula and expanding international cooperation and mobility are more strongly shaped by specific national rationales and problems than by a single "logic" of globalization or internationalization of higher education.

3

The Department of Foreign Affairs and International Trade (DFAIT), Canada: Providing Leadership in the Internationalization of Canadian Higher Education?

Roopa Desai Trilokekar, Ontario Institute for Studies in Education/University of Toronto

Introduction

"Can Canada Gets Its Act Together in International Education?", the title of Robin Farquhar's speech at a Canadian Information Centre for International Credentials (CICIC) event, aptly captures the sentiment among Canadian international education researchers and administrators.[1] The lack of a national international education strategy for Canada is lamented, especially given the growing importance of such a strategy to a nation's prosperity and economic agenda in the twentieth century. Farquhar states, "Canada lacks a vision and an agenda for international education, even though there is a growing awareness that both are urgently needed,"[2] and, like many others, suggests that this gap or lacuna is the primary responsibility of the federal government, more specifically the Department of Foreign Affairs and International Trade (DFAIT).[3]

The literature on the internationalization of higher education in Canada is critical of the Canadian approach, and numerous reports elaborate the many ways the Canadian federal government could take a lead by substantially increasing fiscal allocations for international education activities, developing a flagship program and establishing a nationally coordinated initiative, thus enhancing a strategic approach towards the internationalization of Canadian higher education.[4] The government itself, by commissioning several reports and studies in the last ten years,[5] has acknowledged the importance of internationalizing higher education. A few studies have looked at the influence of Canadian federalism on foreign policy[6] or the federal role in international education,[7] but most of the literature on the internationalization of Canadian education is prescriptive. There has never been an analytical study of internationalization from the policy perspective of the Canadian federal government.

This chapter draws from my doctoral dissertation[8] that intended to fill this research gap through an in-depth historical case study of the International Academic Relations Division within the Department of Foreign Affairs and International Trade (DFAIT).

The 2005 brochure for this division, now called the International Education and Youth Division, states that it is "responsible for the management of Canadian foreign policy in the international dimension of education and learning opportunities." The roles of the division are closely aligned with the objectives of international education and, in the context of this book, the internationalization of higher education.[9]

Definitions

International Cultural Relations (ICR), International Education and the Internationalization of Higher Education

Joseph Nye first coined the term *soft power*, which refers to "the ability to get what you want by attracting and persuading others to adopt your goals. ... A country may obtain the outcomes it wants in world politics because other countries — admiring its values, emulating its example, aspiring to its level of prosperity and openness — want to follow it …. This soft power — getting others to want the outcomes you want — co-opts people rather than coercing them."[10] Most nations, recognizing the importance of soft power, have developed international cultural relations (ICR) policies and, as a component of ICR policies, international education policies to support their foreign policy objectives. In this context, departments of foreign affairs have typically been involved in international education in that they "link people and educational institutions across national boundaries" through international education cooperative agreements, academic mobility programs, international scholarships, technical and development assistance programs and international curriculum studies.[11]

There is a link between international education in the context of a nation's foreign policy and the internationalization of higher education. As Knight suggests, international education comprises a wide range of activities, and the internationalization of higher education is the process associated with integrating all of these various activities. She defines internationalization "as the process of integrating an international, intercultural or global dimension into the purpose, functions or delivery of post-secondary education,"[12] and outlines distinct rationales for internationalization: namely, academic, cultural, economic and political. Under each of these rationales, specific objectives such as national cultural identity, citizenship development, foreign policy, national security, technical assistance, peace and mutual understanding link closely with a country's ICR policy objectives.

For the purposes of this study, *internationalization of higher education* is considered a strategic national policy on international education influenced by national interests and resources, developed within the context of a nation's foreign policy agenda and *in response* to the forces of globalization.

Methodology

A case study analysis and an historical approach were considered to be the most appropriate methodological tools for this research study. The primary sources of data were the archival and working files of the DFAIT Cultural Bureau and the International Academic Relations Division and sixteen interviews, eleven with current and retired officers from the International Academic Relations Division and/or the International Cultural Relations Bureau and five with individuals from the nongovernmental organization (NGO) sector or other government organizations that have been directly involved with the division/department in policy and/or program coordination. The interview data complemented and filled the gaps in chronology in the archival texts and helped in data interpretation and analysis. Secondary data were gathered from Council of Ministers of Education, Canada (CMEC) files. The data collected provided a fairly complete historical case study of the International Academic Relations Division within the department.

History of the International Academic Relations Division: Policy and Program Approaches

The historical data can be categorized into three distinct time periods, 1967-73, 1974-89 and 1990-95, each corresponding to a specific set of policy and program approaches.

Building Relations with the Domestic Academic Community (1967-73)

The Academic Relations Section was first established by the Department of External Affairs (DEA) in 1967 within its Information Division.[13] Its creation was a response to criticism from academics in Canada who, "sympathetic to the left and increasingly politicized by such contentious issues as the American war in Vietnam and growing US investment in Canada. ... openly challenged Canadian foreign policy and those who ran it."[14] This new section was established under Prime Minister Lester B. Pearson and Secretary of State for External Affairs Paul Martin Sr. to build better relationships with the academic community.

In policy and program development, it is interesting to note that the department looked primarily to the US State Department model and adapted several of its program initiatives such as the Resident Visitors program, contracting with faculty for research and study in international affairs, commissioning a comprehensive report on international and area studies programs at Canadian universities, sponsoring seminars and conferences on foreign policy and lending department personnel as resources or speakers for academic conferences. It is even more interesting to note that, in establishing such programs, the department rejected the appropriateness of certain US State Department initiatives such as their in-house Foreign Service Institute and their direct engagement of faculty either as consultants or as employees in their foreign-service institute. Although the US approach was recognized as one that enabled the State Department to engage the academic community as experts in government programs and policy, there was a concern that in Canada, such approaches by the federal government would be viewed as too direct.[15]

The department did, however, consider financial support for the study of international relations and area study programs at Canadian universities as a logical development to further the department's foreign policy objectives: "We think it might be possible for the Federal government to become involved in contributing to the support of schools of international studies — a field in which only the Federal government has a direct and immediate interest — by making grants available to universities, on the basis of criteria set by the Federal government in order to fulfill a national requirement."[16]

Several initiatives were considered to support the development of international academic programs at Canadian universities, such as support to studies in fields such as International Law and Strategic Studies, and to area study programs. The department even provided a special grant to support the Centre for Asian Studies in Vancouver, BC, to strengthen the knowledge and understanding of Asia-Pacific countries. Eventually, however, the department avoided any other large-scale initiatives in higher education. This is because direct or indirect federal support for academic programs and research in international affairs was considered inappropriate within a Canadian context. At one level, there were concerns that direct government involvement in academic matters would interfere with the principles of institutional autonomy and academic freedom. At another level, there were concerns about intruding on policy areas within provincial jurisdiction. At yet another level, the government was cautious of establishing a policy of providing financial support on the scale provided by the US State Department.

Projecting Canada's Cultural Image Abroad (1974-89)

In the second period, the policy orientation of the Academic Relations Division changed radically. In 1974, the government emphasized the promotion of Canadian culture and of cultural diplomacy, significantly expanding its foreign policy orientation and scope.[17] Academic Relations thereby developed an entirely new mandate, "to develop an informed awareness and a more balanced understanding of Canada ... and to facilitate the development of more productive contacts and cross fertilization between Canadian and foreign scholars."[18] During this period, the first blueprint of the Canadian Studies Program Abroad (CSPA) was established with four main objectives: "to expand the influential [scholastic] community and keep them informed about and favorably disposed towards Canada; to raise awareness of Canadian realities overseas; to foster productive exchanges between Canadian and foreign universities; and to thereby improve Canada's bilateral relations."[19] The CSPA became the primary program of the Academic Relations Division, its raison de être, aligning the division more closely with the department's foreign policy objectives.

In developing the CSPA, the department avoided a one-size-fits-all approach and was sensitive to the local needs and nature of individual universities and educational systems in different countries; for example, Canadian Studies was developed in Japan, with the DEA supporting the translation into Japanese of introductory texts in Canadian government, economy and history. The DEA also considered it important to develop local scholarship and hence supported foreign faculty so that they could teach Canadian studies courses themselves rather than be dependent on Canadian faculty. In general, the Academic Relations Division's CSPA was considered to be "well managed on the basis of clearly defined objectives which flow naturally and logically from the objectives endorsed by the government for the cultural relations program as a whole, and ... better attuned to foreign policy considerations."[20] The CSPA was perceived as a less direct and intrusive approach, as it did not in any way intrude on issues of jurisdictional authority, institutional autonomy or academic freedom within Canada, and hence an approach that the government was more comfortable in adopting. It seemed a win-win situation for the DEA.

In the late 1970s, the integration of the Academic Relations Division with the Bureau of International Cultural Relations resulted in new divisional responsibilities such as administering the Government of Canada (GOC) Awards program, coordinating cultural agreements with educational components and representing Canada's interests at international education conferences. To coordinate international education matters, the division worked closely with the CMEC and the provincial ministers of education and established a set of protocols for participation and representation at international conferences.[21] CMEC and the DEA also jointly established the Federal-Provincial Consultative Committee on Education-Related International Activities (FPCCERIA) to facilitate reciprocal communication and help develop recommendations on matters of growing mutual interest in international education between the federal government and the provincial ministers, an example being issues around hosting foreign students in Canada.[22]

During this period, the division was criticized by Canadian academics for not supporting Canadian educational initiatives and for providing travel/study grants to foreign academics at the expense of Canadian faculty and students. The International Academic Relations Division strategically decided against duplicating the mandates of other domestic cultural organizations and fully committed itself to providing support to foreign institutions to develop the Canadian Studies Program. By the late 1970s, the division's earlier role of working with the Canadian academic community had disappeared, and the department's interest in supporting area studies and international study programs had also dissipated.

Developing a Policy Framework for the International Dimensions of Canadian Higher Education (1990-95)

The early 1990s was a period marked by austerity and severe budget cuts within External Affairs. Fiscal pressures raised recurring questions about the appropriate structure and mandate for international cultural relations (ICR) and caused inconsistency in policy and program approaches within the government. In response, several reviews and consultations on ICR were commissioned by the government; each recognized the division's coordinating role, called for the department's enhanced commitment to the ICR program and requested greater stability in resources.[23] In spite of this support, there was a parallel move in the early 1990s to remove the

ICR function from the DEA altogether. Bill C-93 proposed a merger of the Social Sciences and Humanities Research Council of Canada (SSHRC) with the Canada Council, as well as a plan to shift cultural and academic activities, including the international cultural and academic bureau, out of the department and into the proposed new organization. The 1990s was thus a period of contradictions.

Fortunately, the proposed Bill C-93 was defeated in the Senate and, under Prime Minister Jean Chrétien's comprehensive review of Canadian foreign policy in 1994, culture was reinstated within the department's foreign policy objectives. In fact, "Canada in the World," the government statement published in 1995, identified three key foreign policy objectives, and the projection of Canadian values and culture was recognized as the third pillar of Canada's foreign policy.[24] The reinstatement of the importance of culture in a context which recognized the growing importance of a "knowledge based economy," and the need for education and training for improved domestic *and* international competitiveness,[25] resulted in a broadening of the department's agenda. Within this context, the call for an increased international dimension to higher education became pertinent, and the terms *international dimension* and *internationalization of higher education* were incorporated into the government's vocabulary. These terms were used in no previous government documents. DFAIT pursued extensive consultations with various constituencies, including the provinces, and produced a paper titled "The International Dimension of Higher Education in Canada: Collaborative Policy Framework."

In this paper, a five-point strategy was recommended: strengthening the policy dialogue with provincial governments; increasing networks and collaborations among higher education institutions in priority areas of research; student and faculty mobility; developing stronger partnerships between public and private organizations and higher education institutions; and supporting marketing efforts by Canadian higher education institutions.[26] As a direct result of this initiative, the department invited CMEC, the provinces and other federal departments to participate in several meetings and round tables to discuss strengthening cooperation in the internationalization of higher education. As a first step, it began negotiating educational cooperation programs with the European Union (EU) and North America as well as with the Asia-Pacific region to support institutional links, strengthen partnerships in science and technology and provide opportunities for student mobility. It reinforced existing programs such as Canadian Studies and initiated new projects such as the opening of ten international educational centres (Canadian Education Centres) to support the marketing of Canadian educational services.

Thus, in the third and final phase, the mandate and role of the Academic Relations Division expanded considerably and, as was noted earlier, this was when the term *internationalization of higher education* first came to be used by the department. The division came to be known as the International Higher Education Division, albeit for a very brief time during this period.[27] While the importance of the division's coordinating role was identified in several reports, it is interesting to note that the department was in no position to take the lead in developing or implementing any policy decisions or initiating any new programs in this arena. In the case of international student mobility programs, for example, an entirely new federal ministry, the Department of Human Resources and Skills Development Canada (HRSDC) made the necessary fiscal investments and took charge of program administration.

Discussion

A review of the three time periods establishes the department's engagement in the internationalization of higher education, although the specific policy and program approach within each period was distinct and the formal reference to internationalization was only made by the department in the 1990s. The department's interest in investing in international study programs during the first phase of its history is most closely aligned with Knight's definition of internationalization, "integrating an international/intercultural dimension into the teaching, research and service elements of an institution"; yet there is no reference to this departmental interest in the current literature, nor has the department itself reverted back to its interest in this aspect of internationalization in subsequent years.

During phase two, the policy orientation of the division was most closely aligned with Canada's ICR and Canadian foreign policy goals, and the CSPA represented a highly strategic and symbolic policy initiative. In this sense, this time period represented an anomaly in the department's history. Also, in developing the CSPA, the department established a set of unique and distinctively Canadian principles for its program approaches. These program approaches have not been fully appreciated by the current Canadian literature on internationalization.

During phase three, the division's policy interest shifted; it is best described by the department as *intermestic*[28] as it included a wider range of both domestic and international activities associated with the internationalization of higher education.

Culture was formally recognized as the third pillar of foreign policy, reinforcing the federal government's conviction that ICR objectives are best met within its own structure rather than through an arm's-length agency. Yet the government steered away from any broad-scale policy decisions or large funding commitments to support either existing or new ICR initiatives. Nonetheless the department took a proactive role in bringing several stakeholder groups together and in identifying core components of the internationalization agenda. Marketing and commercial interests, such as the recruitment of foreign students, permeated more traditional international academic exchange approaches.

Each of the three time periods in the history of the division are marked by distinctive policy and program imperatives; however, together they raise some fundamental questions regarding our understanding of the internationalization of higher education within a Canadian context.

Is the CSPA Canada's Flagship International Education Program?

The literature on the internationalization of Canadian higher education suggests the absence of a flagship program and advocates a substantial government investment of funds towards a new initiative. This study reveals that, in the department's view, the CSPA is its flagship program, one which it has strategically developed and has protected, as much as possible, against funding cuts. For the past three decades the divison has spent close to half of the Academic Relations budget on this one program ($5.4 million out of a total budget of $12 million in 2002-03 as verified through interview sources).[29] Unfortunately, the CSPA and its unique policy approaches have been largely overlooked by the internationalization literature.

The CSPA has the most direct link to the foreign policy objectives of the department and, since it deals directly with academics and higher educational institutions, it fits well within the mandate of the Academic Relations Division. It enhances Canada's image internationally through the study of Canadian content rather than through the use of more direct cultural propaganda strategies. Through this program, the division is dedicated to developing and enhancing host country resources rather than transplanting Canadian expatriates to universities abroad for program development. Another very important feature is the ability of the program to leverage funds from third countries and private sources. By encouraging investment from the host country and its institutions, the division is ensuring the viability and sustainability of the programs abroad. The CSPA approach is also one that respects Canadian values of academic freedom and institutional autonomy. The divisional officers are cautious not to interfere with either the content of or approach to the study of Canada. The CSPA is first and foremost considered an academic activity, as reflected in the initiatives supported: curriculum development, research, library acquisitions and academic seminars.

The policy and program approaches for Canadian studies ensure geographic balance within foreign policy objectives, including those related to overseas development assistance (ODA); emphasize non-imperialistic or noncolonial approaches; aim to empower local communities and ensure reciprocity in program development; enable the academic arena of Canadian Studies to be developed by "foreigners"; enhance available resources through leveraging funding opportunities; build sustainable and viable program models in terms of funding and structure; and encourage entrepreneurship. These characteristics merit the status of uniquely Canadian principles of practice in international education.

Is There an Absence of Policy Strategy and Coordination?

The literature criticizes the department for not being proactive in coordinating a national policy strategy for the internationalization of higher education. The history of the division reveals that this has not always been the case. The department has been responsive, albeit in different ways, during the course of its history; for example, it jointly established a protocol for Canadian representation at international educational conferences with CMEC in 1977, 1982 and 1987, and also established the FPCCERIA in 1986. One of the most comprehensive policy coordination efforts was made in 1994, when the department published the paper on "The International Dimension of Higher Education in Canada: Collaborative Policy Framework." It is clear that the department has attempted to support communication and coordination among various stakeholder groups. The real challenge has been to establish any large-scale uniform national policy initiatives.

One of the primary challenges to policy coordination has been the department's or the government's own reluctance to engage fully in this policy arena. This could be a result of several factors. The department's responsibilities for ICR overlap with those of other federal departments such as the former Secretary of State and with other domestic cultural and educational councils such as the Canada Council and the research councils as well as the Canadian International Development Agency (CIDA) and HRSDC. As a result of this overlap, the department's mandate in ICR is at times contested by other federal departments challenging the department's understanding of its distinct role vis-à-vis other departments.[30]

Besides the challenges from within the federal government structure, the department has confronted recurring policy coordination issues as a result of Canada's federal structure: the jurisdictional separation between the two levels of government (federal and provincial) in education and the lack of policy coordination mechanisms between them. A classic example of this challenge is DFAIT's relationship with CMEC. While the department views CMEC as a central coordinating agency for educational matters, CMEC does not view itself as representing provincial interests and has often refused the division's attempts at involving CMEC on boards or committees for that purpose. In CMEC's view, the department ought to approach each of the ten provinces individually for any policy or programmatic input; it should not expect a centralized national response. Fiercely protective of provincial jurisdiction in education, on various occasions CMEC contested the need to establish a national policy framework on international education matters. CMEC questions the role of DFAIT in international education, suggesting that it has a better capacity than DFAIT to respond directly to requests from foreign governments or international organizations on matters concerning Canadian education. The result of this constant tension between CMEC and the provinces on the one hand, and the department on the other, was that, on several policy matters such as the signing of international cultural agreements, the department began to avoid coordinating with CMEC and the provinces and moved towards cultural ententes that did not require formal provincial approval. On a broader scale, this resulted in the department's reluctance to invest in this policy area. This situation is best captured by interviewees participating in this study who confirmed that, whereas no Canadian diplomat would deny the relevance of international education or cultural affairs to a country's foreign policy objectives, lobbying for investment in this area is not something to expect from diplomats. In the Canadian context, both culture and education are best left "untouched" as policy areas for the federal government, given that the domestic dynamics within Canada are heavily dominated by tendencies to resist any attempts to centralize policy matters in education or culture, be they domestic or international in orientation.

The federal government's role in Canada is determined largely by whether or not an issue is considered "educational" and therefore a provincial responsibility. The federal government may or may not face challenges in policy coordination, depending on where the initiatives originate and how they are framed; in this context, DFAIT may always play a limited role in matters concerning international education. Sheffield suggests that the federal government's powers are clearest with respect to education and training as related to economic growth, while the provinces tend to focus on cultural and individual development.[31] In this context, HRSDC's responsibility for the international mobility programs is largely accepted.

The Central Challenge in Policy Coordination: Structure, Funding or Foreign Policy Context?

The literature critiques the poor funding allocations made to international education by the department. Reports identify Canada's investments as being among the lowest among several developed countries and also suggest that Canada is lacking the structure of a well-established centralized organization such as the United States Information Agency, the British Council, the German Academic Exchange Service and the Goethe Institutes, EduFrance and the Alliance Française network, the Netherlands Organization for International Cooperation in Higher Education (Nuffic) and the Japan Foundation, to name only a few.[32]

It is difficult to attribute the government's low levels of funding and structural commitment exclusively to the federal challenges within Canada for national policy coordination. The department's relatively weak position within the federal government and its limited foreign policy approach equally affect the government's ICR approach.

Cohen provides an excellent account of the history of Canada's international role and its steady decline and invokes the department's overall profile within the federal government[33] to explain the low priority and poor funding of the International Academic Relations Division.

Subsequent to a relatively brief period of prosperity, or what Cohen refers to as Canada's golden years in the 1950s, the department's status within the government has been steadily declining. Pierre Elliott Trudeau is considered responsible for this downward trend, which began with his foreign policy review in 1970. Trudeau's approach emphasized the importance of national priorities and also tied foreign policy closely to Canada's economic development. He restructured the department, merging External Affairs with the Trade Commissioner services. This emphasis on trade was further strengthened by Chrétien, and the department was renamed the Department of Foreign Affairs and International Trade. During this period, the marketing of Canadian higher education, recruitment of foreign students and the link between culture and trade took on importance. Canada's foreign policy became synonymous with its trade policy, restricting its pursuit of other political or cultural interests. In Cohen's terms, cultural diplomacy in the Canadian government's foreign policy is considered more as an "after business hours [initiative] not as part of an overall policy [direction]."[34] The focus in Canadian foreign policy has been to connect Canada to some of the world's fastest-growing markets, and, as the US is Canada's largest trading partner, this reality further restrains the need for any major international outreach initiatives.[35]

Another challenge for Canada is its domestic rationale for international cultural diplomacy. It is very important to remember that the Canadian federal government established a cultural relations division within the department in 1965 largely in response to Québec's role in international affairs.[36] This rationale is distinctly different from those of other nations who have ICR policies to serve their international political, economic and/or cultural interests. As Cooper states, "The underlying problem with Canadian cultural diplomacy was in its origin. Because it arose out of specific domestic circumstances it was narrowly defined and strictly focused. While this restricted approach may have been sufficient to meet the immediate goal vis-à-vis Québec, in the long run it raised serious questions about the rationale for Canadian cultural activity overseas in terms of both Canadian foreign policy and cultural policy." As a result, Canada has never had a very strong rationale for ICR.

The specific characteristics of Canadian federalism and its foreign policy have directly shaped Canada's approach to ICR and, subsequently, to international education.

Conclusion

This study confirms that DFAIT has always been engaged in one or more components of internationalization although the specific policy and program orientations have changed dramatically over time. DFAIT has always expressed its commitment to ICR and, although the recurring issues of structure and funding have remained

unchanged, the government has steadfastly ensured that ICR structure and functions have remained part of its own portfolio. It has
resisted any attempts at establishing an arm's-length ICR agency.

The Canadian literature on internationalization of higher education suggests that Canada lacks a flagship international education
program; however, in the department's view, the CSPA is its flagship
program. The literature also suggests that there is a lack of policy
coordination in this area and it identifies DFAIT as the lead agency
for national policy coordination. The department's history indicates
that it has made numerous attempts to coordinate national policy
in international education. While it has achieved a few successes, for
the most part the department has faced several challenges that have
limited its policy coordination abilities. The study confirms that
funding is a major issue and that both the department and the division have been poorly resourced because ICR has a limited place in
Canadian foreign policy and Canada's investment in international
affairs is highly restricted to trade and economic initiatives. Thus,
both Canada's highly decentralized federal structure and its foreign
policy orientation pose serious challenges to any national coordination on the part of DFAIT for international education.

What is the future for Canada? As Farquhar asks, can Canada get
its act together in international education? In my perspective, our
understanding of the department's role in the internationalization
of Canadian higher education is rather simplistic. It is not sufficient
to lobby for policy development for the internationalization of
higher education. Of equal, if not greater, importance is to understand internationalization as a broader higher education policy issue
and to give recognition to the different rationales, strategies and
challenges among the different stakeholder groups.[37] It is essential
to recognize the link between national characteristics and policy
outcomes. Also of central importance are policy coordination
mechanisms and the impact of policies on higher education systems
and structures. In Canada, foreign policy has a limited ICR focus;

it is highly trade-oriented. Further, the absence of a federal ministry of education challenges the notion of any national policy initiatives in education. ICR provides the base for internationalization policies; however, in most countries, the policy agendas for the internationalization of higher education are driven by their respective ministries of education, not their foreign offices.[38] Similarly, the process of policy decision-making and policy coordination differs greatly across federations. Canada epitomizes a highly decentralized, uncoordinated federation. The few coordination mechanisms that exist, such as the FPCCERIA through CMEC, have served as mechanisms for information exchange, not as effective policy-making or policy coordination mechanisms.

Given this unique Canadian context, I question the fundamental assumption made by the literature that DFAIT should provide leadership in developing a national strategy on the internationalization of Canadian higher education. Instead I suggest that other federal departments such as HRSDC and the research councils, with a primary domestic agenda, have a far stronger potential to influence Canada's investment and approach to the internationalization of higher education. First, they have the funding and the resources to influence policy albeit they are likely to face similar challenges in coordinating national policy. Second, they are in a better position to play a potential role in influencing internationalization policy as it is understood in the present context.

I agree with Enders when he suggests that the internationalization and globalization of the higher education agenda has more of an icebreaker function for national reform agendas, rather than being part of our traditional notions of international academic relations.[39] If this were not the case, then such countries with strong ICR policies and substantial investments in international education as Germany would not feel the pressure to internationalize their higher education. This is evident within Canada's own policy orientation. From the third pillar of foreign policy in 1995, the internationalization of higher education is now referred to in the 2005 international policy statement as "Getting the Domestic Environment Right." It is outlined under "Commerce," as a government strategy to "help workers upgrade their skills ... to make sure their qualifications are relevant to the needs of globally competitive business and to provide options for communities and individuals grappling with economic change; we will promote the internationalization of education through academic networking among Canadian colleges, universities and international partners and through student exchange programs to build our education and cultural assets."[40] Here, internationalization of higher education is perceived in the context of human resource development priorities and has little connection to Canada's place in the world in the sense of ICR and the old or traditional internationalism of the Pearsonian era.

In recommending the role of other departments, I am not denying the importance of DFAIT or its role in international education. Most certainly, higher levels of investment in ICR will produce bold results as suggested for several years by John Ralston Saul, an avid proponent of culture and cultural foreign policy. There is also the potential for the department to revisit its original interest in supporting and strengthening international study programs and thus contribute to the internationalization of Canadian higher education. As well, the Canadian Studies Program Abroad could be expanded and strengthened to benefit both the international and domestic academic communities. But how feasible are these policy directions given Canada's foreign policy orientation? And is it likely that, given the trade focus with DFAIT, with increased investment, Canada's international education policy orientation would resemble that of Australia: more market-driven, less academic; more competitive, less cooperative; and more in terms of trade and less in terms of cultural understanding? DFAIT certainly has the potential to play a niche role in this arena, but should it, could it, be one of national policy leadership in the internationalization of Canadian higher education?

Provincial Internationalization Efforts: Programs, Policies and Plans in Manitoba and Alberta

Christine Savage, Simon Fraser University

Introduction

Higher education plays an important role in bringing about change and progress in societies. The internationalization of higher education is one of the ways to prepare students with the international and intercultural knowledge, skills, abilities and attitudes necessary for living and working today and into the future. Public sector support through educational policies and programs, in concert with committed and engaged institutions, has the potential to be an important catalyst in transforming the educational system to proactively address global realities.

Increasingly we are seeing governments' involvement in the internationalization of their education systems. Countries such as the United Kingdom, Australia, the United States and New Zealand have recognized the importance and value of international education and have established a range of programs, plans and policies to support and enhance the internationalization of their education systems. Key approaches have included providing for international student scholarships; study and work abroad opportunities for teachers, faculty and administrators; branding and strategic marketing of educational products and services; internationalizing the curriculum; conducting research; ensuring quality measures; providing professional development and coordinating efforts across stakeholders.[2]

In Canada, we are also witnessing a growth in involvement in internationalization, both nationally and provincially, although this development has been fairly ad hoc. Federal departments and provincial governments have implemented a range of approaches from formal policy to the delivery of programs and services. However, within the last decade, a number of concerns have been expressed about the lack of a strategic approach to internationalization, the absence of effective coordination and collaboration amongst the various stakeholders and the overall impact that this is having on the progress of internationalization in Canada.[3]

Provincial governments can and do undertake a number of roles in supporting the internationalization of the post-secondary education system within their jurisdictions. They have the capacity to facilitate coordination and collaboration amongst the provincial international education stakeholders and to unify and strengthen provincial efforts internationally by promoting their education system and the province as a whole. This is important, given growing international competition, the absence of a strong national marketing approach and the complexity of Canada's education system. The provincial governments can also play a role in terms of knowledge management and of facilitating the sharing of information, research, outcomes and best practices provincially. This can be an efficient method of sharing resources and can contribute to the development of innovation and to strengthening quality. Through the development of standards and policies, governments can create a framework for internationalization to occur within their jurisdictions,

provide a strategic focus for activities and emphasize the importance of internationalization and the role it plays in positioning the
province for the future. Government's involvement in supporting
research or commissioning key studies can contribute to the knowledge base. It provides resources for the benefit of the system as a
whole, and this is particularly beneficial in a relatively new area of
research such as internationalization. Provincial governments can
support positive provincial and federal relations by providing ongoing information to federal government departments on key
developments in internationalization, ensuring that they link and
connect to federal initiatives and create opportunities for ongoing
dialogue and discussion around internationalization and how to
support the process effectively. Finally, provincial governments can
play important roles in designing and developing programs to support key aspects of internationalization that require strengthening
and currently are not being supported, through other initiatives
such as study-abroad programs and internationalizing the curriculum.

As indicated earlier, a number of provincial governments have
identified internationalization as a growing priority and have either
implemented or are in the process of implementing a range of
approaches. For the purposes of this chapter, two provinces have
been selected, Manitoba and Alberta, as they have recently intensified their internationalization efforts. The history of their
involvement in internationalization, their current activities and
their future directions for internationalization are highlighted in
the following two sections.

Manitoba

Overview

The post-secondary system in Manitoba is composed of seven publicly funded and five private institutions that offer undergraduate,

graduate, preprofessional and professional degree programs and certificate and diploma programs in a broad range of disciplines. In 2005-06, there were approximately 43,000 full-time students in Manitoba's universities and colleges.

Manitoba Advanced Education and Literacy, the government department responsible for higher education, works in partnership with its post-secondary institutions and the Council of Post-secondary Education, an agency that promotes excellence and cooperation within the post-secondary sector to provide an education system that is of high quality, affordable, accessible and responsive. In 2005-06, the government allocated over $380 million to support post-secondary education in the province.

History of Government Involvement in Internationalization

The Manitoba government's structured involvement in internationalization began in 1999 with the creation of a new position, Director of International Education, which reported directly to the Deputy Minister of Education. This was followed by the submission and approval of a proposal to the Community Economic Development Committee of Cabinet for the creation of a new International Education Branch, which was established in 2001. The primary rationale for this development was the government's desire to enhance the economic potential of international education, and the submission served as a quasi-strategy for international education in the province.[4]

Current Internationalization Activities

The International Education Branch is now located within the Department of Competitiveness, Training and Trade. It has four broad objectives that focus on developing the global competencies of its citizens, increasing the economic impact of international education, encouraging a broad and deep approach to internationalization and enhancing the profile and recognition of Manitoba internationally. The branch works in collaboration with a range of departments, such as Education, Citizenship and Youth and Advanced Education and Literacy, to coordinate international activities.[5]

As noted earlier, Manitoba has a strong focus on strengthening the economic impact of international education with broad objectives of increasing the number of international students, the number of international education projects and contracts and the number of offshore programs. The branch is working to achieve these objectives by distributing promotional materials, launching a provincial Web site, participating in targeted missions abroad, hosting incoming delegations, undertaking focused advertising activities and conducting familiarization tours.[6]

This economic focus, however, is supported by a commitment to enhancing the academic outcomes of internationalization activities as well as the quality of the programs and services provided. This means that consideration is being given to how particular initiatives can be structured to encourage the international learning experiences of both international and domestic students and how they can be structured to maximize success. Through ensuring access to information about opportunities to study and work abroad, the branch encourages the international mobility of Manitoba students, faculty, teachers and other educational staff. Furthermore, through the delivery of professional development sessions and advice, the branch promotes the importance of connecting internationalization activities back into the classroom and across the campus and the importance of providing programs and services that are of the highest quality.

A component of the government's strategy is to enhance collaboration amongst the players within the province as well as beyond. An important responsibility of the International Education Branch is to coordinate international activities among provincial departments such as Advanced Education and Literacy; Education, Citizenship and Youth; and Labour and Immigration. It also works closely with schools and post-secondary institutions in the province and the Manitoba Centre for International Education, a provincial non-profit organization established in 1999, to provide a forum in which institutions meet, discuss issues and collaborate around international education. Federally, the branch liaises with and/or sits on a range of advisory committees for Citizenship and Immigration Canada and the Department of Foreign Affairs and International Trade.[7]

Future Directions

The focus on collaboration is formally recognized in Manitoba's *Reaching Beyond Our Borders*, the framework for Manitoba's international activities which creates the template for enhanced coordination, cooperation and synergy in its international efforts — provincially, nationally and internationally. The framework has specific objectives focused on 1)ensuring a more strategic and corporate approach to the province's international activities, 2)increasing the promotion of the province's strengths and capabilities internationally and 3)strengthening involvement in international development and advancing global interests. Of particular note, one of the key areas of focus within the framework is international education.[8]

The government is developing a comprehensive international education strategy, based on consultation and cooperation with Manitoba's educational institutions, which will provide a long-term plan for strengthening international education in the province. There will continue to be a focus on promotion of the province's post-secondary system internationally and increasing the number and diversity of international students as well as international projects and contracts, but with a new strategical focus on selected countries. There will be an enhanced emphasis on areas that have been less developed such as exchange programs, development projects, offshore delivery and internationalizing the curriculum, thus balancing the economic and academic rationales for internationalization. Manitoba will have an ongoing commitment to enhancing the quality of internationalization strategies and contributing to their sustainability through professional development programs, market research, resource materials, best-practice guides and evaluation. The specific role and function that the International Education Branch will play will be identified as part of the development of the new strategy.[9]

Alberta

Overview

There are twenty-eight post-secondary institutions located throughout Alberta, operating under the authority of the Minister of Advanced Education and Technology: four public universities, fourteen public colleges, the Banff Centre, two technical institutes and seven private institutions accredited to offer specific degrees. These institutions offer a broad range of doctoral, master's, bachelor's and applied degrees, university transfer, diploma, certificate, academic upgrading and apprenticeship programs to over 140,000 full-load-equivalent students (2004-05).

Alberta Advanced Education and Technology works in partnership with post-secondary institutions to provide an accessible, flexible and responsive learning system. In 2005-06, the post-secondary education budget was $1.7 billion.

History of Government's Involvement in International Education

While the Alberta government has a relatively long history of involvement in international education, a significant focus of the activities has been on the Kindergarten–Grade 12 sector, with the exception of one long-standing initiative, a post-secondary student awards program to support cultural relations with sister provinces, foreign states or countries. However, there is now a growing focus and emphasis on internationalization at the post-secondary level.

In terms of policy directions, the provincial government launched *Alberta's International Education Strategy* in 2001;[10] emphasizing the importance of international education, it outlined a vision and series of objectives for internationalizing the province's education system and facilitating a more coordinated approach across the entire sector. As stated in the document, "important objectives [were] to promote the internationalization of education curriculum to support Alberta's school jurisdictions and post-secondary institutions in providing international services and in accessing international markets, and to expand the range of international opportunities (economic and humanitarian) available to Albertans."[11] The strategy outlined a range of activities that were being undertaken by government and proposed a number of additional initiatives for the future.

In 2004, the Alberta government launched a twenty-year strategic plan that lays out a long-term direction for the province, focusing on providing the province and its residents with new opportunities. It is based on four key pillars: unleashing innovation, leading in learning, competing in a global marketplace and making Alberta the best place to live, work and visit.[12] Given this new provincial strategic plan, it was determined that it was timely to review the international education strategy initiated in 2001 and to develop a detailed action plan for the future.

An important starting point for the development of the new International Education Action Plan was to determine the status of internationalization in Alberta's education sector and to provide participants with the opportunity to contribute to the development of the action plan. A survey was conducted, and its results were analyzed and presented in a *Profile of Alberta's Post-Secondary*

International Education Sector.[13] Key highlights are:

- The majority of surveyed institutions have been involved in internationalization for more than two decades.
- The main rationale for internationalization is to provide students with international and intercultural knowledge, skills and abilities.
- Program areas of activity include international student programs, study-abroad programs, international education projects and international partnership agreements.
- There is a more limited focus on internationalizing teaching/learning practice and faculty/staff development programs and services.
- In the next five years, most institutions anticipate being involved in a wide range of internationalization activities, the top three areas being international partnership agreements, international student programs and faculty/staff exchanges.

The survey provided a number of opportunities for participants to provide feedback on key challenges and to make recommendations for governmental involvement to strengthen provincial post-secondary international efforts. Feedback identified the need to strengthen the promotion of the sector, profile the importance and benefits of internationalization, enhance coordination and collaboration, strengthen the expertise of the sector and implement a range of programs to support internationalization.

Current Internationalization Activities
In November 2005, Alberta Advanced Education tabled the *International Education Action Plan* in the legislature during

International Education Week. The plan provides a framework to position the international education sector competitively, facilitate the internationalization of the province's education system, and support and strengthen the 2001 International Education Strategy. The *International Education Action Plan* renews the government's commitment to internationalization and the important role that it plays in helping Albertans acquire the international and intercultural knowledge, skills and abilities needed to participate effectively in an interconnected world. The action plan links international education with the province's twenty-year strategic plan in terms of its contributions to diversifying the economy, increasing the relevancy of the education system, improving international competitiveness and creating a vibrant cultural mosaic. It argues for a sustained, strategic and comprehensive approach to internationalization that is undertaken with a spirit of cooperation and collaboration with key stakeholders within the province, across the country and around the world. Finally, there is an acknowledgement of the need for adequate resources, collaborative leadership, a commitment to ensuring quality and the need for ongoing evaluation of outcomes.[14]

The objectives identified in the *International Education Action Plan* focus on developing the international and intercultural knowledge, skills and abilities of Albertans; promoting Alberta as a destination of choice for international students; increasing the competitiveness of the education sector internationally; enhancing provincial, national and international collaboration and cooperation; and raising awareness of what internationalization is and why it is important.[15]

Alberta Advanced Education has identified a range of programs required to ensure a sustainable, integrated and comprehensive approach to internationalization in the province and will implement these, contingent on the availability of resources. Initiatives that have been implemented to date focus on promotion, professional development and mobility. A new range of marketing materials has been developed, including brochures, a Web site and a provincial booth display. In order to strengthen educational connections between Alberta and Mexico, an Alberta Education Centre in Guadalajara was officially opened in September 2005 during a ministerial-led mission of twelve post-secondary institutions to Mexico. An awards program to highlight the innovative approaches of faculty in terms of internationalizing their teaching and learning practices was implemented during the launch of the *International Education Action Plan*. An ongoing series of forums for international educators is provided so that the government and institutional stakeholders can share information, discuss issues and provide advice for future activities. Finally, a new Alberta-Smithsonian internship program will provide opportunities for fifty students from Alberta's post-secondary system to gain valuable international experience at one of twenty-eight Smithsonian centres throughout the world.

Future Directions

Alberta has identified a commitment to strengthening the quality of internationalization strategies by sharing of good practice, professional development and resource development. A number of programs have been identified that will support the achievement of the objectives outlined in the *International Education Action Plan* and these will be developed as the availability of funds and the government's strategic priorities permit. Alberta Advanced Education and Technology will continue to examine ways to enhance coordination and cooperation provincially with such departments as International, Intergovernmental and Aboriginal Relations; Education; and Employment, Immigration and Industry. The internationalization objectives are multipronged, with the intention of implementing a range of activities to support a broad and deep internationalization process.

Summary

From the two case studies, we see that both provinces have undertaken or are in the process of undertaking the development of a strategic planning approach to enhance the internationalization efforts of their post-secondary system. In addition, these plans have been positioned within the broader context of other key governmental strategies with an emphasis on enhancing collaboration and cooperation provincially as well as nationally — encouraging a whole-of-government approach. Finally, the plans are or will be based on consultations with institutional stakeholders, providing important opportunities for them to contribute to the development of the strategy and ensuring that the plan builds on and enhances the internationalization foundation already in place.

While there is certainly an economic rationale for both governments' involvement in internationalization, there is also a communicated commitment to the importance of developing the international and intercultural competencies of students. This suggests a more comprehensive approach to internationalization that might provide some balance between academic and economic aspects of internationalization. The commitment is supported to a certain degree in both jurisdictions by the provinces' involvement in or profile of a range of internationalization mechanisms.

There is a focus on ensuring the quality of the programs and developing the capacity of the system through a range of professional development initiatives. Through the evaluation of outcomes, these governments are in a position to examine the effectiveness of various approaches and determine the outcomes or impact of the initiatives implemented. It is not simply a question of how many students are sent abroad but whether the experience contributed to the development of the international knowledge, skills and abilities identified as one of the goals of the program. Furthermore, ensuring innovation and quality requires a commitment to research and professional development. Opportunities to share strategies and best practices and to engage in discussion about various aspects of internationalization, as well as the development of practical resources to help develop and implement various internationalization activities, reflect an interest in and commitment to knowledge management.

Conclusion

Internationalization research provides some guidelines that are important for governments to consider as they examine and develop their approaches to internationalizing their higher education systems. The term *internationalization*[16] has undergone significant discussion and debate. While there may not be widespread agreement on the exact meaning of the term, some aspects are perceived as critical. Francis, Knight, McKellin and de Wit[17] perceive internationalization as a process which is ongoing and dynamic. Infusion of the international dimension into programs, policies, procedures and plans is key and facilitates the sustainability of the process. Finally, internationalization achieves greater stability when a number of different activities, programs and initiatives work in mutually strengthening ways.

The same researchers[18] outline a series of mechanisms for achieving internationalization focusing on students, faculty, curriculum and the community, ranging from integrating an international dimension across the curriculum to creating opportunities for students and faculty to study abroad. While recognizing the value of a range of internationalization programs, these researchers have also noted the importance of a number of organizational factors necessary for effective internationalization. These include the support and commitment of senior administration; a critical mass of faculty and staff who are supportive, committed and involved in the process; integration of internationalization into the planning, budgeting and evaluation systems of the institution; a central office or coordinator to facilitate communication, linkages, focus and support; adequate financial resources to support the process; and professional development programs for faculty and staff. The selected literature advocates for a comprehensive process of transformation and change through the infusion of internationalization throughout programs and across organizational processes, as it is through this broad and deep approach that internationalization will be sustainable in the long term.

Given this framework, important considerations for provincial governments developing their internationalization approaches might be:

- Creating a vision for internationalization by involving key stakeholders in a dialogue and discussion about the rationale for internationalization, developing clear internationalization goals and objectives with measurable outcomes which are integrated with the plans and/or strategies of core government activities.
- Raising awareness about what internationalization is and why it is important, and developing a broad-based understanding about internationalization within the bureaucracy and across the education system.
- Providing adequate financial resources and implementing a range of integrated internationalization programs that achieve the overall goals for the process building upon positive practices already established within the system and supported by appropriate policies, plans and procedures.
- Creating a framework that facilitates collaborative leadership amongst provincial and national stakeholders and recognizes that internationalization is a complex process involving a wide range of players

engaged in a broad range of roles and responsibilities.

- Ensuring the ongoing quality of programs through a commitment to evaluating and assessing outcomes, supporting the professional development of faculty, staff and administrators and enhancing the capacity of the system to deliver leading-edge programs.

- Committing to ongoing environmental scanning to understand the broader context within which internationalization occurs and to become aware of new trends and developments and their implications for existing plans and programs.

The expressed commitment to internationalization by Manitoba and Alberta and their indications of support for long-term planning, collaboration, quality, professional development, advocacy and comprehensiveness are a positive development in Canada. The significant challenge for these jurisdictions, and for other jurisdictions exploring their role in internationalization, is turning their rhetoric into reality. The time is right, given the growing interest in and involvement by governments internationalization, to broaden the discussion and dialogue concerning rationales, strategies and outcomes for provincial involvement in internationalization and to engage in research in this area.

5

The Internationalization of Québec Universities: From Public Policies to Concrete Measures

France Picard, Université Laval
Diane Mills, Bishop's University

Introduction

Surveys of all Québec universities conducted by the Conseil supérieur de l'éducation[1] [Québec Advisory Council on Education] have shown that most institutions consider internationalization a priority and engage in a relatively high level of activity in this field. What are the main reasons for this trend found in Québec universities? What support does the Québec government provide for the implementation of internationalization initiatives? These are the basic questions addressed in this chapter.

The first section outlines the historical events underpinning the political and institutional guidelines for university internationalization, up to and including the challenges and issues of today. The second section describes the changes in public policy that have influenced the development of internationalization at Québec universities. The third section presents an overview of current initiatives pursued by Québec universities.[2] The fourth and last section discusses an innovative measure designed both to increase the mobility of Québec students and to promote studies outside Québec.

Historical Milestones, Current Challenges

University internationalization has been linked to geopolitical events that have influenced not only public policy in the area of international relations but also the nature of international exchanges between universities and the structure of the network of partner countries. The challenges and issues that universities are currently facing in this field thus stem from historical events in addition to current social, political and economic contexts.

It is important to note that in Québec, the university system has developed over the past 150 years, with major expansion occurring in the late 1960s. As a result, Québec has a relatively young university system, and its activities in the field of internationalization have taken place mainly since the 1970s, the period selected as a starting point for analysis of the various phases of public policy.

The Origin of Québec's University System and Ties with Europe

McGill University and Université Laval, Québec's first two universities, were both founded in the nineteenth century. During this period, the European higher education model was being exported to colonies in the Americas, Africa and Asia, and international exchange was centred in Europe. In the twentieth century, following the two world wars, the international initiatives of universities were based on the political objectives of peace and mutual understanding between nations.[3]

The Expansion of Québec's University System and International Assistance Initiatives

During the Cold War period of 1946 to 1991, following the lead of universities in the United States, university cooperation with developing countries emerged in an attempt to counterbalance the influence of the Soviet Union.[4] This occurred also in Canadian universities, and they were supported in their activities by grants from the Canadian International Development Agency (CIDA). Canadian universities played a major role in international cooperation activities.[5] From 1968 to 1983, Québec's university system expanded as ten French-language universities, located throughout the province, were established to create the Université du Québec network.[6]

At that time, French universities opened their doors to students from French-speaking African nations. The fall of the Berlin Wall in 1989 heralded the end of communism, and the Soviet Union fell two years later. Funding of international assistance initiatives for universities continued at the same level until the mid-1990s, then declined as CIDA grants were scaled back.

Québec Autonomy on the International Stage

Historically, Québec has affirmed its autonomy to act on the international stage in areas of its jurisdiction. In 1961, La Maison du Québec was opened in Paris, later to become a General Delegation. Today, Québec has approximately thirty delegations or offices located in eighteen different countries. In 2002, the Ministère de l'Éducation[7] adopted an internationalization strategy for all educational levels. This strategy stated Québec's intention to continue its involvement in education at the international level. In May 2006, the Québec government signed an agreement with the Canadian federal government[8] allowing Québec to be part of the permanent Canadian delegation to the United Nations Educational, Scientific and Cultural Organization (UNESCO). At the end of the same month, in collaboration with the Canadian government, Québec established a new international policy reaffirming its autonomy with regard to international exchanges to support the international promotion of the French language and the major role played by

Québec within La Francophonie.[9]

The Affirmation of Québec's French Culture and Its Influence on the University System and International Exchange

In the wake of the Quiet Revolution, given that Québec constituted a French-speaking enclave within North America, several laws centred on the preservation of the French language were enacted. The timeline is as follows:

- 1969: passing of Bill 63, the Act to Promote the French Language in Québec, among other things promoting the use of the French language in elementary and secondary schools.
- 1974: passing of Bill 22, the Official Language Act, proclaiming French as the official language of Québec in business and government.
- 1977: Bill 101, Québec's Charter of the French Language, gave concrete expression to the aspirations contained in previous legislation and went further by introducing the notion that French in Québec should be "predominant," an objective pursued by the Parti Québécois, which had come to power in 1976.[10]
- 2002: the Charter of the French Language was amended. French-language universities in Québec were required to advise the Minister of Education of their policy on the use of French, whether as a language used to communicate with outside organizations, as the working language for their employees, or as the common language for teaching and research. For their part, English-language universities were required to specify how French was used in their communications and to name the procedures

used to teach French as a second language.[11]

All this legislation reflects the importance placed on French-language schooling over the years while the language rights of Anglophones were preserved. The requirement that children be schooled in French at the elementary and secondary levels does not carry over into higher education, but access to French-language universities is clearly promoted by the fact that fifteen out of eighteen Québec institutions in the university system use French as the teaching language. In the field of internationalization, the teaching language plays a role in the universities' recruitment and attraction of international students, as discussed below; for example, access to higher education in English is one of the aspirations of Asian students and their families,[12] whereas most students who come to Québec from French-speaking countries prefer to study in a French-language university.

Current Challenges

The current context for the development of internationalization activities by Québec universities is rooted in these historical milestones. However, new challenges are emerging. For higher education systems everywhere, internationalization raises major concerns, primarily regarding:

- the brain drain/brain gain balance of students, professionals and researchers;
- the enrichment of the education experience for domestic students;
- quality assurance in education;
- national security;
- the reciprocal benefits pursued by partners through their participation in joint international projects.

In addition, Québec universities face specific challenges. Firstly,

Québec largely depends on immigration for its social and economic development. Although Québec, like Canada, saw an increase in the number of young adults (aged 20 to 29) between the late 1990s and 2004, the demographic situation of this age group remains tenuous following a decade of continuous decline. Given that a certain number of international students will eventually choose to settle in Québec, their recruitment could help fill the number of high-level research and professional positions needed by Québec society. International students represent a select category of immigrants under Canadian and Québec immigration policies. However, the delicate question of brain drain among international students from developing countries is crucial, as it has ethical ramifications at an international level that must be addressed.

Secondly, Québec's ongoing influence in Francophone countries is an integral part of its public policy in the field of international relations, and its French-language universities have a role to play in this field. This is reflected, for example, in cooperative projects that historically have brought together universities in Québec and France and have led the former to welcome students from French-speaking Africa. Given a global context where English is the common language of internationalization, Québec's French-language universities have had to increase their efforts to maintain an active output of scientific publications in French, as well as to improve the language skills of French-speaking students not only in French but also in English or another language to prepare them for global competencies.

Thirdly, research is, by its very nature, international. Yet no country, however affluent, ever has sufficient resources or expertise to conduct scientific research independently in complex areas such as climate change, genomics, nanotechnology, world population growth or multiculturalism. Moreover, given that Québec's industrial base largely consists of small and medium-sized businesses with limited research capabilities, Québec universities play a pivotal role in the province's research commitment. Therefore, university research is a critical factor in innovation and economic development, and the internationalization of research has become a means to reinforce the performance of Québec's universities. For instance, international research collaboration provides faculty members and students at the postgraduate level access to international expertise and state-of-the-art laboratories.

Public Policy in the Field of Internationalization

Public policy guidelines on the internationalization of Québec universities reflect major social realities. Before examining the main guidelines, it is instructive to consider the place of Québec universities in the Canadian system as a whole.

In keeping with its demographic rank within Canada, Québec has the second-largest university system, after Ontario's. In 2003-04, Québec's universities recruited approximately 26 percent of all university students in Canada. Of this number, one-quarter attended English-language universities, and three-quarters attended French-language universities. University funding policy in Québec promotes access to higher education; over the years, the Québec government has subsidized its universities to a greater extent than is the case elsewhere in Canada. This policy has resulted in a freeze on tuition fees for Québec residents since 1994. In 2005, tuition fees were approximately $1,700 for a total of ten three-credit courses per academic year.

With regard to public policies adopted since the 1970s, five main phases are evident. The **first phase** centred on international assistance for developing countries, which increased during the Cold War. The funding provided to Canadian universities by CIDA supported the development of this type of international activity.

The **second phase** involved the striking of a new balance between international students in Québec's English-language and French-language universities. At the end of the 1970s, as English-language universities accounted for 75 percent of international students in Québec, the Québec government decided to support French-language universities in recruiting international students. To this end, in 1979, international students from Francophone countries, including France and French-speaking African nations, were exempted from an increase in tuition fees for international students that had been implemented the previous year. This strategy was designed to favour French-language universities in the recruitment of international students.

During the **third phase**, public policy with regard to the influence of Québec universities within La Francophonie was less evident. In 1983, restrictions were imposed on the exemption from increased tuition fees through the establishment of a quota for each country, with the exception of France. In addition, the exemptions were extended to include other countries outside La Francophonie. In other words, the objectives of the exemption program were modified. During this phase, development assistance initiatives declined.

The **fourth phase,** beginning in the mid-1980s, saw the consolidation of cooperation with other industrialized countries in order to boost economic growth in Québec. In accordance with this objective, some of the exemptions from increased tuition fees were also used to attract promising students, particularly those at the postgraduate level, and students from the United States, Japan and Europe.

During the **fifth phase**, beginning in 2000 and still ongoing, the Québec government introduced several policies focused on internationalization.[13] These policies led to a range of measures at both the provincial and federal levels to support student mobility, as follows:

Since 2000, $10 million has been allocated annually to help Québec university students study abroad. The Programme de bourses de courts séjours d'études universitaires à l'extérieur du Québec (PBCSE), a bursary program for short periods of university study outside Québec, has been established by the ministry. This measure will be detailed in the last section below.

Since 2000, the Politique des droits de scolarité aux étudiants internationaux, a policy on tuition fees for international students, has set the following general guidelines:

- Tuition fees remain frozen for Québec residents to improve accessibility to higher education for students from Québec, and fees for Canadian students from outside Québec are based on average Canadian tuition fees. For international students, tuition fees are set at a higher rate but are still below the average cost of each student enrolled, in order to keep Québec universities competitive with the North American market.
- In order to increase the number of foreign students enrolled in universities in outlying regions, the ministry grants additional tuition fee exemptions to these universities.
- International students at the postgraduate level have priority for additional tuition fee exemptions, and postdoctoral researchers from abroad can benefit from tax exemptions.
- To redress the imbalance between incoming and outgoing students participating in short study periods abroad, the ministry has introduced parity-based university funding.
- A support program has been established for international initiatives in the fields of research and innovation.
- The programs of some Québec research funding agencies now include an international component.
- Québec's recently adopted International Policy out-

lines various actions to promote university internationalization, including integrating universities into the mainstream of international networks,[14] recognizing the qualifications of workers trained outside Québec, providing accreditation programs in collaboration with professional orders,[15] and placing priority on knowledge, innovation and education in internationalization initiatives.[16]

- Various federal government measures also support international students. As of 2006, international students can work on or off campus with a work permit. In addition, some of the formalities for obtaining study permits will be streamlined following changes adopted by Citizenship and Immigration Canada.

Highlights of the Internationalization of Québec Universities

Certainly, Québec universities have developed their internationalization activities to varying degrees, and there are also differences among them in terms of strategies adopted to support or promote internationalization and the values on which it is based. The size, location and language of instruction of each university are determining factors in the advance of internationalization. Beyond the apparent differences, several trends can be noted:

- **Administrative reorganizations have taken place in recent years to make internationalization a priority of Québec universities**. The role of the international office has changed. Twelve out of eighteen universities in Québec have now set up an international office.[18]
- **International student enrolment in Québec has increased**, particularly since the year 2000, slightly

more than the average in Canadian universities. The number of international students with study permits in Québec universities has tripled in just over twenty years, from 6,500 in 1982 to almost 20,000 in 2004. In 2003, McGill University and Concordia University reported 44 percent of all international students enrolled in Québec universities — a higher percentage than their relative weight within the university system — while Université de Montréal, Université Laval, Université du Québec à Montréal and École Polytechnique together reported 39 percent of international enrolment. International students represent 7.7 percent of all university students in Québec,[18] a percentage that is slightly above the Canadian average. In 2003-04, Québec recorded 30 percent of the international students enrolled in Canadian universities,[19] slightly more than its relative share given the size of its university system compared to those of other provinces.

- **Both universities and government are working to increase the international mobility of Québec university students**. The data available to measure this trend are incomplete, as is the case in many other university systems around the world. For Québec, it is estimated that fewer than 1 percent of students enrolled in a Québec university in the fall of 2003 had taken part in a short education session abroad. In some universities, where the mobility of domestic students is more pronounced, it is estimated that between 10 and 15 percent of graduates had completed an education session abroad during their program.

- **Historically, Québec's French-language and**

English-language universities have defined their networks of partner universities differently. English-language universities tend to accept more students from the United States, the Middle East, Asia and Oceania, a pattern resembling that in the rest of Canada. By contrast, French-language universities accept students mainly from France and French-speaking Africa, as well as from Central and South America and the Caribbean.[20] However, a survey of university administrators carried out by the Conseil in 2005 revealed that both English and French-language Québec universities are in the process of redefining their partner universities abroad; for example, as current agreements expire, decisions will be made to maintain existing partnerships or develop new ones, depending on the strategies of each university. One of the goals is closer affiliations with North America; another is access to new markets, including Asia. The nature of the exchange has changed: Québec universities are attempting to develop ties with partner universities with which they can establish integrated curricula, in order to promote student mobility, and they are also attempting to broaden the scope of the partnerships to cover other international activities such as joint research projects.

- **International research collaboration, an established tradition, is continuing to increase, both in terms of knowledge production and dissemination.** With regard to research, a survey of faculty workloads conducted in the spring of 2003 revealed that half of all faculty members, regardless of subject, considered their involvement in international research activities to be

"very" or "quite" important.[21] However, it has been
shown that this involvement in international research
activities did not necessarily lead to an equivalent
degree of participation by Québec faculty members in
research projects subsidized by international agencies.[22]
In natural sciences and engineering, the percentage of
publications by Québec faculty members in collaboration with foreign researchers did increase gradually
between 1981 and 2000, from 20 to 40 percent.[23]

In this brief overview, it is important to note that student mobility, along with international research collaboration, represent the
primary activities in the internationalization of Québec universities.
These two types of activity are also key action points for future
development, according to university administrators. Few Québec
universities have become involved in cross-border education. However, according to observations made by Jane Knight,[24] this
situation is expected to change in the coming years within Canada
and internationally. Québec universities have also withdrawn from
internationalization initiatives pertaining to development assistance
for developing countries, a trend that reflects a decrease in CIDA
funding since the mid-1990s. Only five of eighteen Québec universities continue to consider development assistance as a priority in
their ongoing internationalization.[25]

Bursaries for Study Abroad

Québec universities and the Conference of Rectors and Principals
of the Universities of Québec (CREPUQ) lobbied vigorously for
student mobility funding in the late 1990s. At a Youth Summit in
the winter of 2000, the former Parti Québécois Minister of Education, François Legault, announced the creation of a $10
million-a-year pilot project, Programme de bourses pour de courts
séjours d'études universitaires à l'extérieur du Québec (PBCSE),

with the first Québec students slated to leave for their host universities in the fall semester. The objective of the three-year program
was (and continues to be, since its regularization in the provincial
government's budget in 2006) to promote the internationalization
of Québec universities, to encourage both undergraduate and graduate students to complete part of their degree program in another
Canadian province or abroad, and to develop competencies and
skills for success in an international context. What are those competencies?

   The preferred definition of intercultural competence (considered
by many businesses to be at the core of global competence) is
"Knowledge of others; knowledge of self; skills to interpret and
relate; skills to discover and/or to interact; valuing others' values,
beliefs and behaviours; and relativizing one's self. Linguistic competence also plays a key role."[26] Dr. Darla Deardorff, who teaches
cross-cultural courses at Duke University, has created a model for
intercultural competence, defined as the "ability to communicate
effectively and appropriately in intercultural situations based on
one's intercultural knowledge, skills and attitudes." Students need
to begin with the requisite attitudes of respect (valuing other cultures and diversity); openness (withholding judgement); and
curiosity and discovery (tolerating ambiguity). Students need to
acquire knowledge and comprehension (cultural self-awareness,
deep cultural knowledge including contexts and impact of others'
world-views) and sociolinguistic awareness. Combining these with
skills to listen, observe, interpret, analyze, evaluate and relate, students can then develop "internal outcomes" of adaptability and
flexibility and an ethnorelative view as well as empathy for others.
The depth of intercultural competence will depend on the levels of
attitudes attained, knowledge/comprehension and skills acquired.
The desired "external outcome" is for the student to be effective
and appropriate in communication and behaviour in intercultural
situations. [27]

Administration of the Bursary Program

Each university in Québec receives an annual grant from the ministry based on the full-time enrolment of Québec students. For some of these institutions this represents an amount in excess of $1 million for student mobility. Bursaries are awarded to students who demonstrate academic excellence and meet the criteria established by their respective university for the CREPUQ or bilateral exchange programs, international development projects, co-op work internships, or research for a thesis, which all represent course credits that can be transferred to their degree program in Québec. To ensure that the requirement of excellence for those participating in the PBCSE bursary program is respected, the ministry recommends that students who return to their home university within two weeks of their departure, or those who fail all their courses abroad, refund the bursaries in full. Under this program, a student's decision to participate in education experiences abroad should be linked to their professional and career goals, with advisers and career counsellors providing information to assist them in articulating the skills and competencies they have acquired.

To be eligible for a bursary, students at the undergraduate level must have completed one-third of their ninety-credit program, while students at the graduate level must have completed nine credits. Students can go abroad for a minimum of two months and a maximum of eight months (two semesters), with a minimum of six credits and maximum of thirty credits transferred to a degree program at their home institution. Students can apply for two bursaries and make two trips of two months' duration each. Master's or doctoral degree students can research, write part of their thesis, or work abroad within the context of their academic program, after their course requirements have been met. The bursary can be complementary to another scholarship, including travel awards offered by the Office Franco-Québécois pour la jeunesse to Québec students going on exchange to a university in France or to participate in a co-op degree work program. Students are awarded $1,000 per month to study in the United States, European Union, Australia, New Zealand, Japan, Norway, Switzerland or Iceland; $750 a month for another province in Canada and all other destination countries, with a maximum amount of $8,000 for eight months to one year. At their discretion, universities can decide to offer a lesser amount to each student, which has been the case for those institutions whose budget allocation from the ministry is no longer sufficient to fund the number of students leaving their campus (Bishop's, for example). Several universities make the PBCSE bursaries payable in two, three or four instalments, and some wait until final marks are submitted before providing final payment. Also at the discretion of each university, students receiving funding from other mobility programs may be denied a bursary in order to enable the greatest number of eligible students to have the opportunity to study abroad.

In the first year of the program, $50,000 was spent on advertising; $25,000 was spent in the second and third years. Universities were allocated 10 percent of their first year's budget to promote and administer the bursary program. This was then reduced to 5 percent for the subsequent years after the program was regularized. Bishop's, for example, uses part of its administrative fee to pay membership fees to the National Student Exchange program in the United States. Due to the success of the program and the near-tripling of the number of students participating, requests have been made by Québec universities to the ministry to increase this fee amount to 10 percent or more, to provide an adequate level of funding to support students preparing their study experience abroad both administratively and academically.

Most offices responsible for exchange programs did not hire additional full-time staff, with the understanding that the funding was temporary and resources and infrastructure were already in place. This has meant a significant increase in workload for those who assist students in preparing to study abroad, for faculty who pre-approve courses and for the university financial aid offices that issue the bursary cheques to the students.

Universities submit annual reports and financial statements to the ministry on November 30 of each year for the previous three semesters (fall, winter, summer), including the names of all participating undergraduate and graduate students, where they went, how long they were away and how many credits they transferred to their degree programs in Québec. The remaining $11.7 million of initial pilot project funding for 2000-03, not allocated in these first three years, was recouped from Québec universities' budgets by the ministry in January 2006.

Numbers of Students Receiving Bursaries for Study Abroad

In the five years after the implementation of the program at the beginning of the 2000-01 academic year, the number of students receiving PBCSE bursaries more than doubled, increasing from 1,094 to 2,504 in 2004-05 alone. An example of this increase can be seen at HEC Montréal, whose international office had received 455 applications (approximately 4 percent of their student body) by the January 2006 deadline to participate in their bilateral exchange programs for 2006-07, compared to 120 applications three years earlier. Université de Montréal sent 485 students to study abroad in 2005-06, while Laval sent nearly 1,000 of its 36,000 students.

Internationalization and Competencies: Initial Results

The dynamic process of the internationalization of Québec universities has seen both the restructuring and the creation of international offices, including two new positions responsible for study abroad programs: Vice-Provost, International Relations at

Concordia and Vice-Principal, Research and International Relations at McGill. CREPUQ established a Vice-Principal's Committee for International Relations in December 2005 to direct the development of the PBSCE program, and its first meeting was held in March 2006.

The value of the program to the students is reflected in some of the comments made by students from Université Laval:

> I've learned to be concerned with the economic and social development of countries and regions, and I intend to be involved in alleviating poverty in Québec. (a business exchange student in Mexico)

> Other cultures are no longer abstract concepts to me. By making friends with students from five continents, I've personally embraced several cultural concepts. (a literature exchange student in France)

> The change which I appreciate the most is a feeling of independence and openness to the world. I now have the capability to take initiatives myself in the future. (a business exchange student in Mexico)

As mentioned previously, the program's main purpose is the development of competencies which students can use in their future professional careers or further education, to succeed as global citizens in a workforce that is increasingly interconnected in the twenty-first century. The value of study abroad to employers is students' demonstrated skills and competencies gained through their experience — but not education abroad in itself.[28] Students must learn to identify and to effectively market competencies they gain through education abroad experiences. To aid in this process, universities and colleges could begin to develop specific indicators of intercultural competence, thus making it measurable as a learning outcome. For students to function more effectively in our integrated world, they need to interact appropriately with people who have other cultural identities.

Québec universities have proven that providing students with funding increases the number that participate in either exchange programs or other academic and research activities abroad. This innovative commitment to internationalization has given thousands of students the opportunity to benefit personally and professionally from their experience in living and studying in another country and culture, being immersed in a different educational environment with a different world view on their subject of study. Only longitudinal studies concerning long-term impacts on employment and career paths will provide real data on how this study abroad has affected students in the global economy.

Conclusion

Based on the CSE survey of Québec universities, the following key elements of internationalization emerge:

- increased internationalization activities over the years;
- consolidated internationalization initiatives aimed at meeting the objectives of individual universities;
- strengthened cooperation with partner universities abroad;
- explicit recognition of international aspects of the missions, management tools and organizational structures of Québec universities.

However, within the university system and in the development of public policy, additional effort is still needed to address difficulties arising from the expansion of internationalization activities. Work has begun to recognize the prior learning and qualifications of foreign students, to rethink short-term student mobility agreements, also known as "CREPUQ consortium agreements," and to improve the procedure for issuing study permits. The development of internationalization activities also raises the challenge of ensuring that the quality of the education provided reaches international standards.

In addition, the recommendations addressed by the Conseil to the Minister of Education, Recreation and Sports emphasize several essential principles to guide universities in the development of their internationalization activities:

- university internationalization must be based on a harmonization of national and global interests;
- exchanges and partnerships that result from internationalization activities must comply with the principle of reciprocity;
- successive rounds of negotiation for the General Agreement on Trade in Services will eventually require universities to formalize general policy guidelines regarding cross-border education;
- internationalization must be founded on established values, including the enrichment of peoples around the world through the promotion of sustainable development, the progress of democracy, the respect for fundamental human rights, a reinforcement of social cohesion and a culture of peace.

Contrastive Rhetoric and the University Classroom

Linda Steinman, York University

If everyone conforms to one style in academic writing, then where is the richness of writing?

— J. Liu[1]

There is genius in every language.

— N. Thiong'o[2]

I have worked in the presence of multilingual speakers and writers for decades as a teacher of English as a second language and an educator of teachers. I kept my practice fresh, and generally I was satisfied with what I did concerning academic writing and with how my college students produced — in many cases, *re*produced — what was expected of them.

And then I began doctoral work in second language education and my equilibrium became upset. For my thesis, I examined autobiographies by those who have crossed languages and cultures; these

154

powerful first-person accounts led me to question my attitude and practice with respect to teaching North American academic writing conventions. The multiliterate learners/narrativists in my corpus underscored the significant effects that our language histories generally and writing histories more specifically have on our present and future actions. I learned much about what it *feels* like to write in a second language, and what is involved in writing in languages other than English. I explored and was strongly affected by research literature on contrastive rhetoric, which is the study of writing conventions and writing values and how they vary across cultures. I began to understand the many implications of these values — textual, contextual, cognitive, emotional and political. I reconsidered from a pedagogical and human point of view what it was that we in the English for Academic Purposes professional community and specifically what *I* have been expecting multiliterate students to produce, and how I was requiring them to suppress rather than draw on a powerful personal resource — their first language writing.

Why, I began to wonder, did I work so hard to mainstream, to mould the written expression of my students when, on many occasions, their particular and unfamiliar take on a topic startled me into paying attention, even as I evaluated it into submission: "Their [writers' from other cultures] texts and interpretations can challenge us to recognize our own rhetorical prejudice and to reconceptualize our perspectives on academic discourse — a mutually enriching process."[3]

I began asking my English-as-a-second-language (ESL) students what it felt like to conform to a new writing style. In addition, I had my graduate students interview multiliterate writers for their experiences on writing across languages. I was as fascinated and sobered by the findings as I had been by my doctoral data. The connections between writing and identity are powerful. Dislocation, geographical and rhetorical, has consequences. It has become important to me that we in the academic community reexamine what it is and why it is that we maintain such a prescriptive view of what is acceptable in academic writing. I argue that we have a lot to learn by becoming more flexible and open readers or evaluators of texts authored by those who are writing in a language other than their first. I hope the following discussion of contrastive rhetoric will provide useful information and heighten awareness of what international students may be experiencing as they write their knowledge.

Contrastive rhetoric "is an area of research that has identified problems in composition encountered by second language writers, and by referring to the rhetorical strategies of the first language, attempts to explain them."[4] Connor (a multilingual person herself) is a leading researcher in the field of academic writing and contrastive rhetoric. I do question her use of "problems" in this definition. I would prefer the word *features* or *characteristics*. Awareness of contrastive rhetoric is important for those who teach, write and read in the university community. I recommend that faculty familiarize themselves with the writing conventions that students bring with them and help students to achieve balance between those conventions and the academic writing conventions that are favoured in North America: "A broad range of the world's people adopt models and norms diametrically opposed [to Western notions of voice]: they foreground subtle, interpretive, interdependent, non-assertive and even non-verbal characteristics of communicative interaction."[5] I argue that international students who study and write in Canadian university classrooms are likely to continue to be commuters among literacy communities and therefore will need a portfolio of writing skills, a repertoire of literacy personas appropriate for their various contexts. Total adaptation or capitulation to North American academic rhetoric can no longer be a goal of the university: "While the [*teaching*] profession celebrates heteroglossia, and difference, most rhetoric instruction remains monologic and ethnocentric."[6]

Some international students come to our campuses of their own volition while others are actively recruited in the drive to globalize our classrooms, to enrich our understanding of other worlds, other words. These individuals learned to write in particular places and ways and they are more than likely to value the writing expectations of their first culture. What happens then, when multiliterate students are asked to write their knowledge in our Canadian classrooms? What happens when a professor or a teaching assistant receives a paper that is shaped in unusual and unexpected ways? The following features (or irregularities, from a Western reader's point of view) may be present:

- The thesis or main point appears at the end of the text rather than up front.
- Maybe the language has more passion than the reader feels comfortable with.
- The progression may appear circular or digressive rather than linear.
- The readers seem to be expected (respected?) to draw their own conclusions.
- The writer cites people from the past — much more than five years earlier — perhaps many decades or centuries in the past.
- The authorial voice presents as humble rather than assertive.
- There may be no meta-discourse — no roadmap telling the reader where the writer is going or reviewing where she/he has been.

How is this work read? Is it read? How much is skimmed because it is not presented in the way in which native English speakers are programmed to read? What comments are noted, what suggestions are made (or criticisms leveled)? How welcomed are multiliterate international students and their take on the world into the Western academic community of practice?

I offer the following points to consider:

1. No language is neutral.[7] all writing styles are constructs and represent ideology.

2. Our writing histories/writing cultures shape how we write (and how we read) in ways big and small.

3. Insights into what it means to write in a new rhetorical style are to be found in both theoretical literature and first-person accounts.

4. Multiliteracies and critical theory are two theoretical frameworks that underscore the influence of contrastive rhetoric.

5. Changes in practice at the university should result from a serious consideration of contrastive rhetoric.

Textual conventions — what is enacted, expected and valued in the writing of a culture — are local and ideological: "Conventions governing academic discourse are partisan."[8] What native speakers of English in North America (hereafter referred to as the West) consider be logical and clear and effective is only one culture's notion of logic and clarity and effectiveness. In 1966, Robert Kaplan, an applied linguist, wrote a seminal paper on contrastive rhetoric.[9] In this often-cited article, he used rough diagrams to represent how some cultures tend to shape their written discourse. For example, Western writing was illustrated as linear in organization; Oriental writing as circular; and Semitic writing as a series of parallel constructions that are more often coordinated than subordinated.

Those who came after Kaplan, and indeed Kaplan himself, criticized the 1966 paper and its claims for a variety of reasons: it was simplistic, even essentializing; many languages were omitted from the initial study; distinct language groups were oddly grouped — the classification of Oriental languages, for example, covered Chinese and Korean but not Japanese; and only organization was studied, not other variables of writing. As well, Kaplan's early work was called ethnocentric: it presented English patterns as the standard and viewed the writing patterns of other cultures as being more *something* than English or less *something* than English. I recently came across the term "ethnic rhetoric"[10] — which focuses less on the differences (contrasts) among rhetorics and more on the descriptions. But critical theorist Mao argues that current studies on ethnic rhetoric do continue to valorize English norms rather than describing each rhetoric on its own terms: "For example, Asian-American rhetoric ... must be Asian-American enough so as to be different from any other ethnic rhetoric. [Yet] ... its own rhetorical uniqueness and visibility will not become completely accepted unless it has been compared to, if not adjudicated against, Western rhetorical traditions."[11]

Since 1966, the field of contrastive rhetoric has expanded dramatically. In fact, in a recent text edited by Panetta,[12] *Contrastive Rhetoric Revisited and Redefined,* contrastive rhetoric was broadened to include not only writing conventions and values across language groups but also writing across geopolitical borders, gender borders, sexual orientation borders and economic borders. Furthermore, research is being done on writing conventions not only between English and other languages but also across varieties of English — across English*es*, if you will. Not dealt with here, but interesting areas of study, are discipline-specific (writing in the sciences versus writing in business contexts, both within a single culture and across cultures) and genre-specific contrastive rhetoric (variations between newspaper writing, or annual reports across different cultures). To complicate the subject even further (or to make it even more intriguing), contrastive rhetoric is an area of research housed, currently and concurrently, in applied linguistics, composition studies, education, anthropology, cultural/identity studies and, more recently but quite firmly, in critical theory. I have recently been examining how contrastive rhetoric can be described from a sociocultural perspective, which views communication as co-constructed, interactive, negotiated and "dialogic,"[13] rather than a series of rules or prescribed moves.

Another sociocultural theorist, Wertsch, acknowledges the tension that occurs when one uses a new tool, or means, to act upon the world. The new mediational means for an international student are the English language and western academic style of writing: "New mediational means transform mediated action.[14] ... The introduction of a new mediational means creates a kind of imbalance in the systemic organization of mediated action."[15] However, my focus in this chapter is contrastive rhetoric as it affects academic writing in the university classroom and I speak from my position as an applied linguist and a current teacher of English for academic purposes. I address my remarks particularly to faculty members in Canadian universities.

I will present a few of the dimensions along which writing may vary across cultures. These dimensions of potential difference include purpose, organization pattern, reader responsibility/writer responsibility, evidentials and authorial voice. Readers of this chapter may well have noticed some of these features in their own writing, if they are multiliterate, or in the writing of their multiliterate students or colleagues.

Purpose

Writing may be considered a vehicle for individual self-expression, as in the West, or as a medium for expressing solidarity and shared social purpose, as it is in Japan, according to Carson.[16]

Organization Pattern

Korean texts seem to be characterized by indirectness and nonlinear development, and the four-part pattern of Korean prose is transferred to writing in English.[17] There is a delayed introduction of purpose[18] and the main topic appears at the end of the text.[19] Clyne[20] describes German writing as digressive and propositionally asymmetrical, while longer sentences and greater elaborations are present in texts authored by Spanish writers.[21]

Reader Responsibility/Writer Responsibility

Hinds[22] notes that, in Chinese writing (as in English writing), the onus is on the writer to make things clear, whereas Japanese writers are more likely to expect the *readers* to make their own sense of the text — the intent being to stimulate the readers rather than to convince them. This is a feature of English writing that many of my own students find difficult to understand — the need to spell everything out explicitly for the readers, telling them what to think, rather than allowing them to reach their own conclusions and interpretations.

Evidentials

What counts as evidence in writing? Kaplan notes that cultures have different notions of what constitutes evidence, "the optimal order in which evidence is to be presented and the number of evidentiary instances that need to be presented in order to convince the reader."[23] Leki notes that personal experience simply does not count in some cultures: "Quoting famous people is what constitutes evidence."[24] She also observes that conventions of argumentation in English call for facts, statistics and illustrations; other cultures, however, "rely heavily on analogy, intuition, the beauty of the language, and the opinion of the learned of antiquity."[25]

Authorial Voice

Atkinson defined voice as "the cult and culture of personal opinion."[26]

This seems to me to be a particularly Western notion of voice. What happens, I ask, when a person's first culture and writing conventions of the first language train him/her to background personal opinions? Is this absence of voice, or a difference in concept of voice, of textual self?[27] Shen, one of many translingual writers who have written moving accounts of their indoctrination into English academic writing, points out that "the 'I' must be buried in writing in Chinese."[28] He describes the lack of sensitivity on the part of Western faculty to the enormity of the task facing those presented with a new rhetorical style.

Research indicates that first-language writing practices, and importantly, writing values, influence second language writing.[29] Insights are also provided by first-person accounts as multilinguals write about the dissonance and confusion and sometimes resistance that occur when writing values collide. Kamani from Bombay wrote: "In America I was expected to come clean on information, feelings, ignorance, speculations, judgment — largely taboo in India and considered bizarre."[30] Keizer, whose first language is Dutch, cynically entitled his essay "Circus Biped" and described how he resented having to "perform" in English in order to have his ideas accepted: "Writing in English first felt to me like trying to plough stretches of marble: an ungainly procedure ruining some pretty nice material."[31] Resistance was Brintrup's reaction when she came from Chile to be a doctoral student in the United States: "To be more effective and efficient academically I received advice like this: 'Forget everything you learned in the past and start again.' Why this necessity of washing off my mind...? I felt like something had been taken away, like my skin and my verbal conception of the world."[32] Canagarajah[33] wrote evocatively of the criticism he received from both of his writing communities as he composed in Tamil and in English. He spent many years identifying and then learning to use North American discourse conventions. When he applied that style to a text he wrote in his Sri Lankan academic community, his colleague and his students reacted strongly and negatively. His writing seemed "pompous" and "overconfident": "My cocksure way of beginning the essay — announcing my thesis, delineating the steps of the argument, promising to prove my points conclusively — left a bad taste in the mouths of the local readership. They said that this excessively planned and calculated move gave the impression of a 'style-less,' mechanical writing."[34]

Canagarajah has become sensitive to using American discourse style when writing about what he refers to as periphery concerns. "Thanks to my colleagues from Sri Lanka, I have become alert to the contradictions of representing periphery concerns and subjects in a discourse that is so alien to their interests and traditions."[35] He laments his capitulation to western modes of writing: "Perhaps I shouldn't have gone to such lengths to suppress my ethos and my feelings in my early journal articles. My strategy has been to write myself out of my texts." He now uses and calls for hybrid, heteroglossic texts: "I am now constantly trying out ways of reconciling the competing discourses in a manner that is more satisfying to both my politics and poetics."[36]

Zamel expressed concern over the reductionist and formulaic expectations and results when teaching/acquiring academic discourse. Students struggle as they "defer to the voice of the academy ... and disguise themselves in the weighty imponderable voice of acquired authority losing themselves in the process."[37] Further, Zamel suggested, what is reified as academic discourse is not as well-defined as one thinks. Multiliteracies (a philosophy and practice of teaching discourse which I will discuss in the next section) also suggests that teachers cannot really claim to know what discourse communities they are preparing students for. In five or ten years' time, much of the communicating may be in multimodal format or otherwise quite unlike the nature and models of communicating today.

There is a dilemma then. How, and to what extent, should

international students be socialized into the Western academic writing community? I argue for a flexible, additive intent rather than a prescriptive, subtractive one. The goal of academic writers today should be to build writing repertoires, or "everchanging portfolios of skills,"[38] so that as international citizens, they may move from writing culture to writing culture easily. Code-switching is a term generally reserved for moving back and forth between languages in spoken discourse. The switching happens perhaps on the basis of topic, of audience, of solidarity, of linguistic environment and the like. Code-switching could refer as well to movement back and forth between written discourse conventions. The beginning of the title that Canagarajah gave to his literacy autobiography, written as an essay, is "Shuttling Between Literacy Communities."[39] If our students are, similarly, to be literacy commuters, it seems imperative that faculty present Western rhetorical conventions as just that — not the ultimate in logic or clarity — but simply what Western readers expect and like to receive. I argue that universities are preparing students, and students are preparing themselves, to operate in multiple literacy communities. Mao acknowledges the inevitability of border crossings in rhetoric: she describes "rhetorical borderlands where creative heteroglossia becomes the norm."[40] As globalization flourishes, the likelihood increases that readers of our students' texts will be speakers of other languages, or speakers of English as an additional language. One-size writing will not fit all: "Diverse readership implies diverse notions of what constitutes good writing."[41]

I present two theoretical frameworks that support contrastive rhetoric quite powerfully: multiliteracies and critical theory.

Multiliteracies

The New London Group refer to creating meaning as *design*, and call for using all available designs — sound, distance, gesture, different modalities (not only print) — when representing knowledge. The first-language writing pattern is one of those designs, I would argue. According to the New London Group, "We are both inheritors of patterns and conventions of meaning while at the same time active designers of meaning,"[42] and they argue against canons: "Productive diversity ... the multiplicity of cultures, experiences, ways of making meaning, and ways of thinking — can be harnessed as an asset."[43] There should be no standard that cannot be negotiated. Here, in my view, is where sociocultural theory meets multiliteracies in a mutually supportive way: "To be relevant, learning processes need to recruit, rather than attempt to ignore or erase, the different subjectivities, interests, intentions, commitments and purposes that students bring to learning,"[44] leading to transformation not only of new users of English but of native users of English.

Critical Theory

Whose discourse is dominant? Whose knowledge counts and whose does not? Critical theory examines the hegemony involved in devaluing someone's form of self-expression and attempting to erase it: "We must be humble when claiming to know."[45] Identity construction, destruction and reconstruction through text were dealt with at length by Canagarajah in his 2002 text, *A Geopolitics of Academic Writing*, and by other critical theorists such as Kubota and Lehner,[46] and Pennycook.[47] Critical theory, multiliteracy pedagogy and contrastive rhetoric meet in a call for constructivism in the classroom; that is, knowledge is co-constructed. Emerging text replaces reproduced text. Zamel suggests that, rather than emphasizing what students must change, "what they must become in order to accommodate our discourse, we work to sustain and extend the histories and abilities that students bring with them."[48]

Shi[49] wrote of Chinese writing teachers who returned from training in the West having been sold on Western academic writing and planning to pass on this rhetoric format to their students. Clearly, English and its rhetorical style were viewed as "linguistic capital," to use Bourdieu's term.[50] There are implications — personal, linguistic, sociocultural and political — for this adoption of the conventions of another, and there is resistance on the part of some multilingual writers: "A moth is drawn to the light and ultimately consumed by it. I do not want graduate school to be such an experience for me. The question hovers: How close to the light can I get and not be drawn into destruction? I must be cautious ... I must survive, wings and spirit intact."[51]

I suggest some implications for practice, and invite readers to add some of their own:

- We become aware of and acknowledge the powerful resource in our classrooms that is first-language writing. Multiliteracies with its respect for multiple sources and multiple (re)presentations is both a reality and a goal. We raise for discussion in class the constructed nature of rhetorics and invite students to consider what features they will hold on to from the writing conventions of their first language and what they will incorporate from the writing conventions of their second language in order to best achieve their personal goals.

- We proceed cautiously and sensitively when commenting on the writing practices of international students. Ballard and Clanchy found that, "when faced with writing that falls out of their own notions of acceptable style and pattern of argument, [teachers] pepper the margins with 'irrelevant', 'incoherent', 'illogical'."[52] Instead, we could ask, "Is the writing disorganized or differently organized? Is it illogical, or differently logical?"[53] As our students add to their writing repertoires, we in the Western academic community need to add to our reading repertoires. Research indicates that multiliterate writers are themselves more skilful at interpreting a wider variety of writing style. Monolingual readers are accustomed to receiving their academic information in very particular ways. Stepping out of our zone of comfort would be good. Can we only shape or are we willing to be shaped?

- We might reconsider the particular demands we make in writing. We might reprioritize what really matters with respect to the intelligibility of a text. If we are members and invite members of the international community of practice, then we must become familiar with and appreciate hybridity of texts, and accents in writing.

At the beginning of this chapter, I provided two quotes and, for symmetry, I end with two quotes, one by Zamel and Spack and one by Lloyd, penned more than fifty years ago:

> One way to enable students to find their way in the academy, we believe, is for us to accept wider varieties of expression, to embrace multiple ways of communicating. This is exactly what we are asking students to do.[54]

> If we find anything that we have to change — and we do — we know that we are touching something that goes deep into students' pasts and spreads wide in their personal lives. We will seek not to dislodge one habit in favor of another but to provide alternative choices for a freer social mobility. We seek to enrich, not to correct. By respecting students' traditions and the people from whom they come, we teach them to respect and to hold tight to what they have as they reach for more.[55]

7

Internationalization, Social Transformation and Global Citizenship: An Evaluation of Global Health

Lori Hanson and Madeline Johnson
University of Saskatchewan

1. Introduction and Background

In 2000, I was offered the opportunity to teach an innovative inter-disciplinary undergraduate course entitled International Health. The course was the brainchild of a group of Saskatoon community and academic activists seeking ways to increase the capacity of students to understand the links between the health determinants of marginal-ized peoples of Saskatchewan and communities abroad by having students engage in and reflect upon community health and develop-ment efforts locally.[1] The underlying teaching philosophy and pedagogy guiding the class is transformative education, and the guid-ing theoretical frameworks draw from human-centred development and primary health care. I have since taught that class six times. Although the course has metamorphosed in content and name and has expanded to include a sequel six-week course in Nicaragua, the underlying philosophies, basic structure and goals remain constant.

During the same time period, the University of Saskatchewan

engaged in the process known as internationalization. As part of that process, a "University of Saskatchewan Internationalization Mission Statement"[2] and an ensuing foundational document[3] required that each college add an international dimension to its programs. Transformative learning, global health teaching and the internationalization process synergistically connected when I was asked to write an internationalization strategy and to assume leadership of the process for the College of Medicine (COM). The growth and nature of internationalization at the University of Saskatchewan and in the COM in particular is not the focus of this chapter, although it is important as background and context in which an evaluation of current global health teaching becomes both relevant and timely.

The evaluation described here considers the nature of actual versus intended transformations of students and our collective communities/world, and it probes the question of whether and how such social change objectives might be integrated into internationalized curricula. A more persistent question regarding "educating for social change"[4] also underpins the evaluation. Broadly, that question asks: Can we as educators in a university setting create internationalized curricula that catalyze personal and social transformation and fosters global citizenship? If so, how?

This chapter has as its modest goal not to ascertain but to propose answers to such queries. It is organized in three main sections: a brief description of internationalization models, the COM's social transformation model and curricular implications; an outline of concepts underlying the teaching of global health; and the methods, findings and discussion of the follow-up class evaluation.

2. Internationalization Models

Globalization is a multifaceted phenomenon, and one of its major components is the international-

> ization of education. The increasing pace and
> complexity of global knowledge flows, and the
> accelerating exchange of educational ideas, prac-
> tices and policies, are important drivers of
> globalization. Higher education is a key site for
> these flows and exchanges.[5]

Given that the term *internationalization* became popular in the globalization era, the internationalization of higher education is often considered to be the institutional process in which universities compete for students globally and the educational process that prepares students for a competitive and globalized world by providing international opportunities to students and faculty to prepare them for securing competitive global market advantage.[6] Warner identifies these characteristics as pertaining to the *market model* wherein internationalization is centrally about increasing the global advantage of academic institutions through strengthened competitive position.[7] Emphasis in this model is on standardization rather than innovation in educational programs.[8] While there is reason to suggest that this model — and its underlying neo-liberal philosophy — is the most established in North America as a whole, many Canadian sources trace the evolution of internationalization in higher education to the tradition of development assistance and student cultural exchanges.[9]

The *liberal model* explains those intercultural internationalization activities. It suggests that internationalization should be centrally about global cooperation and international and intercultural understanding.[10] The AUCC *Statement on Internationalization* illustrates the liberal model by using principles of collaboration, cooperation, contribution to development assistance, and idea sharing among members of the "global village" to describe the intended nature and goals of internationalization.[11]

The *social transformation model*, while sharing some of the features of the liberal model, sits in contrast to the market model, as it is purposefully oriented to social change. The principal difference between the emphasis on cross-cultural understanding embedded in the liberal model and the social transformation model is that social transformation adds the dimension of critical social analysis.[12] It calls for recognition of the reality that globalization, while benefiting a few, leads to increased marginalization of significant groups of people around the world. Hence, operationally the model suggests that internationalization is or should be centrally about pursuing those activities that seek to increase knowledge and awareness of inequity and to decrease the inequalities both within and between nations. Further, recognizing that significant groups of people everywhere are working to redress inequities, a social transformation model also suggests that internationalization research and education activities should be guided by principles of mutuality and reciprocity and should be established through networks or partnerships.

2.1 Internationalization in the College of Medicine

The internationalization initiative of the College of Medicine at the University of Saskatchewan considered the overall mandate on internationalization exemplified in the foundational documents "Globalism and the University of Saskatchewan"[13] and the "Internationalization Mission Statement."[14] But these documents, like most internationalization foundational documents in Canadian universities, are purposeful yet vague. Ironically they provide room for the institution to offer, with one hand, internationalized programs that seek to address inequities, while with the other hand to create programs that foster global competition and support neo-liberal policies from which inequities arise. Given that potential and given the known adverse effects of globalization and inequities on health, the COM internationalization initiative chose to seek a values-explicit approach in line with the social accountability vision of medical schools[15] and thus adopted the *social transformation model* of internationalization.

By implication, internationalization in the COM would "support a range of activities beyond traditional international engagements (of discipline-specific research and teaching) into interdisciplinary teaching and research approaches that seek socially just and sustainable solutions to the massive North-South divide in health and development, through close, capacity-building collaboration with partners in developing countries." Further, internationalization was to be "a *reciprocal* process, where communities and institutions locally and internationally seek to share insights and knowledge and to learn from the experience, cultures and research of each other."[16] Ultimately, internationalization would "foster personal and professional development of capable, globally responsive and caring citizens."

The idea of bringing the many and disparate international activities of faculty members in the COM into the fold of internationalization began in earnest only three years ago, but already much has been accomplished. Certainly one cannot say that all activities have contributed to social transformation and global citizenship, or even that the majority have, but the proposed model did give impetus to the solidification and expansion of the health sciences curriculum and co-curricular activity in ways consistent with the chosen model.

2.2 Internationalization of Curriculum: A Social Transformation Model

Broadly, the COM vision of internationalization and social accountability supported processes by which the medical curriculum could be enhanced or transformed and, in that way, it echoed the vision of the Association of Universities and Colleges of Canada (AUCC) wherein internationalization was "a necessary, vital and deliberate transformation of how we teach and learn ... essential to the future quality of higher education in Canada, indeed to the future of Canada."[17] The 1995 AUCC statement is important as it provides impetus for internationalizing the curriculum and including programs of study with international foci but also because it prompts new conceptualizations of internationalized curriculum in line with social transformation as described above.

Bond and Scott offer such a conceptualization.[18] They propose that internationalized curriculum can challenge traditional knowledge paradigms and intentionally seek transformation of the academy by infusing an international dimension throughout the curriculum, using an interdisciplinary approach, emphasizing experiential and active learning, integrating and coordinating with other international activities and encouraging self-reflection on Canadian culture and the way it influences our cognition. Internationalized curriculum so conceived counters a naive tendency toward the promotion of what they call "intellectual tourism," involving the application of traditional academic knowledge and practice to new cultures with no attention to critical self-reflection or the discourse of development. Blurring rigid disciplinary boundaries, validating alternative epistemologies and engaging in self-reflection are all consistent with social transformation but radically differ from other models in terms of operationalizing the idea of "internationalized curriculum," and the implications are wide-ranging. Instructors might be called upon to reexamine disciplinary boundaries and their own culturally situated knowledge paradigms. Departments and the wider institution would need to actively offset the overzealous uptake of the notion of "internationalizing curriculum" by countering the idea that it means simply adding "global examples." Engaging internationalization in this way in fact challenges some very fundamental academic thinking about education, and it suggests a strategic use of critical and transformative pedagogies. Yet, from a cursory reading of the internationalization literature available, it would seem that examples that adopt the pedagogies of transformational education in the process of internationalizing curriculum in Canadian universities are few. The example of global health classes at the University of Saskatchewan is offered here, prefaced as follows by the necessary background — the key concepts and assumptions underlying global citizenship and transformative education.

3. Global Citizenship, Transformative Learning and the University

3.1 A Rationale for Global Citizenship

As Byers states, "Citizenship is as much about obligations as it is about rights."[19] That the era of globalization has intensified the gaps between the rich and poor is hardly disputable. In the world's richest countries, the income gap between the top and bottom quintiles sits at a ratio of 74:1, a change from the 60:1 ratio in 1990 and an incredible jump from the 30:1 ratio thirty years earlier; while globally, according to the World Bank, the number of very poor in the world rose by 10.4 percent from 1987 to 2001.[20] In health, the gap between developed and low and middle-income countries mirrors this trend. The gap in child mortality, for example, increased from a tenfold to fourteenfold difference between 1990 and 2000[21] and, with the global spectrum of poverty-related diseases such as HIV/AIDS, there is now an alarming forty-eight-year discrepancy between life expectancy in the richest and poorest nations on earth.[22]

The requirement of social and economic change to arrest these trends is thus immutable, yet strategies to engage people in thinking and working for global health equity remain somewhat elusive, and the role of post-secondary education is not clear. The lack of clarity stems in part from the reality that globalization has increasingly shifted the balance of power from public to private interests and from national to supranational domains resulting in an emerging social order that excludes or oppresses certain groups of people and makes targets of change appear to rest far away from civic influence.[23] In addition, the West's enduring legacy of individualism impinges on both community capacity and individual willingness to respond to the need for change as those who "have" get caught up in the mystifying web of *busy-ness*, consumerism, cynicism and the unending race to the mythical top while those who "have not" are caught in a disempowering struggle for survival — overall contributing to weakened links of community and human solidarity.[24]

Educators who consider their work to be about and for global social change are thus immersed in a challenging project. Critical analysis of the realities of growing social, economic, gender and cultural inequalities in the world is vital, but so are empowering affirmations to our students that engaging in personal and social change is both possible and desirable.[25] Fostering the growth of global citizens is therefore a daunting task.

As used in this chapter, a global citizenship perspective involves not only recognition of global interdependence, "but also awareness of and commitment to societal justice for marginalized groups, grassroots empowerment, nonviolent and authentic democracy, environmental care, and North-South relations based on principles of equity, respect and sharing."[26] Global citizenship further involves the ability to view the world and its inhabitants as interacting and interdependent, with concern for the survival of the environment and human race and capacity to act to advance both one's own enlightened self-interest and the interest of people elsewhere in the world by understanding the interconnection of all living things.[27] Indeed, as Byers notes, members of a global community need not give up special affiliations and identities but must work to make all human beings part of the community of dialogue and concern. One might ask, then, what might a university do to foster global citizenship?[28]

3.2 Stewarding Global Citizenship: Social Change and the University

Edwards and Sen pose that all social systems rest on three bases:

1) a set of principles that form an axiomatic basis of ethics and values; 2) a set of processes — involving the functioning mechanisms and institutions that undergird the system and 3) the subjective states that constitute our inner being — our personal feelings and intuitions in the deepest sense. Each base has within it a system of power; together they combine to create a "social order." Edwards and Sen suggest that change toward a more equitable social order and toward sustainable paths of human development requires all values-based organizations to acknowledge the interconnections. Further, they note that only an integrated approach will work to construct the kind of global citizenship and solidarities needed to confront the collective problems of the twenty-first century, for "we cannot compete our way to a cooperative future." Rather, social change requires "those who gain power to make room for those with less; and all to use the power they gain in more responsible ways — not submerging their own self interest entirely, but modulating it."[29]

Universities, as public entities, are values-based organizations immersed in the project of human development. They can provide processes which facilitate change to the social system and social order through the foundational principles, policies and programs they adopt and support. But their ability and willingness to do so effectively, especially in the context of internationalization, depends in part upon their culture and whether they choose to "foster, support, and reward creative innovation."[30] One of the most difficult innovations involves how university education is to attend to the personal "subjective states" that, as Edwards and Sen suggest, are required to sustain the momentum of social change. Transformative education innovatively addresses both personal and social change and thus holds great potential to meet the challenges of fostering global citizenship in the classroom and beyond.

3.3 Transformative Education

According to the renowned critical pedagogue Paulo Freire, as a programmed approach to learning, education is never neutral.[31] It can either have an instrumental or an emancipatory purpose; by implication, the teacher either engages in the reproduction of the status quo or encourages questioning, challenging and, ultimately, changing it.

Transformative learning theory and transformative education (TE) shares much with Freire's approach to education; however, it diverges in emphasis. TE considers self-reflection of individual learners on their values, beliefs and behaviours as necessary prerequisites to change, whereas a learner's critical reflection on conditions of oppression is a starting point for Freire. In other words, TE "addresses the other side of the coin, direct intervention by the educator to foster the development of the skills, insights, and especially dispositions essential for critical reflection — and self-reflection — on assumptions and effective participation in critical-dialectical discourse (reflective judgment) — essential components of democratic citizenship."[32] The assumption is that the development of such disposition engenders a drive to expand personal capacity to act.[33] Kasl and Elias point out some of the capacities TE is believed to foster, such as "the ability to balance divergence and convergence, reflection and action, chaos and order, and the ability to challenge uncritical subjectivity, manage unaware projections, and sustain both authenticity and open boundaries."[34]

Personal and social transformation, global citizenship and transformative education, taken together, have been the rationale and guide for the teaching of global health classes. The following section explores some of the outcomes and the potential of this kind of teaching by reporting on a small follow-up evaluation of those classes conducted in late 2005.

4. Global Health & Local Communities (GH-I) and Global Health II: Selected Issues in Nicaragua (GH-II)

4.1 Background

Global Health and Local Communities: Issues and Approaches (GH-I) is a fourth-year undergraduate interdisciplinary class offered by the Department of Community Health and Epidemiology. It is a prerequisite for Global Health II: Selected Issues in Nicaragua (GH-II), which is taught as a six-week study abroad program. GH-I also effectively functions as a prerequisite for various study-abroad practica offered by the Colleges of Nursing and Medicine and is considered a senior elective for the International Studies Program. In other words, GH-I is one of the most interdisciplinary classes offered on campus and in any given year has approximately twenty students from at least four different colleges and more than six departments. The class content includes an introduction to global health issues: a framework of population health, people-centred development and primary health care. Links between health and development issues and approaches common overseas and in Saskatchewan are emphasized. The class roughly simulates the idea of praxis — or reflection and action cycles. Students volunteer with community organizations and read both conventional and nonconventional academic literature to flesh out the "theories in action" of the approaches used. In class, they reflect on the meaning of experiences through interdisciplinary class discussions, participatory exercises, case stories, videos, guest lectures and creative class evaluations. Many class activities involve students in self- and critical reflection on alternative paradigms and epistemologies. Such activities are purposefully inserted to disturb the boundaries of learned disciplinary, professional, class and gendered ways of seeing. Hence, "active learning" in the class tends to be more intense and personal than most group problem-solving activity.

Global Health II continues the trajectory of GH-I with Nicaragua as the site of a six-week experiential field study program. The course is structured in a similar way but with an in-depth focus on Nicaragua's particular health and development trends and issues.

Students take Spanish classes and live with home-stay families for three weeks as they are oriented to Nicaragua's history, politics and culture. Following the home stay, they spend three to four weeks in cycles of active and experiential learning and reflective sessions, by, for example, volunteering with community organizations and non-governmental organizations (NGOs) and being immersed in the life and work of a rural community, then holding challenging reflection sessions using participatory techniques and lectures. Students can stay on to volunteer for up to one month following the formal class offering. I have taught Global Health II three times to groups of five to seven students per year.

4.2 The Study — Goal and Questions

A post-course outcome evaluation was conducted in late 2005. The broad goal of the study was to explore whether and how participation in the classes and the use of transformative education philosophies underpinning them have fostered global citizenship and personal and social transformation — as expressed in students' discourse and in their tangible or planned post-class involvement in local and global community health and development initiatives or organizations. Further, the study sought to discover whether and how these classes might serve to model an internationalized curriculum within a social transformation approach to internationalization in an academic institution.

The evaluation was guided by these three specific questions that attempt to provide clues to the above queries:

- In what ways is the personally transformative potential of GH-I and GH-II a) discussed/identified and b) manifested by students who have graduated from the class?
- How do GH-I and GH-II contribute to global/local citizenship?

- What elements of the classes appear to matter most?

4.3 Methods

The study used multiple data-gathering methods, including reviews of three years of mid-term in-class evaluations and five years of final teaching and course evaluations, two tape-recorded focus groups, several individual written submissions and one telephone interview. In each focus group, participants responded to guiding questions and exploratory prompts. Outside submissions responded to similar questions.

One of the criteria for participation was that at least one year must have passed since the individual had completed either GH course. The means of contacting a participant was the e-mail address originally provided in class, of which many were now non-functional. The focus groups were held over two weeks. In spite of a small number of participants (thirteen), the responses were rich and complex. The non-functional e-mail addresses and a quick turnaround, as well as logistical factors (students had moved, were working, etc.) impeded convening many additional interested participants in the same location at the same time.

Ethical approval for the study was granted by the University of Saskatchewan Behavioural Ethics Board. To ensure anonymity and confidentiality, the research assistant contacted students, led the focus groups and presented only summary information to the researcher (given that the researcher in this case was the instructor). Permission was sought for the use of key quotes; those used herein were extracted after most identifiers were removed, although participants were aware that their identities could not be protected fully because of the small numbers in the potential pool of participants (approximately 120) and the close relationship of students with the professor during the class. Basic qualitative analysis assisted the categorization of responses outlined below.

4.4. Study Limits

The study findings are generally consistent with the information available on written post-class evaluation questionnaires completed by all students on the last day of class, although the focus groups in this study are richer in depth and allow the additional perspectives on class impact that only time can grant. The study participants included students from at least four different disciplines, from at least four different years of the program and from both GH-I and GH-II. However, the study involved a small number of highly motivated people. The study does provide a snapshot or collage of student perceptions on their learning and is a useful learning tool; however, both post-program evaluation and outcome evaluation without a baseline are designs which cannot discern cause and effect. Nor can they identify or ascribe the impact that the class independently has on students, for there is always a complex inter-play of factors affecting learning and behaviour change. Collectively, these are the parameters that delimit this study.

4.5 Results

Results are organized under three main categories of responses — personal transformation, global citizenship and teaching and class-room matters. Extensive quotes from many participants attempt to represent some diversity of opinion and to ensure that participant voices are heard. Direct quotes or portions thereof are given in ital-ics. The last category of responses (class elements) suggests some differences among those who took only GH-I and those who took both GH-I and GH-II in Nicaragua.

4.5.1 Personal Transformation

The category of "personal transformation" comprised expressions and perceptions of persistent rather than transitory emotional states. Proxy indicators of personal transformation thus involved reference to ongoing change or shifts in one's values, beliefs, behaviours, skills, insights and particularly one's overall disposition to critical reflection — together with self-reflection.

Evidence of personal transformation so defined existed among all participants, with some variation in degree of intensity. The following examples illustrate expressions of a disposition for conscious and critical reflection and, in some cases, for growth of self-confidence:

> I am more likely now to question why things are
> the way they are and to challenge the status quo in
> a number of areas.

> [The class] helped me to not feel self-conscious or
> shy about advocacy — this helped give me more
> confidence personally.

> The most valuable part of this course is not what
> we read or what we hear. It is the encouragement
> to improve our skills of critical analysis and reflec-
> tion, to not accept everything at face value and to
> dig deeper to find the underlying reasons why
> things are the way they are.

A number of participants noticed that the class initiated or catalyzed a *feeling of awakening and self-awareness that was not there before* — and some participants spoke of changes in terms of feeling/being *transformed*. A *growing self-awareness* also provoked a good deal of *discomfort* and for some, *an ongoing struggle to find or make meaning of events* that had occurred since or because of the class.

> I felt more confused after the class about what my
> role should be. I ended up questioning everything.
> Now I feel clear, but at the time I felt
> overwhelmed.

Disrupting personal comfort zones left some students feeling confused at the end of the course, although for some *it all came together.*
Examples where participants were engaging their new perspective by connecting the personal with the big-picture realities were numerous. *I had been to Central America before* [but on return after the class] ... *I was able to see things differently than on my first trip. The class allowed me to make big-picture policy connections to the personal realities of life.* The category of personal transformation included shifts in career or academic paths and, for some, altered career paths were among the most enduring legacies of the class.

> I remembered from the course — "you only know your world. You can go and visit another person's world, but they know that world best, and they're the best people to decide what's best for them." So I said, "what do I know and how can I contribute?" So I was thinking Saskatchewan and what can I do here? So that's why I went into nursing.

> This class is why I decided to do my Master's in Community Health and Epidemiology and why I started volunteering in Saskatoon.

4.5.2 Global/Local Citizenship Contributions

"Contribution toward global citizenship" encompassed responses that included community/global awareness and interconnection and involvements in health and development events, campaigns and organizations. As discussed earlier, global citizenship involves both inward and outward components. Acts of seeking critical sources of global and local knowledge and critical reflections on roles/rights/obligations and on interconnections were considered inward dimensions. Outward expressions involved actual and planned community involvements, whether local or global.

Students also reflected on the meaning of the term *global citizenship*, and examples of their comments are included. Taken together, participants' responses overwhelmingly indicate that GH is contributing to global and local citizenship as defined.

Examples of responses that show an inward commitment to global/local citizenship — in particular, those relating to seeking and using information *to stay aware* — revealed both promise and shortcomings. Students use mainstream news sources such as the CBC, *Globe and Mail* and CTV News; and mention many kinds of alternative news media, such as the *New Internationalist*, the David Suzuki Web site, *Planet S*, the Saskatchewan Council for International Cooperation (SCIC) bulletin, *Prensa Libre* online, or local community agency listservs and *keeping an ear to the ground*. Noted shortcomings included a lack of integration and either too much global or too much local focus: *I feel less informed about Saskatoon goings on than the rest of the world.* But for most people the biggest problem appeared to be that there *is just too much information out there.* While several made comments such as *good global citizens need to be informed before becoming involved*, more frequently students reported tensions between the acts of "knowing" and "doing" and some reported frustrations on how to connect the two.

> It is hard to be a good global citizen. There's too
> much information and you need to find a balance
> between being realistic and acting meaningfully.
> You can't be paralyzed by all that can go wrong.
> I want to "do" and not just examine others' efforts.

Interestingly, the high level of critical commentary on community action, or lack thereof, was not matched by the actual and planned level of community involvement and there were ample examples of volunteering and involvement by participants. Most, though not all, participants suggested the class was a significant catalyst for that involvement. For some, a disposition to engage in community action existed prior to the class, but an opportunity to engage was lacking.

> Making volunteering with local NGOs a part of
> the class requirements ... really did break the
> "can't participate" barrier for a lot of people.

> It's so awesome to work with the community and I
> probably wouldn't have if not for this class.

Community volunteering during the class occurs primarily in sites on Saskatoon's "West side,"[35] an experience which in and of itself presents new perspectives on issues for many and for some is beyond their comfort zone. Although volunteering for class involves a minimal commitment of five hours per month, the experience often appears to catalyze a much longer and more intense period of volunteering, and, for a few, includes plans for the development of complex programs:

> I was apprehensive at first, but now I have lots of
> experience. It began a huge line of volunteerism
> for me.

> I grew up in a small town and I never spent time
> on the West side. When I volunteered at the Good
> Food Box, I really saw the difference. It was an
> essential eye-opening experience.

> I continued to volunteer at my community place-
> ment for one-and-a-half years after the class and
> then went to South Africa to work in an HIV
> clinic for eight months.

> I want to work with young people and possibly
> create a global education program in Saskatoon
> under the Red Cross humanitarian issues program.
> I am still interested in refugee and immigrant
> issues, which is a direct result of the class.

Additionally, global citizenship is reflected in the nature of personal decisions and obligations and, again, there were numerous examples:

> I think more about the businesses I support. I now
> recycle and I make conscientious purchasing deci-
> sions.

> I am manifesting my values on a daily basis. I try
> to reduce harm socially and environmentally and
> help others to do the same.

The following items are reflections on the role of a "good global citizen" — a role some say was initiated and others say catalyzed into action by taking GH-I and GH-II:

- Involved locally (neighborhood, region), nationally, and internationally.
- Conscientious, informed, and educated about issues
- "Think globally, act locally."
- "Be the change you want to see in the world"
- One who reflects personally is open minded and realistic about their capabilities.
- Exhibits environmental and social responsibility
- Shares in the burdens of others and is an advocate alongside the oppressed.

4.5.3 Class Elements that Matter Most

Both post-class-questionnaire and focus-group responses suggest a marked difference between this class and almost all other university classes and illustrate an impact on students' lives well past the termination of the class. This final category of responses from the evaluation speaks to the elements of the class that stood out as most important. Some are small details, such as readings that help people see things from new perspectives: *The white privilege article made me think in a new way I hadn't before.*

Other elements mentioned frequently were volunteering and community involvement. But in addition, what enables a fuller engagement in reflective praxis, i.e., the integration of theory with practice needed to enable students to make meaning of the experience and take away transferable lessons, are the active learning methods: *not pencils and paper, but seeking to involve the mind and heart;* the critical and self-reflection encouraging students to *think outside the box and question assumptions and biases;* and the openings provided by changing the role of the instructor, although recognizing that to do so is difficult in the university system:

> If we see profs live out their philosophical stances, this makes a huge impact. She did not set herself up at a higher level than her students ... I saw her as a fellow learner ... She encouraged participation in class which overflowed to participation in Saskatoon communities.

> [For the instructor] it takes a lot of energy to be participatory in the class. It takes far more teaching time and focus to do that. It's always a new experience. You can't just give the same lecture over again. So I think it's a lot more challenging. They [the university] don't allow time. You have to

> go crazy above board … to be able to make this
> impossible goal of trying to be participatory a real-
> ity for teaching. So, it's hard.

In the GH-II class in Nicaragua, especially, participants felt that the way the class was taught resulted in *lots of learning without realizing it*. The experience of the class in Nicaragua was in various ways distinct from that in Canada. The course, being a more concentrated amount of work and energy in a short time frame, required much of students. Though the class elements that stand out for participants were similar, there were several added dimensions. Volunteering, the community speakers, the home stay experience, the village stay and *the non-class time of just "being" in Nicaragua* all provided a more in-depth under-standing and expanded capacity for critical reflection. But there, all experiences become "fodder" for class discussion — *There was no separation between home life and school life*. Full immersion in the lives of those who are marginalized within the country also extended and deepened awareness in ways that volunteering cannot:

> The overnight stay in the rural community will
> always stand out for me. I will never forget that
> you can't really know a place or appreciate how
> things are if you don't immerse yourself and try to
> live like they live (even if it's just one night).

4.6 Discussion
4.6.1 Evaluation Methods
Individual participant responses varied in kinds and degrees of per-sonal change noted, in kinds and levels of active participation in communities, and in ways the classes were associated with changes

mentioned. This variation reflects the probability that the class (and the moment of the evaluation) catches each person at a different place in their own lives and also the reality that the impact of any learning intervention depends on an array of factors and complex synergies.

The evaluation was based on several data sources — focus groups, review of post-course questionnaires, and written submissions. In general, there was consistency among the data in terms of both content areas and direction of responses. However, more complex responses became available through the focus group sessions, which often served to contextualize and make sense of some of the shorter replies in the post-course evaluation questionnaires. As well, some of the participants had graduated as many as four years prior, presumably giving them enough time and life experience to enable them to evaluate the classes' impact from a longitudinal perspective. Overall, although the study was modest in scope and lacked baseline data, the evaluation of the classes provided some important lessons that will be useful for improving the class.

4.6.2 Lessons Learned

The lessons particularly relate to the lack of attention to issues of integration of class learning with post-graduation reality. The evaluation illustrated that students do not necessarily stay connected with critical sources of information, although most try. Many appear to notice that something is amiss with the lack of integration of local and global issues, but do not always act on the implications of that. Many were also frustrated by the lack of or overabundance of information, and how and when to turn information into action. The evaluation points to a need, therefore, for better preparing students to balance necessary critical information and understanding with personal learning and political action — especially once they have graduated and entered the work world.

The evaluation raised a second hypothetical problem associated with the idea that the class left some feeling confused and with a need to *question everything!* Entry into the liminal space that often foreshadows transformational learning moments creates vulnerabilities that require both time and ways of working themselves out — often supported by a learning mentor or engaged group learning process.[36] What the class currently provides of these may be insufficient for some students.

The study was also useful in providing an illustration of the potential of transformational education in the context of the university — which may be of particular interest to those seeking to operationalize the idea of "internationalized curriculum" in a social transformation model. Indeed, some students already considered it a model of *what universities are trying to do — service learning, community speakers/perspectives, making connections.*

The results of this study support other research that points to the effectiveness of participatory approaches in fostering adult learning in general, as compared with traditional university lectures. It also suggests that some of the teaching and learning issues raised are relevant to internationalized curriculum in a social transformation model; however, continued innovation and evaluation research is needed in other specific communities and university contexts. Further, advocacy for such approaches will be required, given the reality that such approaches remain at the University of Saskatchewan, as elsewhere, "counter-normative in higher education."[37]

4.6.3 Global Citizenship, Transformation and Internationalization

This chapter attempts to draw together various ideas related to internationalization and social transformation. The course evaluation herein offers an illustration of a university course that appears to catalyze students' personal transformation and foster global citizenry. It is appropriate to return to the threads connecting these ideas.

Global citizenship involves empowered people participating in decisions concerning their lives and "is expressed through engagement in the various communities of which the individual is a part, at the local, national and global level. And it includes the right to challenge authority and existing power structures — to think, argue and act — with the intent of changing the world."[38] The example of GH-I and GH-II illustrates a way to encourage students to be and act as engaged and critical citizens in the communities of which they form part — including the university community. In so doing, GH-I and GH-II challenge the traditional academic distance between professors and students and provide a space in which students can freely challenge authority — or *think, act and argue* about alternative visions of the world. Having professors become co-learners and facilitators rather than lecturers is vital to transformative education and spawns insightful "learning on learning," which is a highly useful skill for helping professionals — be they from global studies, medicine, community development or adult education.

Most authors agree that we can see glimpses of human transformation in the discourse associated with events that radically alter consciousness or cause shifts of awareness.[39] In this study, certain events, such as community volunteering, were highlights for students, but in analyzing student discourse we see how they make meaning of such experience. Evidently it is not one event but various synergistic effects of community involvement and critical and self-reflection — in addition to changes of the role of instructor — that are key to the lasting impact of the learning and the catalyst for personal transformation — also called "transformative learning":

> Transformative learning involves experiencing a
> deep structural shift in basic premises of thought,
> feelings, and actions. It is a shift of consciousness
> that dramatically and permanently alters our way
> of being in the world. Such a shift involves our
> understanding of ourselves and our self locations;

our relationships with other humans and with the
natural world; our understanding of relations of
power in interlocking structures of class, race and
gender; our body awareness; our visions of alternative approaches to living; and our sense of
possibilities for social justice and peace and personal joy.[40]

In the context of the social transformation model of the internationalization of universities, transformational educational
pedagogies are highly relevant in fostering personal transformation
and global citizenship. But to engage them is to *openly* recognize
that neither education nor institutions are ever neutral. Further, it
is to recognize that critical thought and analysis — while vital to the
life of the academy and to the educational preparation of professionals — are insufficient to fully prepare professionals to act, or
"deal critically and creatively with reality and discover how to participate in the transformation of their world."[41] Accordingly,
engaging in transformative education within the system of universities requires educators to work "tactically inside and strategically
outside of the system," necessarily embracing the tension between
critically examining what is and posing what could be; engaging a
language of critique and a language of possibility.[42]

5. Conclusion

Although the study was modest in scope, it has provoked both
learning and new questions that will be utilized to improve future
classes and for further research. The chapter is useful in providing
an illustration of the potential of transformational education in the
context of the university — which may be of particular interest to
those seeking to operationalize the idea of "internationalized curriculum" in a social transformation model.

It would seem that a social transformation model of internation-alized curriculum involves thinking beyond any one particular innovative educational method or intervention. Community engagement is not enough. Problem-posing education is not enough. Service-learning is inadequate. Neither critical analysis nor self-reflection is sufficient alone. Rather, we need to move transfor-mative and engaged methods from the periphery of education to the centre — synergistically combine and experiment with them, listen to and evaluate their impact on students and then modify them to fit our own contexts and communities. As we do so, we too will be challenged as educators to reveal ourselves as co-learners with our students.

Such shifts in the way we teach may require completely new par-adigms, new roles and new skill sets. As Mezirow suggests: "Creating the conditions for and the skills of effective adult reason-ing and the disposition for transformative learning — including critical reflection and dialectical discourse — is the essence of adult education and defines the role of the educator, both as a facilitator of reasoning in a learning situation and a cultural activist fostering the social, economic and political conditions required for fuller, freer participation in critical reflection and discourse by all adults in a democratic society."[43] In other words, our role must shift to one of *facilitator of epistemic reasoning* and one of *citizen-activist* model-ling opportunity for engagement, for critical reflection on and for soulful participation in the creation of a new discourse and a trans-formed global social order. Without this shift, meaningful change in our universities and our local and global communities is unlike-ly, and internationalizing curricula may remain a vague concept and ineffectual process.

Reframing Internationalization in a (Post)Colonial and Diasporic Context: Two Initiatives at York University

Deborah Barndt, York University

> [The] general liberal consensus that "true"
> knowledge is fundamentally non-political (and
> conversely, that overtly political knowledge is not
> "true" knowledge) obscures the highly organized
> political circumstances obtaining when knowledge
> is produced.[1]

I was born in the US at the end of World War II, when the term *international* was used to promote a more hopeful vision of world peace (at least in the "free world") as the United Nations was formed by the victorious world powers to foster collective security, and the Bretton Woods international institutions (the World Bank and the International Monetary Fund) were crafted to rebuild the international economic system and to facilitate post-war reconstruction. These institutions were integral to the promulgation of a particular economic model of "development," one which Arturo

Escobar, in deconstructing development, suggests turned peasants, women and nature into objects of knowledge and targets of power under the gaze of western experts.[2]

I, too, was shaped by and participated in the dissemination of this ideology as a graduate student at Michigan State University (MSU) in the late 1960s and early 1970s. MSU had become a centre for international education, with Everett Rogers, author of the classic *Diffusion of Innovations*, part of a pioneering department of development communications. I was invited to join the staff of a series of communications workshops, a service that MSU had been contracted by the Agency for International Development (AID) to offer for foreign scholars before they returned home. These were the élites of the "third world," as we called it then in the context of the Cold War, whose education had been financed by the US government. They were required to complete this training in communications, to consider how they would apply the ideas and technologies they had learned in the US to their own contexts. We tried to move them in the direction of Rogers' "diffusion of innovations" — offering communications techniques for propagating ideas formed in US universities.

Around the same time, I was also involved in cross-cultural communications training developed at the University of Pennsylvania and promoted by a network of scholars and practitioners in the Society for International Development preparing US students to go "overseas," as we described it then. We developed activities to help them deal with "culture shock" and adapt to different value systems.

By 1972, I was living in Canada and found myself once again involved in cross-cultural training — developing materials and activities for international cooperants[3] of the Canadian International Development Agency (CIDA) who were taking up posts of "technical assistance." I also worked with Canada World Youth in its infancy to apply the pedagogical principles of Brazilian educator Paulo Freire to its educational programs.

All of these experiences would have fit under the rubric of international education at the time and reflected close and complex links among governments, universities and nongovernmental organizations (NGOs). Even though, in the Cold War context, *international* referred to the US-dominated free world, in that period we used the term with a pretension of neutrality and universality. In the past decade, however, post-colonial theory has offered me a useful tool of critical analysis for revisiting the context, meaning and impact of these early internationalizing experiences. The words of Edward Said, pre-eminent post-colonial scholar, that knowledge is always produced under "highly organized political circumstances" resonate as I consider the political, economic and ideological climate within which foreign élites were being educated in Western knowledges, some of which might contradict or devalue the local knowledges of their people and context.

Post-colonial scholars argue that, despite the decolonization and national liberation of colonized nations in Africa, Asia and Latin America, these nations remain in positions of economic inequality and subordination to Europe and North America. One of the consequences of the restructured global economy, seen by many as a continuation of colonialism, is the increasing displacement of people from their lands and countries of origin; there are over twenty million refugees in the world today. In the context of corporate globalization, internationalization is often conflated with the economic, political and cultural integration promoted by neo-liberalism, free trade and greater movement — not only of goods and services but also of labour, of bodies compelled or coerced to leave their countries of origin for reasons of war, famine, poverty or repression.

Toronto as a global city of the twenty-first century epitomizes this increasing movement, as its diasporic population makes it perhaps the most multicultural city in the world, with almost half of its residents considered visible minorities. York University was founded in 1959 in part to respond to the expanding diversity and proclaimed its commitment to social justice values. Its mission statement emphasizes its multicultural context:

> York University is part of Toronto: we are dynam-
> ic, metropolitan, and multi-cultural. York
> University is part of Canada: we encourage bilin-
> gual study, we value tolerance and diversity. York
> University is open to the world: we explore global
> concerns.

One only needs to walk through York's main entrance hall to witness the presence of the diaspora in our midst. We do not need to go anywhere to have intercultural experiences and encounters with difference. This has been recognized by the York International Internship Program, which includes not only locations abroad but Canadian NGOs in its placements. It was also evident in the orientation for those students chosen for international internships and being prepared for the "culture shock" they might expect to encounter. When I asked them how many of them had been born outside of Canada, or had had experiences in a cultural context very different from the dominant Canadian culture, everyone raised a hand. "Diversity" is not only a moniker for York University but a source of pride.

Yet what difference does this diversity make in what and how we teach and learn at York? If we were to reframe internationalization as post-colonial and intercultural, our classrooms would be seen as sites for intercultural learning, for probing the richness of an internationalized university. Yet if we apply a post-colonial analysis to Western academic institutions, then we must also recognize how they have been shaped by Eurocentric world views, notions of knowledge, and of what it means to learn, to know, to act.

As post-colonial scholar Robert Young suggests, "Most of the writing that has dominated what the world calls knowledge has been produced by people living in western countries in the past three or more centuries, and it is this kind of knowledge that is elaborated within and sanctioned by the academy, the institutional knowledge corporation."[4]

Just as international development theorists and practitioners have been challenged to rethink the value of local knowledges "so long rejected as primitive" yet essential to questions of sustainable development, for example, so too we can offer broader and deeper learning experiences to our students if we tap into the diverse epistemologies present in our midst. And there is also a scholarly literature which we can draw upon, as "feminists and other holders of subjugated knowledges such as Indigenous scholars and critical race theorists have for some time been delineating 'ways of knowing' and of researching that challenge Enlightenment epistemologies and methodologies."[5] Yet we must also be open to the challenges of these "insurgent knowledges that come from the subaltern, the dispossessed, and seek to change the terms and values under which we all live."[6]

With this reframed notion of the international as post-colonial and intercultural, I would like to reflect on two recent experiments at York University, two initiatives that are still very much in process. One is the consideration of the use of Aboriginal languages in postgraduate work; the other is the transformation of university curriculum through an intersecting analysis of power, as articulated by Patricia Hill Collins and Egla Martinez Salazar, that addresses diversity and equity in both the content and process of our teaching.[7]

These two initiatives suggest a couple of complementary and perhaps challenging processes towards internationalizing the university, what we might call *Aboriginalizing* and *Diasporicizing* the university as part of a process of decolonizing Western academic practice. They offer an implicit critique of a notion of internationalization that focuses only on exchanges between universities in the North and South, programs that privilege mainly élite students and that are aimed primarily at furthering global economic integration, ultimately benefiting corporate interests and maintaining Western cultural hegemony.

Aboriginalizing Postgraduate Work

A post-colonial analysis would first of all acknowledge the European origins of the university and would probe, for example, the indigenous history of the land on which we stand, teach, learn and research. It would ask, what is the historical relationship between First Nations communities and Canadian universities? And how can we move towards a relationship of greater respect?

It is one of the tragic consequences of European colonization of North America that universities have been neither accessible nor culturally appropriate for First Nations young people, for the original peoples of this land. In recent decades, as Aboriginal communities in Canada have claimed more control over their own educational processes, as part of a broader movement for self-determination and sovereignty, there are more Aboriginal students and faculty in Canadian universities. York University established an Aboriginal Education Council in 2001 and hired its first Aboriginal counsellor in 2003. Beyond providing support for Aboriginal students in university, the council has also undertaken an audit of programs and courses offered that address Aboriginal history, ideas and practices. At a deeper level, Aboriginal faculty and students have compelled us to consider how Aboriginal ways of knowing and learning can be acknowledged and allowed to coexist with Western epistemologies and pedagogies within the academy.

Within the Faculty of Environmental Studies, there has been a steady stream of Aboriginal students, particularly in our master's and Ph.D. programs, due in part to the individualized nature of our graduate program, its interdisciplinary orientation and holistic

pedagogy. Recently our regulations were challenged by two graduate students, both Mi'gmaq, one completing a Master of
Environmental Science (M.E.S.) degree on the promotion of the
Mi'gmaq language through new technologies such as the Internet,
the other in a doctoral program on the history and politics of his
community in the Gaspé. Both students offered compelling arguments for completing the culminating work of their degree
programs in their mother tongue.

Like many Aboriginal students, these two graduate students see
their primary loyalty as being to their communities, many of which
have sent their young adults to university precisely to be able to better serve the needs of First Nations communities. Being
accountable to the community means being accountable to one's
view of and relationship with all of creation.

The issue of language is not only a matter of communications,
even though it is important that the results of their research be
accessible to people in the community who may not speak English.
The loss of indigenous languages is one of the great concerns in
Aboriginal communities, because as these languages disappear, so
too do cultural world views, ways of thinking and being. The loss
of linguistic and cultural diversity is a global crisis.

Cultural cosmovisions[8] and ways of knowing are embedded in
language. One of the shameful legacies of the government and
church-sponsored residential schools that took an entire generation
of First Nations children away from their families and communities
and prohibited them from speaking their native language was their
contribution not only to a cultural but also to a linguistic genocide.
The healing processes and resurgence of Aboriginal communities
claiming self-determination include addressing the loss and recovery of native languages. As Peter Cole, an Aboriginal professor at
York University, has expressed:

Aboriginal/indigenous languages are inseparable

> from their respective cultures; they are part of
> Aboriginal/indigenous ways of knowing. Conse-
> quently, recovery of traditional cultures and
> languages is a project of renewal and revitalization.
> It is an educational and self-empowerment project.
> It is — rather than a process of decolonization —
> one of Aboriginalization.[9]

Thus, to use one's own Aboriginal language in graduate work is to contribute not only to the sharing of knowledge with one's community but also to the continued viability of the language and culture itself. Indeed these goals were central to the graduate programs of these two students.

For many Aboriginal students, the community is considered the source of the curriculum, and students are often accountable to community elders who are guiding them in their studies. At the same time, the Western academy has its own system of accountability: at the graduate level, this involves academic advisers, supervisors and Ph.D. committees, all governed by the Faculty of Graduate Studies. As a result, Aboriginal graduate students have a double accountability — to their communities and to their universities and respective faculties.

In 2005, the Faculty of Environmental Studies (FES) took up the challenge to address this double accountability and to recognize Aboriginal students' primary accountability to the Aboriginal community. Because FES pedagogy is built around an individual plan of study through which both the content of the curriculum and the process of learning are elaborated by the student, there was receptiveness in principle to the integration of Aboriginal languages and community advisers into the plan. A small committee worked to draft a proposal that would change our regulations to allow the M.E.S. major paper, thesis, or project report as well as the Ph.D. dissertation to be submitted in an Aboriginal/indigenous language, "if so indicated in the statement of requirements for the Major Project or Major Paper or in the Thesis Proposal or in the Dissertation Research Proposal, and if relevant supervision and sufficient support can be provided."[10]

It is important to note that this process was also the result of ongoing mutual learning between non-native faculty supervisors and Aboriginal students. In defence of the proposal, for example, Anders Sandberg, the non-native dissertation supervisor of an Aboriginal doctoral student proposing to complete his dissertation in Mi'gmaq, articulated his growing understanding of the distinct epistemologies in tension in this effort to change the regulations:

> The motion goes some way in supporting and recognizing what I have come to learn to be a unique First Nations academic discourse that is distinct from the colonial discourse that dominates in Canada today (in different manifestations). The Western discourse is typically based on "rights" that are attached to individuals in the form of the protection of private property, freedom of speech and expression, and universal suffrage in a representative liberal democracy.

> The Mi'gmaq discourse, by contrast, is deeply rooted in a collective belonging and responsibility towards the land and territory of Mi'gmagi, where the Mi'gmaq scholar senses a deep bond and responsibility towards his or her subjects or objects of study. I have come to think about this as a "responsibilities discourse" where an ethic of responsibility and connectedness exists between the scholar, the land that he or she belongs to, and the people, animals, flora, and spirits of that land.

> Scholarly pursuit here becomes an interaction with
> the community where negotiation and respect
> need to exist and prevail at every turn.[11]

It is important not to homogenize the Aboriginal practices, either, and the term *First Nations* emphasizes not only the original inhabitants but also their diversity. In this particular case, Sandberg goes on to argue:

> There is a unique form of Mi'gmaq scholarship,
> stories and knowledge holders (academics) along
> with Mi'gmaq archives, classrooms and universities
> (the land). This Mi'gmaq "academic complex" pre-
> dates the so-called "contact" and needs to be
> recognized, valued, and further developed. It has
> never been replaced or displaced by colonialism
> (though repressed) and many First Nations stu-
> dents now point to this complex as a place where
> they would like to place their studies. Aboriginal
> languages are often an intricate part of that
> process.[12]

Indeed, as Sandberg points out, there is pan-global indigenous scholarship,[13] and Canada's own Social Sciences and Humanities Research Council (SSHRC) has consulted extensively with Aboriginal people about how their knowledge traditions can be more respected, how their research can benefit Aboriginal communities, and how they can have more control over intellectual and cultural property.[14]

While the new regulation was approved by the FES Faculty Council in the spring of 2005, we are still elaborating the ways in which it can be operationalized. The major conditions that must be met include "relevant supervision" and "sufficient support." The issue of supervision, as already indicated, is a complex one. There need to be sympathetic, supportive and "relevant" academic supervisors in the Faculty and academy. There are unfortunately very few Aboriginal faculty members at York, and familiarity with any particular First Nation and language is not assured. Faculty members can, however, offer strengths in certain aspects of the thesis process, while community members can serve as advisers when it comes to the particularity of Mi'gmaq history, politics and language. This means creating a structure of dual accountability and giving equal consideration to the community advisers, their research ethics and cultural protocol.

How does an Aboriginal student get assessed, then, at the stage of the thesis reading and defence? Ideally, an Aboriginal scholar is on the dissertation committee, and the community advisers are also represented at the defence. They can offer their assessment to the committee as a whole. There may be a need for infrastructural support that allows the defence to be conducted in part in the Aboriginal language with simultaneous translation facilitating the process, if the candidate and community members agree this would be useful. Fortunately, in 2004, York University's vice-president research and innovation purchased fifty sets of wireless simultaneous interpretation equipment; resources are needed, however, to hire translators capable of mediating this linguistic interchange.

While the protocols, logistics and financial dimensions still need to spelled out in more detail, we believe that the long-term benefits of this innovative approach will ensure not only that the work of Aboriginal graduate students is relevant and immediately useful to their communities but also that the interchange between academic supervisors and community advisers will enrich the dialogue that is so necessary to a respectful and mutually beneficial relationship between Aboriginal communities and universities.

The so-called international programs of universities such as York can also be enriched by Aboriginalization. Exchange programs between universities in the North and the South could offer specific opportunities to indigenous students, linking them to Aboriginal scholars, communities and practices in their host countries. There is a growing pan-hemispheric movement of indigenous groups in the Americas, for example, which have joined forces in efforts to preserve biodiversity and cultural diversity threatened by the industrial agricultural and exploitative resource extractive practices of corporate globalization. International students with indigenous roots can contribute to these coalitional efforts, a form of continental integration more based on social and environmental justice.

Diasporicizing the Curriculum

I chose to discuss the initiative around Aboriginalizing our curriculum first because I think it is the most marginalized discussion, even more so than the debate about how the curriculum could better tap the rich diversity of the international or diasporic population that make up the majority of our students. More has been done on this latter front, though it is still a relatively new and contested sphere.

At one level, most Canadians historically are part of the diasporic, or what earlier was called the settler, population. Yet the term has most often been used to apply to recent arrivals to Canada as well as to other global cities that have deep colonial roots. In a recent publication based on a York University conference on "Diaspora, Memory, and Identity" in 2004, Anh Hua offers her definition of diaspora as:

> A historical term used to refer to communities that
> have been dispersed reluctantly, dislocated by slavery, pogroms, genocide, coercion and expulsion,
> war in conflict zones, indentured labour, economic
> migration, political exile, or refugee exodus. Diasporic members frequently feel a sense of alienation

in the host country because of systemic racism,
sexism, heterosexism, and socio-economic exclusion. To resist assimilation into the host country,
and to avoid social amnesia about their collective
histories, diasporic people attempt to revive, recre-
ate, and invent their artistic, linguistic, economic,
religious, cultural and political practices and productions.[15]

While countering an assimilationist position, Hua also reminds
us that "it is crucial to remember that diasporic identities and communities are not fixed, rigid, or homogeneous, but are instead fluid,
always changing, and heterogeneous."[16] She also states that diasporic groups are "differentiated along gender and class lines,
generational difference, sexual orientation, language access, historical experiences, geographical location, and so on. [So] Diaspora
needs to be understood as embedded within 'a multi-axial understanding of power'."[17]

In 2002-03, the Faculty of Environmental Studies, in collaboration with York's Centre for the Support of Teaching, initiated a
series of six workshops to examine our curriculum through the lens
of different areas of diversity: not only race and ethnicity but also
disabilities, sexual and gender diversity, Aboriginal perspectives,
class and poverty, and women. While each workshop focused on
one aspect of equity, it promoted an interlocking analysis of power
that acknowledged the ways in which these identities are always
intersecting, one shaping another.

To ensure that this process would engage both students and faculty, we involved all student associations and both the undergraduate
and graduate curriculum committees, as well as seeking advice from
the Centre for Human Rights and Equity along with the Equity
Committee of the York University Faculty Association.

The workshop series had multiple objectives: to educate ourselves, to build a more inclusive community, to develop curriculum diversity guidelines and to propose policy directions. Perhaps most importantly, the six monthly workshops that drew thirty to fifty people for three hours of panel presentations, small group discussions and syntheses of strategic directions broke many silences, creating spaces that legitimized these difficult and self-reflexive conversations about how our curriculum and teaching/learning methods are imbued with the same dynamics of power that permeate the society as a whole.

Among the outcomes of this six-month workshop series was a set of "Curriculum Diversity and Equity Guidelines" for teaching faculty that provide questions about the content, resources and teaching/learning methods to be considered in developing new courses or transforming existing ones. As the workshops had been videotaped, we also edited a series of eighteen short video clips, from two to eight minutes in length, that represent interesting moments, provocative debates and critical questions that emerged in our discussions.

From "Perfect Stranger" to "Creating a New Imaginary"

Two of those moments perhaps best epitomize where we start when we engage in this work and where we hope to move with it. They offer us useful metaphors for the challenge of transforming curriculum in a way that deeply respects the different world views, experiences and knowledges that are represented in our diverse internationalized or diasporicized classrooms. The first framed the workshop presentation by Susan Dion, an Aboriginal professor in the Faculty of Education, who has worked closely with teachers around the integration of First Nations history and reality into the public school curriculum:

When I started working with teachers, one of the

first things I noticed was this — this ease and almost this desire that teachers have. And recently, being involved in the university community, it's not just elementary and secondary school teachers, but it's university course directors and I would argue many Canadians, have this desire and this ease with which to claim a position of being perfect stranger to Aboriginal people.

When I talked to teachers they would say, "Oh, I know nothing, I have no friends who are Aboriginal people, I didn't grow up near a reserve, I didn't learn anything in school. You know I am perfect stranger to Aboriginal people." And there's a way in which this position as perfect stranger allows a kind of innocence and a kind of not being responsible, because that's out there. I am perfect stranger, therefore, I don't need to worry about it … I don't have a responsibility to do it.

… This is something that as educators we need to think about and to recognize that in fact we're not perfect strangers to one another and that we cannot claim innocence on the basis of that relationship because in fact we do have a relationship. Interestingly enough in the work I did for my dissertation project when asking teachers to think more deeply about their experiences with Aboriginal people there comes to the surface key events, stories, experiences that have influenced one's understanding of the relationship between Aboriginal and non-Aboriginal people.

> ... If we want to contribute to a new and better
> relationship, we in fact need to recognize ourselves
> in relationship to that history and in relationship
> to each other.

While Susan was referring to Aboriginal/non-Aboriginal relationships in particular, there are ways in which we tend to deny our relationship to other equity areas as well: I'm white so I can't speak to the issue of racism, I'm heterosexual so I don't have to be concerned about sexual and gender diversity, I'm a man so I have no relationship to gender issues and so forth. Thus, the first step in engaging the diversity within our classrooms in an equitable fashion is to acknowledge that we all have a history of relationships to all of these areas; we have been raised in social contexts that have taught us certain stereotypes, behaviours and prejudices that we have internalized, even if we are not always conscious of them. This is to recognize the systemic nature of discrimination and inequities of all kinds.

The curriculum diversity and equity kit[18] challenges us all to consider our curriculum content and our teaching and learning practices as though we were not perfect strangers; in fact, it asks us to question our own personal experiences as they reflect deeper historical social inequities, and to find new ways to tap the differences that can enrich the learning of students and professors alike.

The DVD with fourteen different video clips can be used in classrooms, professional development workshops and meetings of administrators, to generate dialogue about how we address diversity and equity in the content of what we teach and how we teach as well as at the policy level: how we rethink disciplinary frameworks, hiring policies, and so forth. The accompanying user's guide offers a series of questions that can be discussed following the viewing of the videos. In the section focusing on race and ethnicity, for example, the question is raised, "What classroom ethics can help students and faculty deal with issues of racism?" In the section on disabilities, a discussion question is, "As a student or faculty member with a disability, how can you make your needs known?"

The intersecting analysis of power that framed the workshops and, it is hoped, frames the discussion of the video clips, reminds us that internationalization is not only predicated on differences of national identity, ethnicity and race but also shaped by other elements such as class and poverty, gender, sexual diversity and Aboriginal status.

The curriculum diversity and equity project and kit were meant not only to develop a more critical analysis of our curriculum and teaching/learning practices but also to promote the visioning of positive alternatives. The second metaphor, then, that I would like to leave readers with — "Creating a New Imaginary" — represents where we would like this deep questioning to lead us. In the workshop on sexual and gender diversity, York alumna Sharmini Fernando challenged us to consider how we move outside of and beyond the categories that reflect these historical inequities. She asked:

> How do you address somebody who's racialized
> and a lesbian or homosexual…? How do we
> address diversity from within heteronormativity
> and Eurocentrism? Because both of those areas are
> areas that I grapple with everyday. I deal with
> Eurocentrism as an everyday thing. I don't see any-
> thing of my life ever being reflected anywhere. I
> deal with heteronormativity as an everyday reality,
> because being a lesbian, a dyke, a homosexual is
> not reflected anywhere either … How does that
> get addressed?

Fernando then answered her own question:
> How do we construct a "new imaginary"? How do

> we construct a new imaginary and a new grammar
> that can address [York's] mission statement?
> Because that's what we're asking everyone to do —
> to imagine something different from heteronorma-
> tivity and something different from Eurocentrism
> — that requires not just reading differently or
> writing against the grain but actually imagining
> against the grain.

We have all the elements present at York to engage in the construction of a *new imaginary* that draws on the diverse histories, identities, experiences, knowledges and ways of knowing we find among our colleagues and students, if we only listen and open ourselves to dialogue that moves us beyond our own boundaries, beyond the pretense of being *perfect strangers*. Universities are sites of creative knowledge production and have the potential to embrace this challenge in a post-colonial polycultural world.

As Leslie Sanders, a professor in the Atkinson Faculty of Liberal and Professional Studies, concluded in our workshop on race and ethnicity:

> Curriculum reform is about starting from scratch
> again …. Often these discussions break pedagogy
> into one basket and knowledge into another and
> so the questions becomes how do we make sure
> that all the students in our classroom feel that they
> are represented, feel free to speak, feel comfortable
> to enter into dialogue, but what I've rarely heard
> said is — how about free to make knowledge?

Critically, Sanders brings us back to the question of the purpose of the university, or what might more accurately be called the "multiversity." Is internationalization about creating new knowledge that opens us up to the diversity of epistemologies, cosmovisions and practices that are not just *out there*, but are, in fact, *in here*...in our diasporic academic institution? And is it about recognizing the First Nations on this land, on this very land where we now teach and learn, about recognizing their right to frame their own educational practice in a way that serves their communities and also keeps alive their languages and cultural practices, even as they are constantly changing, as are ours, in a diasporic context? Can the internationalization process include Aboriginalizing and diasporicizing our curriculum and our pedagogies? And can we extend these notions of decolonizing education into programs of international exchange that integrate Aboriginal students and practices so that multiple ways of knowing are honoured?

Promoting Global Learning through International Internships

Svitlana Taraban, York University
Roopa Desai Trilokekar, York University
Tove Fynbo, York University

Introduction

One of the important dimensions in the internationalization of higher education is providing students with learning opportunities to develop cross-cultural competencies, geopolitical knowledge and global awareness. In order to accomplish this task, a number of Canadian universities have designed internship programs that afford students opportunities to work and live outside of Canada. Given that these internships take place in unfamiliar cultural and social milieux, they can provide students with rich opportunities for learning about important global issues, the complexities of global interdependencies and the everyday lives of local communities around the globe.

This chapter starts with the premise that, in today's discourse on internationalization of higher education, critically grounded and academically oriented international internship programs should be considered an important form of global learning. To situate our discussion, we draw on the experiences of a group of interns who participated in the York International Internship Program (YIIP) in the summer of 2005. Our study attempts to understand the meanings that the interns attached to their international experiences and cross-cultural encounters. Specifically, we are interested in the kinds of learning about the globe that took place as a result of these experiences. We hope that this chapter will help to understand international internships not only as a means for developing a skill set for the global market but also as a framework and a context for global learning.

Critical Perspectives on Academic Mobility Programs

Research on the learning outcomes of academic mobility programs has mostly focused on study-abroad programs and student exchanges.[1] A search of the literature revealed that virtually no discussion has taken place with regard to the question of how international internships can help students to understand the nature of global interdependencies, to expand their knowledge of the world and to think critically about global issues and dilemmas. Even when international internships do become the focus of discussion in internationalization literature, they are usually analyzed through the lens of developing cross-cultural skills and competencies demanded by the global market.

This narrow approach to the nature of learning through international internships obscures the complexity of thinking and reflecting on the self, host culture, home culture and the world at large that accompany the experience of working and living in local communities around the globe. The question of critical learning and opportunities to engage global challenges and developments within the framework of international internships is absent in the literature on the internationalization of higher education. Some scholars, however, argue about the need to utilize the experience of international internships to promote global learning. Honigsblum writes: "Internships abroad may prove to be the most efficient and rewarding ways of learning about another culture and ultimately about one's own, and thereby serves a key component in the reform of education in all societies."[2]

Academic mobility programs allow participants to acquire what Murphy-LeJeune terms "mobility capital." In her research on cosmopolitan and mobile students in Europe, she defines mobility capital as a "sub-component of human capital, enabling individuals to enhance their skills because of the richness of the international experience gained by living abroad."[3] While mobility capital does provide students with cross-cultural experiences, it does not necessarily lead to critical thinking, reflective practice and recognition of multiple realities.

In recent years, the assumptions underlying academic mobility programs in North America increasingly have been criticized for their Eurocentric bias and propagation of academic tourism. Major criticisms of academic mobility programs centred on the questions of *who participates* in these types of programs and what *the patterns* of academic mobility are. Some have argued that many academic mobility programs in North America tend to have a narrow geographic focus (predominantly European destinations) and promote a one-way traffic of academic travellers from the North to the South. Commenting on this issue in the US context, McGray observes that nearly half of the American students go abroad to one of four European countries: Britain, France, Italy or Spain. In 2004, for example, Italy received more American students than Africa, Asia and the Middle East combined.[4]

Another criticism of the academic mobility programs points to the fact that many international programs managed by universities are designed in response to the now-popular rhetoric of internationalization without giving serious consideration to the pedagogical rationales of going abroad. With an increasing number of overseas programs that lack reflective and critical angles on international experiences, universities contribute to the proliferation of academic tourism rather than to the facilitation of meaningful learning experiences. This leads to the commodification and commercialization of academic mobility programs offered by institutes of higher education.[5] Several scholars[6] argue that the design of many academic mobility programs lacks insight into their pedagogical and curricular implications and makes no connection between international experiences and student learning. As a result, these programs fail to facilitate perceptual and cognitive changes in the learners and do little to develop the global consciousness and imagination that are discussed in the literature on global citizenship and global identities.

Merryfield,[7] among others, argues that the experience of participating in an academic mobility program does not, in itself, lead to critical thinking and reflective practice related to global issues. She posits that, in order to achieve appreciation of other perspectives and recognition of multiple realities, it is necessary to explicitly examine the connections across identity, power and experience. One way to accomplish this task, in our view, is to develop internship programs that depart from the notion of students-as-tourists and move towards what Singh[8] terms "students-as-fieldworkers." In the following section we draw on Singh's notion of students as fieldworkers in order to outline a framework for organizing global learning experiences through international internships.

Learning about the Globe: Students As Fieldworkers

The experience of academic mobility involves discovering, negotiating and reflecting upon host and home cultures. Several scholars in the field of international education[9] have suggested that this experience has much in common with ethnographic fieldwork, which is centered on first-hand and intensive study of a culture. Like ethnographers and anthropologists doing field work in an unfamiliar culture, students who go abroad are required to engage in intense interactions with the host culture and different ways of being in the world. This experience, according to Geller,[10] can help students develop more complex thinking about cultures and the workings of identity.

As we mentioned earlier, a useful model for conceptualizing cross-cultural learning in international internships could be drawn from the recent work by Michael Singh.[11] While Singh uses the concept of student-as-fieldworker to analyze the experiences of the international students attending Western universities, it can also be applied to understanding the experience of the Canadian students who live and work outside of North America. As fieldworkers in unfamiliar cultural contexts, Canadian students who participate in international internships engage in a variety of ethnographic practices and reflections; for example, through local narratives they learn about the historical and contemporary forces that shape the lives of the local communities. They also develop understanding of local cultural practices and the meanings assigned to them. Some interns learn local languages in order to be able to have more intimate relationships with the new culture. Like cultural researchers in the field, they search for information about the new culture, observe cultural nuances and details and try to develop an understanding of the cultural workings in an unfamiliar milieu.

In order to help students to reflect upon and to learn from their international experiences, Geller[12] suggests that students be provided with interpretive tools that would allow them to recognize multiple realities, to see local-global connectedness and to engage critically with pressing issues. He compared the experience of traditional academic mobility programs to "tasting, without savoring; with only glancing, not seeing." He argued that, in meaningful academic mobility programs, "[s]tudents must be taught to taste. Their eye must be trained to see."[13] Geller suggests that one way to organize international learning is through the use of ethnographic journals, which he considers "a medium through which the student transforms the experience into learning."[14]

As a model for international learning, York University's International Internship Program (YIIP) strives to move beyond merely providing its participants with mobility capital. In many ways, the program aims to respond to the need to connect international experiences to curricular objectives. Through a variety of reflective and critical learning experiences, which are built into the program model (e.g., sharing experiences on a listserv, writing articles, making presentations and supporting student research on an international issue), the YIIP seeks to provide students with a framework for global learning. We will begin our discussion of student perspectives on global learning through the YIIP by briefly describing the inception and the evolution of the program.

Background on the York International Internship Program

The York International Internship Program is an initiative of the Office of the Associate Vice-President International and an integral part of York University's overall internationalization strategy. Announced in January 2004, each summer the YIIP sends a cohort of undergraduate and graduate students to placements abroad or, in a small number of cases, to organizations based in Canada that are devoted to international issues. To date, 125 students have completed the YIIP.

The idea for the international internship came from consultations that the newly appointed associate vice-president international undertook in 2002-03. It was clear that internships could become an important component of the student experience and that faculty, as well as other members of the York University community, had contacts with organizations of diverse types across the globe that would be willing to provide placements. At the same time, it was clear that most of these organizations, especially those in the developing world, could not afford to provide compensation and that most York students could not afford to give up paid employment for a long period of time. These dual realities of accessibility led to the decision that the university would provide a stipend for each placement and that interns would also be eligible to request financial support for their airfare from the existing York International Mobility Award.

The motivation behind the internship program was to increase the number of students at York University undertaking an international experience by providing a greater variety of funded opportunities. The YIIP has produced a substantial increase in the number of students applying for an international experience; both the number of placements and of applications has increased steadily, from 26 and 68 in 2004 to 43 and 97 in 2005 and 55 and 134 in 2006. This increased student interest in the YIIP has been enhanced by the enthusiasm of the returning interns who, upon completing their placements, participate in information sessions and give presentations about their experiences at student clubs, research centres and even international conferences.

The YIIP itself is structured to engage interns in four predeparture program sessions and, on their return, in facilitated debriefing sessions. While away, interns have access to a listserv which allows them to be in contact with other interns and to discuss any problems or concerns. They also complete questionnaires before, during and after the internship which serve as both learning and assessment tools and which offer participants the opportunity to reflect on their experiences in a systematic manner. This cycle — establishing placements, advertising, screening and interviewing candidates, preparing the interns for their placement and debriefing them on their return — has continued. While the YIIP placements do not carry academic credit, a number of students have used their experience as the basis for academic work. Additionally, York has responded to frequent statements by many returned interns that they would like to have further opportunity to reflect on their experience in an extended way by developing and offering a new three-credit undergraduate course entitled "Full Circle: Experiencing the International."

The YIIP model is unique in Canada and perhaps even in North America. First, the Office of the Associate Vice-President International arranges the placements directly with the host organization, in contrast to other internship programs where students typically find their own placements. By taking responsibility for organizing the placements, York is able to develop continuity in the program and to build ongoing, mutually beneficial relationships with the host organizations. Second, the university provides financial support to students, thereby making the program more accessible. In other internships, funding is either provided by the host organization or the costs are borne solely by the student. Third, the placements are established so that students from the widest possible range of academic backgrounds will find something relevant to their area of study: the 2005 cohort represented all ten of York University's faculties.

The Study

Research Questions and Data Sources

This study examines the nature of learning about global issues in the context of international internships. The study is guided by two questions:

1. As transnational actors whose experiences are inextricably linked to the broader contexts of globalization, what do

the YIPP interns (un)learn over the course of international internships?

2. How do the interns think about their experiences and what kinds of questions do these experiences raise for their global awareness and cross-cultural learning?

Four sources of data were used. Demographic information about the interns (gender, status in Canada, academic majors, prior international experience) as well as reasons for applying to the internship program was gathered through the internship applications. The second source of data was the questionnaires which are used as tools to evaluate the experiences of interns and learning outcomes of the YIIP. The third source of data was online discussions on the listserv that was created by internship coordinators to facilitate communication and reflection among the interns. The data presented here came from online discussions that took place in summer 2005. Content analysis methodology was used: printed records of the online conversations were analyzed to identify the themes and issues discussed by interns over the course of the internship.

Finally, the last set of data was obtained through one-year follow-up conversational-style interviews with five interns from the 2005 cohort who responded to a written invitation with interest in participating in the study. The interviews were conducted in winter 2006. The selection of interviewees followed the principle that the sample obtained should be relatively heterogeneous with regard to academic major, gender and prior international exposure. The interviews were semi-structured and open-ended, allowing former interns to think about their experiences retrospectively. All data were coded and analyzed thematically. The analysis of the data from listserv discussions, questionnaires and interviews focused on the identification of emerging themes and recurring patterns.

Participants

A total of forty-two interns participated in York's International Internship Program from May until August 2005. The largest percentage of placements (over 30 percent) were located in the countries of the Latin American and Caribbean region, reflecting the extensive academic links that York faculties have with institutions there. Half of the internship placements were with nongovernmental organizations (NGOs) and another 37 percent were in educational and research institutions.

The majority of the interns (thirty-five, or 83 percent) were female. As a group, the interns had an impressive array of foreign language skills. According to the self-reported language proficiency in the interns' applications, fifteen interns were fluent in two or more languages in addition to English, eighteen interns were bilingual and only eight were monolingual. As a group, the interns were fluent in nineteen different languages.

The majority of the interns from the 2005 cohort reported a high level of prior international exposure in their application to the program. Some of them had participated in exchange programs or international internships funded by the Canadian government. As a group, the interns had extensive transnational educational histories. These findings concur with earlier studies that have shown that students with prior international experience are more likely than average students to participate in various types of academic mobility programs.[15]

While the majority of the interns (thirty-four, or 81 percent) were undergraduate students, there were six master's and two doctoral students participating in the program. The interns showed a great deal of diversity in terms of academic majors. While many were majoring in subjects such as international development studies, international studies or environmental studies having a significant international component, some were studying art history, education, nursing, biology, planning and communication.

Seventeen interns were pursuing double majors.

The interns were also diverse in terms of their cultural and linguistic background and their citizenship status in Canada. While the majority of them (thirty-three) were Canadian citizens, five held permanent-resident status at the time of the internship and four were international students at York University on student visas. Several of the interns were diasporic youth (second or third-generation Canadians). Table 1 summarizes the demographic characteristics of the intern cohort in 2005.

Table 1

Demographic characteristics of the sample (N=42)

	N
Female	35
Male	7
Undergraduate	34
Graduate	8
Canadian citizen/permanent resident	38
International student	4
Prior international exposure	37
Fluency in a language other than English	34

Findings

In this section, we will discuss four interrelated clusters of topics related to global learning that emerged from the analysis of the data. These thematic clusters are summarized in Table 2.

Table 2

Study findings — Thematic dimensions of global learning during the YIIP internship

Themes	Issues discussed
Challenging stereotypes	Representations of places; portrayals of local populations; variations in the social organization of space and time
Problematizing identities	Gender and race in global spaces; self- and other-perception; beliefs and values; identity shifts
Learning about organizations as the agents of development	Issues addressed by host organizations; challenges faced by organizations; complexity of sociocultural and political contexts that underpin the work of development organizations
Questioning the discourse on development	North-South relationships; global inequalities; asymmetry of power; economic exploitation; notions of developed/developing; theory and practice of development work

Challenging Stereotypes

During the online discussions on the internship listserv, several interns commented on gaining significant knowledge about the histories and current situation of the countries in which their internships took place. One intern, for example, wrote:

> I have learned extensively about the Nicaraguan

> historical experience and how that has culminated
> to today's socio-economic and political situation in
> the coastal regions. (female intern in Nicaragua)

A recurrent theme in the interns' reflections on their experiences was a shift in the manner in which they perceived certain places or parts of the world. Several interns reported that the internship has problematized their fixed ideas about countries, regions and groups of people. A female intern who had travelled to more than ten countries prior to the internship wrote:

> I had some preconceived notions about Asian peo-
> ple, which I learned were nothing more than
> stereotypes. I was told that the majority of people
> are very quiet, reserved and introverted. I never
> took into consideration that people behave very
> differently when they are taken out of their envi-
> ronment. When I arrived in Hong Kong I was
> overwhelmed by how outgoing, welcoming, and
> friendly people were, especially the students at my
> hostel. (female intern in Hong Kong)

As shown by many cultural commentators, the tendency to portray culturally distinct and largely unknown places as fixed and unchanging entities often leads to the construction of certain places as backward and inferior to Western locales. The local encounters and opportunities to observe the various aspects of life in local communities around the world afforded interns the opportunity to develop a more complex and nuanced understanding of local places. They learned to understand the difference and diversity that characterize locales around the world and within the same region. By observing differences that might escape the gaze of a tourist but that became apparent to the critical eye of students-as-fieldworkers,[16] the interns expanded and deepened their global outlook. The following excerpts show some of the changes in interns' imaginary construction of unknown countries and regions:

> I learned that seeing Latin America as one homogenous culture is not necessarily accurate. Each country has its own culture and has lived through different processes that make it unique. (female intern in Panama)

> I found that Arab culture can not be generalized. There are many differences that are present. Cultures such as Sudanese, Jordanian, Palestinian, Egyptian etc., are all different although they are all considered "Arabs". (female intern in Jordan)

> I was not surprised to find that the stereotypes about Mexico City don't hold, although I was open to the possibility that they might hold. In any case, it is not impossible to navigate Mexico City. The pollution hasn't killed me, the taxi drivers haven't murdered me, the food didn't make me sick until two months into the trip. (female intern in Mexico)

> There were many things I knew and thought I knew about China. Many of which were reinforced when I came here and many of which were completely debunked when I came here. The opportunity to live in Beijing has given me great insight into modern Chinese society, especially the views of many of the staff and students at Beida. (male intern in China)

Problematizing Identities

As shown in the interns' group profile, they were far from being a culturally homogeneous group. Although formally the identities of all participating interns were collated under the collective identity "Canadian student," in some cases this identity was at odds with the host culture's image of Canada and Canadians. For example, the interns who belonged to one of the minority groups in Canadian society were confronted with the imaginings of whiteness as one of the defining features of Canadian-ness. A female intern of African-Canadian background, whose internship took place in one of the Latin American countries, experienced discrimination and negative attitudes on the part of the local population who routinely challenged her identity as a Canadian. In the midterm questionnaire sent out to all interns, she described her experience in the following way:

> Generally, my ability to adapt and live in a different community is very fluid. Here, in sharp contrast, cultural ideas about me are particularly heinous, thus I struggled against them (even before I knew exactly what they were because the attention felt horrible) …. So now all the time I reiterate that I am Canadian, try and explain my difficulties at being different in this town (what it's like in Canada, how men speak to women, how there are many different kinds of people, etc.) and asked to be called by name not *morena* [term used to describe a dark-skinned person] to those whom I care to. (female intern in Nicaragua)

Similar findings were reported by Taylor,[17] who conducted a study of interculturally competent individuals in the United States. Two African-American respondents in Taylor's study who lived in Latin America attributed their adjustment difficulties to the perception of

them as racially different. This study and our own findings show
that race, along with gender and other attributes of identity, medi-
ate cross-cultural encounters of transnational students. In the
situation of the YIIP intern, we found that the interns did not use
the discussion on the listserv to explore the complexity of "roots
and routes" and to problematize the notion of Canadian-ness.
While interns did offer a number of suggestions on how to handle
the situation, they failed to see opportunities for critical thinking
about the intersections of race and gender not only in terms of
cross-border mobility but also with regard to access to power and
opportunities. The story of the female intern in Nicaragua shows
that, like other transnational actors, the YIIP interns are confronted with the question of how race and gender shape the experience
of cross-border mobility and how race, gender and other categories
of identity are constructed in culturally specific ways.

In contrast to the Nicaragua account, the experience of a male
intern in Jordan shows that he had a much easier time fitting into
the host culture. As an Anglo-Canadian male, he felt comfortable
with his "outsider-ness" and even took pleasure in the fact that, due
to his "Western-ness," he was perceived by the local population as
different and exotic:

> While I doubt that I will ever be able to fit in as a
> Jordanian (people still shout 'Welcome to Jordan!'
> across the street at me!), I have learned to dress,
> behave and even speak similarly to a native. Arabic
> culture has many formal rules, calls and responses
> and set ideas that are very interesting for me to
> learn, and follow. I have found that the greatest
> intercultural skill is the ability to smile, forget any
> discomfort, and follow along with whatever is hap-
> pening. This holds in many situations, whether
> eating the head of a goat, or dancing at a wedding

while someone unloads their handgun into the air.
(male intern in Jordan)

These two distinct identity-related accounts show that some YIIP interns found their Canadian-ness in the host culture to be transparent and uncontested while for others it was routinely challenged. This raises a number of interesting questions related to the subject of identity in the context of international internships. How do race, gender and other categories of identity shape the experiences of Canadian students who participate in international internships? What kind of identity work accompanies cross-cultural experiences of Canadian students who belong to both minority and majority groups in their home country? To answer these questions, more research is needed on the experiences of minority students participating in international internships and the ways in which they make sense of their experiences in global spaces.

Learning about the Organizations as the Agents of Development

Over the course of the internships, participants had the opportunity to learn about the work of various organizations (e.g., international and nongovernmental organizations, educational institutions) that are active in the area of local community development. The interns learned about the issues confronting local communities and the ways in which local organizations work to address them. An intern who worked in a school in Kenya described his experiences in the following way:

The teachers at [name of school] support each
other. We share the few books, paper and pens
that we have, so that together, we have many
resources at our disposal. We ask each other how
we can improve, as teachers, for the betterment of

our students. (male intern in Kenya)

Likewise, another intern became conscious of the difficult conditions in which many organizations located in the Global South operate:

> Like many government departments and NGOs, resources can be stretched quite thinly compared to the objectives they set for themselves and that others set for them. It has been eye-opening to see a small office accomplish quite a bit, however. (male intern in Dominican Republic)

One of the interns who worked with a local nongovernmental organization in Brazil reconsidered his earlier skepticism towards the work of NGOs:

> Because of the very different realities in North America, I often viewed the work of many NGOs as not so sincere and more politically motivated. Here the case is different. NGOs do real work with real objectives of helping real people ... I have personally begun to appreciate much more the need for such work here. I have been so impressed with some of the work being done here that I feel an obligation to maintain a personal connection and offer my assistance on an ongoing basis. (male intern in Brazil)

It appears that interns not only acquired job-related skills but also developed a more complex view of the local contexts and conditions that give shape and meaning to the everyday life of organizations. By observing the day-to-day activities of local organizations and institutions, the interns were able to develop an understanding of how organizations located at the periphery of the profit-driven and consumer-oriented global market strive to serve their communities. For some of the interns, the experience was so profound that they sought to maintain their connection to the organization where they worked beyond the duration of the internship.

Questioning the Discourse on Development

Regardless of their academic majors, many of the YIIP interns reported learning about various issues facing communities around the globe. In their responses to the questionnaires, interns often talked about new knowledge of poverty, inequities, HIV/AIDS and sustainable development that they acquired as a result of the internship:

> The thing I found the most surprising and the
> hardest to look at was the level of poverty in
> Ghana. Although I have traveled to other develop-
> ing countries, for some reason the level of poverty
> in Ghana really was hard to confront. (female
> intern in Ghana)

> At the personal level the internship has put me in
> front of the reality of Latin America; a reality that
> I had not forgotten but one that used to look dis-
> tant. Being here is a reminder that things are not
> always what they look like, especially from the dis-
> tance. The political and economical situation in
> Argentina is quite volatile and I expected that had
> passed. (female intern in Argentina)

> Academically, I learned so much about interlinks
> between social justice and environmental prob-
> lems. I also become more aware of the complex

notion of sustainability. (female intern in India)

For one of the interns, the experience led her to question what counts as knowledge and how knowledge is situated in local contexts:

> I really learned a lot about local knowledge and
> how important that is in the development process. I
> learned about what it means to live in an agricul-
> turally based economy, that people who may be
> illiterate ... have more knowledge of plant systems
> and how food gets put on the table than anyone
> I've ever met here in Canada. These different kinds
> of knowledge, I realized, are all equally crucial to
> making development work relevant for the people
> it's trying to help. Mostly I just learned about what
> all this stuff I'm studying in school really means —
> what subsistence living is, what it means when
> resources are skewed towards the urban centers, and
> what are the real issues and solutions that women
> feel need to be addressed. (female intern in Peru)

What these excerpts from interns' reflections demonstrate is that not just students majoring in international development or allied fields can benefit from the experience of an international internship. When opportunities for learning and reflection are in place, international internships can provide a valuable means for learning about the globe for students in any academic field.

Discussion

The findings of our study show that, while YIIP interns reported improved proficiency in foreign languages and acquisition of new professional skills, much of their learning had to do with the life of local communities around the globe, the nature of global interdependencies and issues of identity. We discovered that interns became more aware of their own assumptions and social locations as transnational actors from the West. Their international experiences made them more aware of the ways in which self-definitions and other-definitions are shaped by positioning in the global economy and access to power and opportunities.

The accounts show that the YIIP interns gained substantive knowledge about other cultures. They learned about historical conditions and current socio-economic situations in their host countries. They also learned about work environments, social relations, the organization of work and leisure and the construction of gender and race in various locales. A specific example of substantive learning reported by the YIIP interns relates two different approaches to the understanding of the notion of time — monochromatic versus polychromatic time — which underpin the social organization of life in North America and Latin America. As a result, the interns developed an understanding that the notion of time and allied notions of punctuality and efficiency are culture-specific and vary across cultures.

In addition to broader cultural learning, YIIP interns deepened their global awareness by learning about the nature of global development and global change and the ways in which they affect specific countries and communities. Through their work with local organizations, they learned specific methodologies and practices (e.g., popular education, the arts for development) related to community development.

YIIP interns also reported changes in their understanding of other cultures and global issues as evidenced by the reflections that suggest a shift towards less fixed and less ethnocentric world-views. One intern explained how her view of Asian people as quiet, introverted and reserved was challenged by cross-cultural friendships with local students that she came to know during her internship in

Hong Kong. Another intern discovered that her view of Arab culture as monolithic was challenged when she started to observe the
differences among various cultures in the Middle East.

Self-understanding and personal development was another area
where students reported significant changes. Many interns reported
increased self-efficacy, independence and maturity of judgement.

One of the challenges of working through cross-cultural experiences and learning, or sometimes unlearning, about global issues
involves the ability to move from descriptive accounts of experience
to analytical reflection. While the internship listserv provided an
opportunity for the YIIP interns to share their experiences, their
online posts were clearly influenced by the intensity and perplexity
of their immediate experiences. As a result, interns' accounts often
were descriptive in nature and lacked the depth that can be
achieved by analytical distancing from the experience and retro-
spective reflection. As Wilson observes, "Persons are more likely to
'learn from experience' when they are prepared for the experience,
engage in educational activities during the experience, and evaluate
the experience."[18] From this perspective, critical examination of
cross-cultural experiences requires opportunities to think about
them afterwards. We will return to this point when discussing pedagogical considerations in developing international internship
programs.

In summary, our findings show that the nature of learning in
international internships is much broader than is typically imagined.
Looking at international internships primarily through the narrow
lens of global skills acquisition leaves out an important dimension of
learning about the globe. In fact, the learning that took place during
the YIIP internship was a significant factor in determining the personal, academic and professional journey of the former YIIP interns.
One of the interns, for example, developed a strong interest in the
issues of gender in Latin America and decided to study this topic
further upon her return. Another intern was inspired to pursue grad-

uate studies in public policy, and applied to the program while still working in her host country. Yet another intern who developed an interest in popular education in Latin America initiated an independent study course that allowed her to explore in-depth the theory and practices of popular education. While it is beyond the scope of this study to explore the long-term impact of York's International Internship Program on former interns, it is clear that international internships that provide opportunities for critical engagements with global issues and developments result in much greater learning about the globe than internships that merely focus on the acquisition of career-related skills.

Implications for Program Development

This discussion reminds us that, while study abroad and international internships provide some of the richest and most powerful critical learning experiences in understanding global spaces, this is not always the case. The international experience, in and of itself, does not provide for critical reflection, learning and knowledge production. This learning has to be structured and integrated into the program design beginning with the program manager challenging his/her own pedagogical objectives and constructing a program design based on sound pedagogical principles. It is equally important to work in partnership with interns to determine intentional learning objectives and to help them identify their own learning paths.

Experiential education provides a core methodology to integrate such experiences into the academic curriculum. The key is to provide a deliberate process of critical thinking and reflection: an opportunity to step back and examine one's assumptions, question one's motives and objectives and examine one's participation (or nonparticipation) in the learning experience. This continuous process — of experience, observation and reflection, theorizing and conceptualizing, and applying the knowledge to new situations — is what defines experiential education and sets apart, in Geller's terms, academic learning programs from programs that encourage the uncritical consumption of international experiences.

An equally important concept for program design is Singh's conceptualization of students-as-fieldworkers and the necessity to pose questions identified by Kapoor[19] for those involved in the field of international development: Who represents? Why represent? Represent whom? How to represent? In understanding global spaces, it is vital for students to examine critically how their representations are intimately linked to their positioning, their socio-economic status, their gender, race, cultural, geographic, historical and institutional positioning, and for them to be highly self-reflective about their engagement in international education and international learning. It is critical that both the project manager and the students question the inherent good associated with international and global learning and ask questions about their role in this learning process. Who is the learner? Who contributes to the experience and for what reasons? Who is helping whom? And who is the "expert" speaking of and speaking about? A critical examination of the academic world and its approach to the "international" has to be integrated into the learning experience. It is also necessary that students be introduced to important concepts and provided the necessary vocabulary to engage in such critical dialogue concerning global spaces, especially as students from a range of disciplinary backgrounds participate in international study and work-abroad programs.

The focus on study and work-abroad programs is largely administrative: institutions set target enrolment numbers for program participation and provide single predeparture orientations largely focused on risk and responsibility matters related to "exotic," "foreign" and often "unsafe" environments, always assuming the inherent value and benefit of the international experiences provided through these program initiatives. Such program structures can be problematic. As international educators, the program managers and study-abroad advisers must themselves engage in a critical reflection of international learning. This requires systematic study and research about international learning, engagement with the politics of difference and its implications for border crossings, and a conscious effort to integrate learning throughout the academic cycle rather than as a one-off program module. International educators must do further research to understand how their position (e.g., race and gender) influences their participation in international learning, how learning differs between structured and unstructured programs and what long-term benefits there are, if any, to study and work abroad. Much work is still required before international learning can go beyond intellectual tourism and global market competencies to build global perspectives and intercultural dialogue and learning and to translate knowledge into understanding.

10

A Student's Reflections on Cross-cultural Learning and the Internationalized University Experience

Nikki MacMillan, York University

Consider my university career as a case study in internationalization. Having developed an early interest in global issues and foreign language learning (I was placed by my parents at the impressionable age of five into a French Immersion program, which I continued through most of my schooling), and having a strong desire to immerse myself in the multicultural metropolis of Toronto, I left the smallish town of Peterborough immediately after graduating from high school and found myself at York University in September 2003, beginning my university career in the field of International Development Studies. My experience was, from the outset, an international one: my courses had a global focus, my professors hailed from all over the world, I started to learn Spanish, I got involved in international student organizations, and for the first time in my life I sat in classrooms where neither the teacher nor the majority of the students were white. As my academic career progressed, I continued to immerse myself in the global dimension of both my studies and the extracurricular aspects of university life. In my second year, I applied to the York International Internship Program (YIIP) and was accepted for my first choice of placement in Peru, where I spent the summer of 2005. Upon my return, I began to reflect on my international experience, and it was during this time that I was first exposed to the idea of internationalization.

Internationalization as a concept was and still is new to me, even though I have arguably been living it for the past three years. I have gradually begun to recognize that the opportunities for international, cross-cultural, or global learning that have and have not been offered to me throughout my university career are deeply shaped by York University's interpretation and implementation of the concept of internationalization that has become so popular among Canadian universities in recent years. York University's Strategic Plan for Internationalization[1] (produced in 2003-04, my first year of studies at York) describes at least four initiatives, considered to be of importance to the internationalization of the university, in which I have participated or by which I have been directly affected. These initiatives include the promotion of interdisciplinary degree programs that focus on the international (International Development Studies being the most recent addition), the encouragement of foreign language learning, the recruitment of international students to enrich and diversify the classroom experience, and the implementation of the York International Internship Program. Evidently, parts of York's internationalization strategy have reached their target market.

Am I a product of internationalization? If so, what does that mean? There are at least two distinct views as to the purpose of internationalizing the university. One perspective equates internationalization with international competitiveness, arguing that internationalizing Canada's universities is about developing students' sense of global citizenship in the global marketplace. The goal of internationalization, therefore, is to produce graduates who are "globally competitive." The contrasting view presents internationalization as an opportunity to promote cross-cultural learning for the specific purpose of fostering global solidarity and social justice. In this essay, I will put forth my own perspective on the matter — a uniquely student perspective, while I can still call myself a student — a process that has required me to look back and reflect upon my university experience as an internationalized one. I do not attempt to speak as an academic expert on this issue, nor do I speak for all students. I speak from my own experience as a person whose academic and personal choices reveal an immediate interest in "bringing the world to the classroom" but also as a student who, despite perhaps already having an "international" outlook or a desire for one, shares many common daily realities with other students — realities such as attending classes, processing/interpreting information, writing and speaking in an academic context, experiencing cultural life at York, and so on, that may impact and be impacted by internationalization in its various forms.

In this chapter, I reflect upon the internationalization process at York University as I have experienced it and offer suggestions as to how to make this process meaningful for students in an institution of higher learning. In the first section, I will discuss my experience as an intern at PROMEB, a basic education project in rural Peru, enabled by my participation in the York International Internship Program in 2005, and the challenges and opportunities this presented in terms of personal development, learning across differences and positioning myself within the global dynamics of power. In the second section, I will argue for the need to actively promote such cross-cultural and experiential learning at the classroom level so that students are able to make sense of their cultural encounters and critically interpret the world in which they live. Through critical reflection on my internationalized university experiences, I have come to realize that for students to emerge from university with a sense of social responsibility and a commitment to global social justice, rather than with a "globally competitive" set of skills that will enhance their employability in a global marketplace that is dominated and controlled by private interests, university internationalization projects need to reach into the classrooms where students can begin to interpret their international experiences; consider the various elements of power dynamics, identity, and human relationships involved in such experiences; and share those reflections with other students and teachers.

York International Internship Program (YIIP)

The York International Internship Program (YIIP) began in 2004, when twenty-six students participated in internships abroad and in Canada. In 2005, I was one of forty-three interns who participated in the program. My fellow interns and I represented all ten faculties at York University, and we were placed in three-to four-month internships on every continent except Antarctica. YIIP placements with nongovernmental organizations (NGOs), educational and research institutions and government agencies are usually arranged through York faculty and staff connections, and each intern is provided with the contact information of their primary supervisor in the field prior to departure. YIIP interns receive a $3,000 award to cover their living costs during their placement and are given the chance to apply for the York International Mobility Award, which typically covers the cost of airfare. As York's Strategic Plan for Internationalization describes, internationally oriented internships offer an alternative to the traditional exchange program model for students who are seeking an international learning experience. In addition, the strategic plan proposes that, "[b]y making interns available to poorly resourced organizations in other countries and by reducing the economic impediments that put the internship experience beyond the reach of many students, internships of this sort would respond to York's commitment to social responsibility and social justice."[2]

The goals of the internship program are not restricted to providing students with valuable international work experience in their field, as with traditional internships. YIIP encapsulates a broader range of objectives that focus on the intern's academic and personal development, cross-cultural learning skills and understanding of global issues. The program attempts to recruit students who see the internship opportunity as more than just a potential point on a resumé (although many interns, myself included, recognize the value of gaining such work experience in terms of enhancing future employability). YIIP is structured in such a way that interns are encouraged to reflect on these multiple objectives and chart progress on their own individual goals before, during and after the internship, through questionnaires and various orientation and briefing sessions.

Proyecto de Mejoramiento de la Educación Básica (PROMEB)

My placement was in a development project called PROMEB (Proyecto de Mejoramiento de la Educación Básica, Project for the Improvement of Basic Education), located in the rural communities that surround the Northern Peruvian city of Piura. Agriteam Canada, a Canadian NGO, manages the project, which is jointly funded by the Canadian and Peruvian governments. PROMEB works to improve the quality of primary education in rural areas, recognizing the vast inequalities in the calibre of education (and other social services) available in rural versus urban areas in Peru. For three months, my home was in the village of San Juan de Bigote, where I lived and worked with Peruvian teachers and children. About four hours away from the nearest city, San Juan de Bigote is a small agricultural community surrounded by rolling hills and rice fields. Other than the paved central plaza, the roads are mostly dirt, such that any truck passing through kicks up clouds of cough-inducing dust. There are power lines, though during my stay the current running through them was unreliable and outages were common. Running water flowed from most taps, but in order to save my *gringa* stomach from infectious diseases, I avoided unpeeled fruits and vegetables and stocked up on bottled water every week. I shared a room with five of my coworkers in a house with a tin roof and a rooster in the courtyard that acted, whether we liked it or not, as our 5:30 a.m. alarm clock.

My official role within the organization was to support the local teachers and PROMEB staff. In practice, my role was defined and redefined nearly weekly for the first half of my internship, as my supervisors, coworkers and I struggled to find a place where my strengths and skills would be of most use. Since I had a strong artistic background, particularly in drama and dance, I endeavoured to bring arts education into a school system that seemed to be lacking in this area. I taught drama in six different classrooms with students ranging from Grade 4 to Grade 6 and in two schools in more isolated communities outside of central Bigote. These one-room schools housed Grades 1 through 6 all in the same classroom, which made it challenging to develop a comprehensive and inclusive drama program in which all of the children could participate. In these classes, as well as in the ones in central Bigote, I led drama activities that introduced the students to theatre techniques, performance, role-playing, character development, and so on; we also worked on several short pieces that focused primarily on environmental themes such as the planting season and the drought that had been affecting the area.

In the afternoons, I ran a Theatre Club for local youth which was more loosely structured for several reasons. Theatre Club took place outdoors, in a courtyard which was also used for day care and general recreation, and so distractions were unavoidable. It was impossible to enforce regular attendance in such an environment, although there was a core group of approximately ten children who showed up every Monday and Wednesday. Still, the best strategy was to run activities that could be started and finished in one afternoon so that

newcomers would not feel lost but at the same time regular participants could build on what they had learned in previous sessions. By
the end of my internship, the regular Theatre Club participants were
teaching their friends the exercises we had done together, and
expressed interest in continuing the club in my absence.

Among the necessary skills listed for the successful applicant to
the PROMEB internship was the "ability to work in a cross-cultural, isolated and challenging environment." Although I was presumed
to have this ability prior to the internship, it was actually in this area
that I learned and grew the most during my time in Peru. Surprisingly for me, though, the "challenging environment" was not
defined by the water I couldn't drink, the mosquito nets, or even the
severe lack of resources in the schools in which I worked. In many
ways I was prepared for this aspect of my internship: I did not arrive
in Peru expecting to find something like a Canadian work setting; I
had met with the previous year's interns and had seen pictures, and
even a video, of the placement; and the nature of what I study in
university prepared me to see poverty and inequality in rural Peru.

What I found more challenging about living and working in San
Juan de Bigote was dealing with the discomforts I felt about my role
and identity there. For a young, Caucasian, North American, university-educated female with English as a first language and enough
money and mobility to travel to that community — and, crucially,
to just as easily *leave* it after three months to continue travelling
throughout South America before returning to a comfortable life in
Canada — issues of culture, identity and privilege seeped into every
aspect of daily life. What was I doing there? What historical circumstances and what current global power arrangements made my
presence there possible and the presence of a Bigoteño in Canada in
a similar internship role unthinkable? How would an "outsider"
such as myself, relatively unfamiliar with the local culture and local
history, be able to "make a difference" in just three months? And
who would decide what kind of "difference" needs to be made?

Narda Razack, in her investigation of international student exchanges in the field of social work, argues that we need to examine how Euro-Western hegemony is produced and reproduced, including through international exchange programs that exist within imperialist frameworks. She points out that the theories and practices of social work (as well as those of international development, I would add) are based in Euro-Western perspectives that historically have dominated the "developing" world through colonialism and imperialism.[3] Colonial and imperial legacies persist through unidirectional flows of knowledge and information, and they are exemplified by international academic exchanges where, in most cases of travel to "developing" countries, there is in fact no "exchange."[4] "We currently occupy structures which were founded on imperialism and colonization,"[5] she says, an assertion that is important to keep in mind when considering my experience in Peru.

My own anxieties about participating in an international internship echo Razack's point about the imperialist foundations of exchanges — and of university internationalization in general. During my placement, I found myself struggling with several different roles, many of which related to questions of power. First of all, my whiteness and Canadian-ness, as well as my imperfect Spanish accent, immediately identified me as an outsider. The amount of attention I received for the colour of my skin was something I had never experienced before: in the first few weeks, I was called *blanquita* (white girl) more often than I was called by name. While this may have made me uncomfortable, my outsider status did not make me a second-class citizen — far from it, especially in a country where whiteness has been associated with wealth, privilege and high social standing since colonial times.

Historically, foreigners (from the West) working in the so-called Third World have been constructed as experts who, whether through colonialism or development aid, are there to help modernize or develop a formerly backward or underdeveloped society. As

Arturo Escobar points out, this understanding of the world portrays Third World people as powerless, impoverished, and "lacking in historical agency, as if waiting for the (white) Western hand to help subjects along."6 This representation, Escobar argues, "is more a sign of power over the Third World than a truth about it."7

My role as an intern and as a teacher added to the pressures of being perceived as a foreign expert. As an intern, it was presumed that I had something to offer the organization and the community, especially since I came from a Western university where I studied international development. As a teacher, I was in a position of authority vis-à-vis the students, and thus perceived as an expert in whatever I was teaching, if only because I might have been standing at the front of the classroom. The interplay of these roles (outsider, intern and teacher — among others) had a powerful impact on the way I felt about my own cultural identity and reasons for being there.

Ironically, in a context where I may have been viewed as an expert, I certainly did not feel like one. I spent the majority of my three months in San Juan de Bigote learning how to live there. In this respect, I learned more from my students than they learned from me. They taught me how to climb onto the back of a truck to hitch a ride to the river. They helped me improve my Spanish. They taught me traditional dances and told me stories about the local and national history. My coworkers from PROMEB — Maritza, Carla, Milagros, Teresa, Armando, Alfredo — also taught me how to get by: how to take the bus to the village, how not to get "ripped off," how to cut meat with a butter knife. This way, I learned to love the community and the people in it, and, whether I was an outsider at the beginning or the whole way through, by the end I felt like this was my home.

Dualisms such as expert/non-expert, outsider/insider and teacher/student imply to me that one can never really get to know the "Other." While my internship experience illuminated certain inequalities in power and opportunity that exist in the world and shed light on how I am a part of that inequality, it also showed me that human relationships, art and always acting like a student all help to break down these barriers to communication and understanding across cultures.

So I may not have changed the world! I doubt that very many Canadian interns participating in a so-called development project in a poor country for a short period of time would come back with the impression that they had "made a difference." This is not to say that it is a futile or depressing experiment; to live and learn in San Juan de Bigote was not an opportunity to change the world but to participate in it. As students of any discipline, we study the world (the world of politics, of science, of mathematics, of philosophy), but rarely get the chance to participate in it. In terms of "York's commitment to social responsibility and social justice," I would argue that the social justice elements of international internships do not occur when York provides capable interns to under funded Southern NGOs but rather when the intern is encouraged to participate fully in life in the host culture and learns to learn across differences.

Canadian universities that offer international exchanges and internships need to keep their own objectives for internationalization in mind when organizing such placements. On the one hand, universities that view internationalization as a means of producing graduates who will fit easily into a globalized world economy need to reevaluate their reasons for sending students abroad, to recognize the consequences of reproducing global inequalities in this way. On the other hand, universities that have a sincere interest in promoting intercultural solidarity and international social justice need to recognize how easily the internationalization project can become trapped in an imperialist framework. As I have shown above, this is hardly just a theory: most students travelling to the Global South will have a hard time avoiding these issues of power and representation. It is crucial to support students as they experience these uncomfortable realities, so that real learning about our place in the

world can occur. The following discussion explores the university's
role in promoting such learning at the classroom level.

Beyond the Global: Internationalization at Home

Clearly, my internship in Peru allowed me to experience world
issues, global power dynamics and intercultural relations in a new
and truly tangible way. But in order to be meaningful for students
in general, internationalization needs to reach beyond these global
adventures and into students' local experiences, to reach those who
are not able to participate in exchanges or internships abroad as well
as enable those who have had international experiences to make
sense of them here at home. At a culturally diverse university such
as York and in a multicultural city such as Toronto, cross-cultural
experiences or encounters occur all the time, and world travellers
are surely not the only ones who have something important or
interesting to say about the world. Similar issues around cultural
identity, power relations, prejudice and stereotypes, and intercultural communication arise here on a daily basis, and students —
whether or not they have travelled internationally — need the tools
that enable them to critically interpret those experiences.

This critical interpretation needs to take place at the classroom
level. Students should be allowed, in fact encouraged, to bring their
cross-cultural experiences into the classroom, where the sharing and
interpretation of those experiences can affect and alter their understanding of what they study. This means that students who are
returning from an international exchange or internship should be
encouraged to make use of their experience in their academic and
personal lives; this may include writing about their experience,
using experiential knowledge that they may have gained, or speaking in their own or their newly-acquired language. It also means
that international students and students of all cultural backgrounds

must be allowed to treat their culture as a legitimate, reliable source of information and knowledge that they can bring into their academic work and writing.

This is not an easy process, though, and it does not occur automatically, even in a culturally and linguistically diverse classroom setting. Despite the rhetoric of "bringing the world to the classroom," students are conditioned from a young age to leave themselves and their culture, background and personal histories out of the academic process. We are told not to use the first person ("There's no 'I' in 'essay'!"); any claims made must be backed up by provable, scientific, objective facts; and even though many decisions in the world are influenced by emotional reactions, subjectivities, pride and prejudices, we are taught that rationality is the only legitimate basis for argument. Small wonder it can be such a struggle to get students to speak with their own voices instead of borrowed academic ones: in many ways, they have been taught that what they think, what they feel and what they say cannot stand on its own, and, to put it more bluntly, is not worth listening to.

The separation of human experience from the academic process has very real consequences. One peculiar outcome is that students can no longer recognize themselves in their work. In September of 2005, I recall hearing a classmate explaining to her friend her fears and insecurities about starting a new school year. She had been looking through an old test from the previous year, and she could not understand what she herself had written. "I didn't even believe that I wrote it. I didn't even understand it," she said. "And there were all these checkmarks down the side of the page, but I didn't even know what I got right."

This alienation from the work we produce is obviously not higher learning. The separation of academia in general from daily life prevents students from engaging in what they study in any meaningful (or even, apparently, memorable) way. As a result, the university's potential for generating new ideas, stimulating activism and inspiring social change is compromised considerably. In a program such as International Development, the study of global poverty and inequality as something "out there," removed from our own experiences here in Canada, means that we do not consider how we are implicated in the very economic, social and political processes that cause poverty and inequality in the first place. How can we begin to work towards social change if we do not even see how we shape and are shaped by these global processes? The role of internationalization at the classroom level should be to bring these issues home.

To promote cross-cultural understanding and social change from within the university, therefore, requires an *active* commitment by staff and students to bring out new ways of knowing and of approaching academic material that makes it more significant for students. A more experiential, self-conscious and reflective learning process must be built into the curriculum and emphasized in faculty training programs. In the classroom, both professors and students need to be willing to accept not only diverse opinions and perspectives but also culturally distinct ways of understanding, thinking and expressing oneself in class and on paper. To take it one step further, university administrators, faculty and students should work together to forge connections between this kind of cross-cultural communication and the prospect of positioning ourselves as agents of social change.

Conclusion

My internship in Peru was an incredibly rich experience which above all gave me a chance to learn and participate in a community that was different from the one in which I grew up. But it is important to emphasize that my learning did not stop when I left the country. In fact, when I think about my experience in Peru, I find it hard to separate those three months from all of the thoughts and feelings I have had since then. Upon my return, I undertook a number of projects that were inspired by experiences, changes in perspective, or new ideas that I came across during my placement; for example, in my first semester back at York, I completed an independent study course on popular education in Latin America which was fueled by my drive to understand the (potential) connections between education and social change. This kind of intellectual engagement with topics and ideas that newly interested me strengthened my ability to reflect on and make sense out of my international experience and to make it both significant and applicable to my life here in Toronto.

I feel that it is important to mention, however, that I took on these post-internship learning projects mainly independently. While recent interest in the internationalization of the university may have allowed me the opportunity to take part in the internship in the first place, most of my reflections and interpretations of my experience took place outside the framework of internationalization, on my own and with the support of family members, friends and some key faculty members at the university. In other words, international internships or exchanges do not *inevitably* lead to a deeper understanding of one's own place in the world, or an increased awareness of the global dynamics of power and privilege.

This is why I am insisting on a more *active* commitment on the part of university administrators to make this process of internationalization applicable to students' lives, whether or not they participate in traditional exchange programs or internships. I have argued that the role of university internationalization should be to promote cross-cultural learning for the specific purpose of encouraging all members of the university community to better understand and get involved in the world in which they live. In this way, for students, faculty, and policy-makers alike, the internationalization of higher education becomes less about fitting in or adapting to an already-globalized world, more about learning how to interpret and change it. And I would be happy — honoured, even — to be a product of this kind of internationalization.

11

Internationalizing Faculty: A Phased Approach to Transforming Curriculum Design and Instruction

Todd Odgers and Isabelle Giroux,
Vancouver Island University[1]

Introduction

Malaspina University-College's commitment to the internationalization of its teaching, administrative and student support
functions is clearly reflected in its strategic plan and institutional
vision, which is to be a leader in international education by preparing students to contribute to a changing world. In order to achieve
this vision, part of the institution's focus has been on changing
teaching expectations and practices through the development,
implementation and evaluation of a faculty development program
on internationalizing curriculum and teaching practices that was
transformative in nature.[2] In this chapter, we present the results of
our research into the effectiveness of the design and delivery of this
multi-phased faculty development and its impact on participants'
ability to integrate intercultural and international dimensions into
the design and delivery of their curriculum. We also present the
theoretical foundations that influenced the project's design to

demonstrate the necessity of developing and implementing faculty development programs to internationalize curriculum that integrate transformative, cross-disciplinary and intercultural relations perspectives as central components of the design.

Theoretical Foundations — Internationalizing Faculty

The core definitions and theoretical foundations from the field of internationalization that influenced this project's design are presented in this section in order to provide a basis for understanding research findings from a focus group with faculty six months following their participation in Malaspina University-College's development initiative on internationalizing the curriculum. The central role played by faculty as curriculum developers and teachers will be analyzed in order to provide a rationale for focusing on the intercultural development of faculty in these types of initiatives. Finally, recent research in the field that can be used to design faculty development workshops that develop intercultural competence as part of the process of internationalizing curriculum will be presented.

Internationalization and Intercultural Definitions and Perspectives

Internationalization is a word used and interpreted so broadly that we now lack a single shared understanding of the term.[3] The most widely used definition is suggested by Knight, who also acknowledges the confusion regarding the meaning of the term, stating that it "is interpreted and used in different ways in different countries and by different stakeholders."[4] Knight defines internationalization as "the process of integrating an international and intercultural dimension into the teaching, research and service function of the institution."[5] By describing this as an act of integration of these two aspects, she is referring to an ongoing effort that infuses these dimensions into the policies and programs of an institution. Knight's most recent work surfaces some issues that she affirms as being important to promoting internationalization efforts. The first issue is the question of how institutions will "deal with the intersection of international and intercultural."[6] These two dimensions are closely related, but, as a recent study from the University of South Australia concluded after a thorough review of current literature, "it is clearly discernable that the two bodies of scholarship remain quite separate."[7] The study attempts to bridge these two areas by stating that the two dimensions can be integrated but that the intercultural is more inclusive and influential to student learning. The researchers state that "inter*cultural* education, as opposed to inter*national* education, is a more inclusive formulation, in that interculturality includes both international and domestic students. All students, regardless of their location, need to develop the capability to contribute in the intercultural construction, exchange and use of knowledge."[8] Bennett and Bennett[9] provide a definition and conceptualization of intercultural competence that integrates well with the thinking of Crichton et al.[10] by linking the international and intercultural components. The authors take an intercultural relations perspective and define intercultural competence in terms of a mindset and a skill set, beginning with the mindset, which refers to one's awareness of operating in a cultural context. This usually entails some conscious knowledge of one's own culture (cultural self-awareness), some frameworks for creating useful cultural contrasts (e.g., communication styles, cultural values), and a clear understanding about how to use cultural generalizations without stereotyping. The mindset (or, better, "heartset") also includes the maintenance of attitudes such as curiosity and tolerance of ambiguity which act as motivators for seeking out cultural differences.[11]

They then continue with a description of the intercultural skill set, which includes the ability to analyze interaction, predict misunderstanding, and fashion adaptive behaviour. The skill set can be thought of as the expanded repertoire of behaviour — a repertoire that includes behaviour appropriate to one's own culture but does not thereby exclude alternative behaviour that might be more appropriate in another culture.[12]

This mindset and skill set definition of competencies is comprehensive and serves as a means for designing a program that promotes the development of these outcomes.

Overall, these perspectives emphasize the need to recognize the influential place of intercultural learning in any discussion of internationalization. These perspectives also contribute a more complex and nuanced dimension to Knight's conceptualization and promote the view that intercultural development should occupy a central place in the internationalization process.

Central Role of Curriculum

Researchers place the curriculum at the centre of any attempt to internationalize higher education. Bond[13] cites Knight's and de Wit's opinion[14] that there are nearly twenty elements to internationalizing higher education and argues that all of these various elements are not equal to the status and centrality of curriculum for actualizing the kinds of changes to higher education proposed. This position is supported by the earlier work of Maidstone, who identified curriculum as being "the primary vehicle for accomplishing internationalization."[15] Paige further develops this perspective by noting how integration is the means for "developing international and intercultural knowledge, skills, and worldviews."[16]

Definitions of an Internationalized Curriculum

The progress towards conceptualizing an internationalized curriculum is reflected in a definition that is shared by Whalley,[17] a Canadian, and Bell,[18] an Australian, and which has its roots in an earlier work by Bremer and van der Wende.[19] The definition proposes that the curriculum will have "an international orientation in content, aimed at preparing students for performing (professionally/socially) in an international and multicultural context, and designed for domestic students and/or foreign students."[20] This definition incorporates the international and multicultural, professional, and social dimensions of the role of education, and links the benefits that this kind of learning provides to both domestic students and those from abroad.

Nilsson proposes a definition with an added level of complexity by describing it as "a curriculum which gives international and intercultural knowledge and abilities, aimed at preparing students for performing (professionally, socially, emotionally) in an international and multicultural context."[21] This definition incorporates the international and intercultural and the development of knowledge and skills, and, more specifically, it includes performance objectives beyond the professional and social dimensions outlined in the earlier definitions to include the emotional. Nilsson's definition of curriculum also serves learners in domestic and global diversity contexts. This perspective is supported by Wachter, who argues that "part of the qualifications and skills passed by universities to the next generation will not only be 'international' but also 'intercultural'."[22] Arguments that support placing intercultural learning at the centre of this kind of curriculum are becoming an increasingly common feature of recent publications and research in the field.

Integrating the Intercultural and the International

Mestenhauser's model of an internationalized curriculum promotes the development of complex, critical, comparative, interdisciplinary and intercultural ways of thinking and being; it represents one of the most comprehensive and provocative views in the field.[23] This metacognitive view is further developed in the collaboration of Paige and Mestenhauser[24] and later in work published by Paige.[25] These scholars point out that curricula need to incorporate an intercultural dimension in order to move beyond teaching facts toward the promotion of new ways of recognizing how cultural variables influence how and what we know. Yershova, DeJaegere and Mestenhauser[26] take this analysis a step further to integrate intercultural analysis, critical thinking and comparative thinking. Mestenhauser notes the importance of the development of intercultural understanding and perspectives: "Virtually every task and function of international education eventually confronts the concept of culture." [27]

The approach to internationalization taken by some researchers[28] is transformative in that it attempts to create a new consciousness on campuses; this is referred to by Paige and Mestenhauser[29] as an "internationalized mindset." They define this mindset as "a way of constructing knowledge that recognizes the significance of cultural variables and understands education itself as a cultural phenomenon" that uses "interdisciplinary thinking"[30] to understand the global forces at work in shaping the world.

How best to develop intercultural competence as part of the internationalization process is problematic. Teekens[31] argues that curricula need clearly defined objectives to develop intercultural learning. She has been critical of past practices that simply placed diverse groups of learners together in hope that some intercultural learning would emerge from the contact. This view is echoed by Otten,[32] who acknowledges the centrality of the intercultural to international education and who argues that intercultural competence does not occur simply as a result of placing students in diverse or international educational contexts; it must be consciously prepared for and delivered.

The above perspectives of Teekens and Otten regarding the need for an intentional integration of intercultural learning in the curriculum are supported by research by Gordon Allport,[33] who created the "Contact Hypothesis" to describe how contact with dissimilar others does not necessarily lead to intercultural learning; he outlined four conditions that need to be present for reducing intergroup prejudice. This has been modified recently by Pettigrew and

Tropp, who investigated how "optimal contact situations"[34] should look and be created. The findings point to the fact that contact between individuals or groups coming from different cultures does not necessarily lead to culture learning or appreciation. Well-planned curricula provide the constructs for promoting understanding and avoiding some of the pitfalls outlined in the contact hypothesis.

Recent work at the University of South Australia provides examples of how an institution can undertake an ongoing internationalization effort that is interdisciplinary, intercultural and transformative in its approach. Leask[35] reported on an undertaking to bring about convergence of both the administrative and the academic practices of that university. In this conceptualization, intercultural competence played an important role. In the words of Liddicoat, a researcher from that institution, internationalization "needs not only deal with newly arriving students from other places, but also with local students who bring their own language, culture and identity to the learning context and who equally need to be able to respond productively to the cultural contexts in which they now find themselves."[36] This approach places intercultural competence as the central outcome for all participants, whether international or domestic students, faculty or staff.

In 2004, Crichton, Paige, Papademetre and Scarino[37] produced a comprehensive work that integrates intercultural perspectives into curriculum and pedagogy. The work outlined intercultural development as an essential learning outcome and benefit for both domestic and international diversity. They argued that all students (and faculty) need to develop the intercultural mindset and skill set as part of their experience at the university. This study presented a set of five principles supported by some detailed approaches that could be used in the design of curriculum and pedagogical approaches.

Models of the Internationalized Curriculum

Many factors, including national, institutional, disciplinary, cultural, and pedagogical, influence the different approaches to internationalizing the curriculum. The faculty who create and teach the curricula are influenced by these factors and also bring their own characteristics and conception of internationalization to the process. The models presented below have all been influenced by intercultural research and they help us to classify the various approaches different individuals and institutions take to integrating international and intercultural dimensions in the curriculum.

Reading through the models we can observe a tendency to place the curricular approaches along a continuum from those that have added international content with a focus on cognitive learning at one end to those at the other that integrate cognitive, affective and behavioural learning that is intercultural as well as international in ways that are potentially transformative. Institutions and faculty can benefit by identifying where they best fit along this continuum.

A variety of models have been conceptualized to help designers plan and evaluate internationalized curricula. Recent work by Bell[38] studied how faculty attitudes towards culture are reflected in how they design and speak about curricula. Bell's "Spectrum of Acceptance of Internationalizing Curriculum" is a four-stage model that adapts Ellingboe's[39] six-stage measure of attitudes toward this sort of initiative. Both of the models by Ellingboe and Bell were heavily influenced by Bennett's six-stage "Developmental Model of Intercultural Sensitivity" (DMIS),[40] which is described in more detail below. Their designs incorporate Bennett's conception of the developmental shift from a worldview that is ethnocentric to one that he refers to as ethnorelative. Ellingboe's six stages are more strictly tied to the six stages of the DMIS than the four stages proposed by Bell.[41]

Morey[42] incorporates a multicultural education model developed by Kitano[43] that classifies domestic curricula into one of three categories depending on whether they maintain or reinforce status quo thinking, incorporate nontraditional with normative objectives and the development of critical thinking, or address the need for transformative and structural change. Morey used Kitano's domestic multicultural model as a way of viewing the curricular change process in the context of international education. She conceptualizes this process "in terms of levels of transformation rather than as a static outcome."[44] The model developed by Kitano has three stages or categories, moving from a status quo perspective referred to as "Exclusive" to a second "Inclusive" stage and finally a "Transformed" stage.[45] The model effectively focuses on both international and domestic diversity as important components of the curriculum.

A model that complements Morey's is Bond's "Approaches to Internationalizing the Curricula."[46] Bond based her design on the thinking of Mestenhauster[47] and Banks,[48] proposing a three-stage model that describes curricular reform approaches on a scale from "Add-on" to "Infusion" to "Transformation." Add-on refers to a curriculum that simply adds new international content "from a culture other than one's own"[49] This approach is the least complex. Bond explains how an infused curriculum is more systematic, begins to change content and assignments, and integrates more diverse content into the core fabric of the course which represents the most common approach. Finally, she observed that a transformational approach is less common because of how it works to change faculty and students in "fundamental ways" in how they "think about the world and their place in it."[50]

Faculty, Curriculum and Instruction

Faculty's Central Role

Faculty are acknowledged in the literature as being most responsible for internationalizing the curriculum. Bond,[51] after reviewing the literature and conducting surveys of Canadian higher education, concluded that there was consensus among faculty that curriculum falls into their domain of responsibility. This is echoed by Teekens, who took the perspective a step further by incorporating not just the content of curriculum but also the act of teaching as a central feature. She affirms, "It is the lecturer who is the core player in the process. It is her or his teaching that ultimately determines the results in the international classroom."[52]

Paige asserts that faculty can model the kind of knowledge, values and behaviours that the "international mindset"[53] promotes but that "parochialism, ethnocentrism and disinterest in international learning"[54] are also possible. Paige's observation regarding faculty preparation raises the issue of who is teaching the teachers to embody and do the work required. Mestenhauser notes that faculty often expect students to experience and be capable of skills they themselves do not possess. He asks "how to teach the teachers" and how international and intercultural knowledge can "be integrated with the disciplinary knowledge."[55] Faculty create this curricular content as they teach their courses, and so the development of each individual faculty member is central to the success of these efforts.

Content and Instruction

As the above discussion demonstrates, internationalizing the curriculum incorporates both content and pedagogy. Paige and Mestenhauser[56] refer to this approach as one that emphasizes the learning process, and it is reflected in various ways in the later work of several researchers who all noted the integration of content and pedagogy as central to the success of this approach to education.[57] Researchers such as Teekens[58] and Nilsson[59] describe the importance of developing outcomes for learners that are both cognitive and attitudinal (affective). This is developed further in works by Otten[60] and Paige,[61] who emphasize that integrated intercultural and international learning outcomes need to develop learners' cognitive, affective and behavioural domains.

Four researchers — Liddicoat,[62] Paige,[63] Leask,[64] and McKellen[65] — took the above discussion a step further and talk about the importance of sequencing in course design. McKellin discusses how transformation demands fundamental changes in teaching, and Liddicoat, in particular, discusses the implications that decisions about teaching and learning have on faculty and learners. Paige[66] elaborates on his earlier work[67] and presents a way for faculty to integrate Bennett's DMIS[68] as a means to identify learner characteristics and needs and then plan and sequence learning activities based on the developmental needs of learners. This will be discussed in relation to training design in greater depth later in this section.

Faculty Resistance to Change

As noted earlier, faculty play a central role in the redesign of the curriculum. Morey[69] highlights the importance that motivation plays in achieving the changes in expertise and values that faculty need to develop. The national cultures of institutions as well as their disciplinary cultures are contexts that faculty are challenged to become aware of and transform.

Maidstone acknowledges the resistance of faculty to the kinds of changes discussed: "Faculty typically understand their discipline or field, and teach it the way they themselves were taught. Transformations of consciousness do not, therefore, come about easily."[70] This kind of shift in consciousness may not be for all individuals or occur to all faculty members at the same time. Mestenhauser notes this pessimistically, observing that these kinds of transformations of national and disciplinary thinking are "unlikely to be taken into account by the mainstream."[71] Nonetheless, he maintains hope that changes are indeed possible and that they will eventually take place as a result of ongoing well-planned and well-executed efforts.

Designing Training for Developing Faculty Intercultural Competence

The earlier discussion of the nature of internationalized curriculum incorporated the idea that integrating the intercultural and international in curriculum and instruction can be transformative. Paige[72] and Martin[73] discuss the decidedly transformative nature of intercultural learning and the implications for the leaders (facilitators, teachers, trainers) responsible for the design, planning, and delivery of this kind of learning. Paige[74] provides a comprehensive set of trainer competencies that cover the knowledge, skills, and program design and execution dimensions for anyone leading a group of learners through an intercultural learning program. This was considered from the perspective of ethics in intercultural development by Paige and Martin,[75] who argue that, because of the risks involved in intercultural learning, trainers or teachers must be highly skilled in dealing with any issue that arises for learners in the process of a lesson or an activity. Paige and Martin affirm that intercultural learning is "potentially threatening to the learner because it challenges existing and preferred beliefs, values, and patterns of behavior."[76] They argue that a trainer or teacher who has the necessary knowledge, skill and experience can better design and conduct programs that will result in positive intercultural learning outcomes.

Recent scholarship by Bennett and Bennett[77] can be used to design and conduct intercultural training using the "Developmental Model of Intercultural Sensitivity" (DMIS). This is also emphasized in Janet Bennett's framework[78] for assisting trainers and teachers to conceptualize appropriate levels of challenge and support in both the content and process dimensions of their program. As noted earlier, the framework conceptualized by Milton Bennett[79] can be used to assess learners and design intercultural programs appropriate to their developmental stage. The DMIS is a six-stage scheme that identifies where individuals fall along a scale moving from ethnocentrism to ethno-relativism. Individual stages of intercultural sensitivity on the DMIS can now be assessed using an instrument known as the "Intercultural Development Inventory" (IDI).

This resembles the approach discussed earlier regarding work at the University of South Australia that integrates intercultural learning in a way that develops intercultural competence for both internationally and domestically diverse contexts.[80] Bennett and Bennett explain how the DMIS can be used with current research into identity development to design training that promotes the development of intercultural competence in international and domestic contexts.

Bhawuk and Triandis[81] produced a model of "Intercultural Expertise Development" that suggests an uncomplicated scheme for mapping how theory and experience could be combined in an intentional way to bring about intercultural expertise. They describe a progression through four stages, including "Lay," "Novice," "Expert" and "Advanced Expert." Individuals progress as a result of lived experience, the study of intercultural theory, and participation in behavioural training. The model represents an acknowledgement of the importance of lived experience in helping learners develop intercultural competence by incorporating the cognitive dimensions of intercultural learning into affective and behavioural learning domains.

These researchers emphasized the importance of appropriate selection and sequencing of materials, concepts and activities to realize the best outcome for learners. Paige,[82] in his analysis of thirty-five instruments used in intercultural training, discusses the application of the "Intercultural Development Inventory" (IDI) to training design, the assessment of personal development of participants, overcoming participant resistance and bridging theory and practice. He found the IDI to be an effective instrument when integrated into intercultural training programs.

Two researchers from outside the intercultural and internationalization field, Mezirow and Cranton,[83] provide useful perspectives related to transformative adult learning. To these researchers, transformation represents a shift in how learners make meaning or create new ways of understanding when questioning and reforming previously held frames of reference. Mezirow, likely the best known of the transformative learning theorists, defines transformative learning as the "process by which we transform our taken-for-granted frames of reference (meaning perspectives, habits of mind, mindsets) to make them more inclusive, discriminating, open, emotionally capable of change, and reflective so that they may generate beliefs and opinions that will prove more true or justified to guide action."[84]

Leask concurs that faculty need to develop their abilities when she affirms that teaching staff need "to develop new knowledge, skills, attitudes and values"[85] in order to create and deliver an internationalized curriculum. Leask invited faculty to reflect on how they think about teaching and learning. Otten also took this position, noting that internationalizing content and teaching requires faculty to reflect on "the implicit cultural patterns of the entire didactic interaction"; this included "the selection of course content and material, design of classroom setting and teaching material, communication with students, and the role of teachers."[86] Leask's thinking on the role of reflection as part of faculty development was influenced by the work of Schon,[87] who identified the use of reflection as important for practitioners of complex tasks such as teaching.

A flexible model that facilitates faculty efforts to integrate newly developed perspectives into a redesigned curriculum can be found in a successful example produced at McGill University, where workshops were offered to help faculty redesign their course curricula and instructional approaches. The design of the workshops was refined over a period of ten years and was published by Saroyan and Amundsen in 2004.[88] These workshops were not necessarily intended for integrating intercultural development, but their format has the potential to accommodate it. This approach is interdisciplinary and consistent with the integrative, comparative and interdisciplinary thinking proposed in the literature on internationalizing the curriculum by Mestenhauser.[89] It integrates an innovative use of concept mapping with interdisciplinary groups of faculty as a central dimension of its design. The structure is flexible and has the potential to be combined with a program such as the following that develops intercultural sensitivity so that intercultural dimensions can be incorporated into a faculty member's curriculum redesign.

Malaspina University-College's Faculty Development Program

Program Overview

"Internationalizing the Curriculum," the faculty development project implemented at Malaspina University-College, placed intercultural competence at the centre of its design. As a result, it followed principles laid out in the previous section and incorporated the Developmental Model of Intercultural Sensitivity (DMIS) as its core framework for selecting, sequencing and facilitating sessions that would best meet the developmental needs of the faculty participants.

In general, the project's multi-stage design (Figure 2) moved from topics and methods that were relatively safe for participants to those that were increasingly challenging and demanding on a personal and professional level. As a demonstration of this principle, the first three-hour session was designed to appeal to a large audience by focusing on how teachers could better understand and interpret the cultural behaviours of their multicultural student body. The session, offered three times to over sixty faculty, introduced participants to how culture influences student behaviour and expectations by providing some introductory theoretical frameworks that faculty could then apply to their own classrooms. This initial three-hour session also introduced the core concept of the central role played by the "self that teaches" which subsequently influences teaching practices and the development of course curriculum. This model was termed the "Three Pillars of Internationalization" (Figure 1). It is important to note that the session was designed not to challenge faculty to deeply investigate how their own assumptions and cultural conditioning influenced what they were experiencing but only to introduce these concepts that were further explored in subsequent sessions.

Figure 1
The Three Pillars of Internationalization

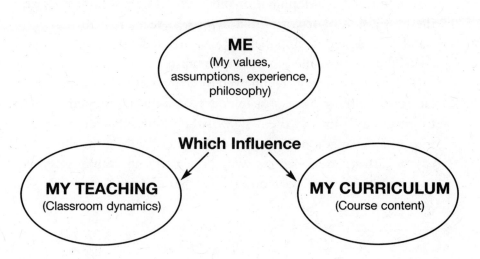

Participants from this first session were then provided with the opportunity to apply for one of ten spaces in an "Internationalizing the Curriculum" three-day retreat. The retreat was based on the application of a transformative design that encouraged faculty to look at how their level of intercultural competence influenced their capacity to interact with and teach an internationally and domestically diverse student body, incorporate various intercultural perspectives, and feel competent designing a curriculum and using/selecting materials that integrate intercultural and international learning objectives.

The retreat was preceded one week earlier by one-on-one "Intercultural Development Inventory" (IDI) consultations to review each participant's assessment results in order to enable them to gain insights into their own intercultural development and what they wanted or needed to work on in the sessions to follow. The IDI results were also used to help the project planners with the design and facilitation of the retreat to ensure it met faculty needs. The retreat was then sequenced into three parts. The first two days focused on the development of intercultural competence through the integration of activities that helped participants better understand the design and potential areas of redesign for a course curriculum they wanted to internationalize.

The first two days were followed by a two-week interval to allow faculty to reflect on the principles explored during the retreat and to integrate them into the design of their new curriculum and to notice any changes in their teaching practice. During the third day of the retreat, these designs were presented and faculty received constructive peer feedback on each of their designs.

Figure 2

Overview of the Complete Program

Teaching and learning in the international classroom	Apply to 3-day retreat	IDI Administration and individualized consultations	Day 1	Day 2	Day 3
• 3hrs • 3 groups of 20		(meetings scheduled to meet faculty schedules)	The intercultural self and the curriculum	Teaching practices and the curriculum	Participant presentations and peer feedback Session Closing
Sept-Jan	Feb-March	April	May	May	End of May

Internationalizing the Curriculum — Results

Procedure

The final stage of the development initiative occurred six months after the last day of the retreat when faculty participated in a focus group session to discuss the results of their participation in the year-long development program. Five of the nine faculty who participated in the initiative took part in this focus group. Its purpose was to gather faculty input on the extent to which their intercultural sensitivity and their ability to teach an internationalized course had changed as a result of participating in the year-long process and how this was reflected in the design and delivery of their curriculum. The questions asked during the two-hour session were formulated to elicit responses in each of these areas.

The Focus Group as a Qualitative Method of Inquiry

The focus group interview was chosen as the primary method of data collection in order to determine participants' perceptions, feelings and attitudes as they related to their involvement in the development initiative. This approach facilitated the creation of a more dynamic social interaction process that enabled the researchers to observe and hear participants talk about their experience as individuals and as a group. Indeed, the aim was to capture the lived experience of faculty in relation to their participation in the year-long process without attempting to quantify the extent of the change or personal transformation that occurred on a measurable scale. The use of this qualitative interview method was also intended to create "a fine-textured understanding of beliefs, attitudes, values and motivations in relation to the behaviours of people in particular social contexts."[90] The social context which represents the focus of this study consisted of faculty members, the individual learning process leading to the development of their internationalized curriculum and the resulting interactions with their students as they delivered the course with new content and an adapted approach.

Results

The focus group discussions revealed that intercultural sensitivity and participants' perception of their overall ability to deliver an internationalized course had increased as a result of participating in the faculty development program which enabled them to develop the necessary attitudes, skills and knowledge.

Individual Change Reflected in Teaching Practices

All of the members found that their approach to teaching had been impacted by the thought process and reflections they had started as a result of participating in the program. When reflecting on the changes that occurred for them on a personal level, the participants in the focus group concurred that internationalizing the curriculum was an ongoing personal development process:

> The more you practise this, the more comfortable you become simply opening up the classroom to experiential learning on a cross-cultural basis.

> I think this whole development process of internationalizing as well as just improving ourselves as teachers on all the various levels is an interpersonal interaction process. ... People who don't want to improve are typically the ones who hide themselves the farthest away from interactions with others. For me personally, I need to go through this process with people who are at different levels to help me keep going, keep the energy up but I greatly appreciate that we were together with ... different perspectives here.

> The thing about internationalizing the curriculum is that we're talking about something that seems to be third party but in effect it forces people to take a look at themselves. If you were to set up a workshop and say, "Hey guys let's get together and talk about our teaching biases," you'd get zero attendance but when you talk about internationalizing the curriculum, it gets around to the same issue.

Outcomes for Students

With an increased awareness of their own underlying beliefs, values and attitudes, faculty incorporated different approaches to delivering their courses which were clearly reflected in the resulting classroom dynamics. All of the participants confirmed the importance of making the differing values and assumptions guiding individual behaviour (including their own) explicit, which in turn increased the students' ability to identify the impact of these variables on classroom dynamics and team dynamics as they completed their group projects. This shift in teaching practices also changed the process of learning that occurred in the classroom, as exemplified by the following statements:

> I've always been focused on inclusion and I realized through this process that I was almost too focused on inclusion and the sameness of us all. Even though I've always understood that people have different beliefs and values, I didn't realize that I wasn't looking as deep as I should have been as to how those beliefs and values play out in the classroom and what my expectations are for students, particularly students from different cultures.

> It probably increased the level of conflict, and I'm viewing conflict in a positive way. So it's made the class more lively, more energetic.

> I probably paid more attention to the process this time around. I've made a conscious effort of being more process-oriented with less emphasis on the marks.

> One of the things I have noticed is that, socially, students are interacting more, especially in our program where no one culture is dominant.

One participant also presented feedback from students which demonstrated how the internationalized course had challenged the students' beliefs and assumptions, encouraged them to think from different perspectives and left them better equipped to articulate their beliefs and values.

New Perspectives on Internationalization

When asked how they would now define an internationalized curriculum as a result of participating in the development initiative, faculty formulated definitions which clearly placed the intersection of the intercultural with the international as a central component of their perspective:

> An international curriculum is one which has seamless connections to all the different cultures in the world and is transparent if there are particular cultural biases where before it used to be built in and assumed.

> It is sensitivity, awareness and curiosity about differences and challenging ethnocentric views of the world so it creates a broader understanding of how we are, where we are.

> I think one of the things it provides learners is an opportunity to challenge their beliefs, values and assumptions and engage them in an exploration that might take them to places that they never expected.

When asked about the relationship between international and intercultural components of an internationalized course, participants clearly placed the intercultural aspects of delivering the course at the forefront:

> The theme that came up for me very strongly last
> spring is that internationalizing means standing
> between nations, the one you come from, and the
> one you're going to or dealing with and respecting
> and understanding them as two different places. I
> tend to see culture as a different thing than nation
> but I also tend to see them as bound up together.

> Nations are lines on a map and culture is about
> the rules of how to operate. For me, trying to
> understand and being sensitive to those rules is an
> important piece.

Next Steps in the Development Process

When asked what the next steps were for them as individuals and
as a group, all participants agreed on the importance of continuing
to meet to share their ongoing learning and insights and to further
the development of their skills and knowledge in the field. A few
participants shared their increased desire to travel abroad, and some
members had already made plans to do so by participating in a faculty exchange initiative:

> I'd like to follow up again in six months or a year
> or at some point just to see [what stage] people are
> at and to share again. Personally, I think we have a
> role in promoting this to other faculty and encour-
> aging other people to participate in these
> experiences.

> I've just scratched the surface. That's what I feel
> like. I've got an increased awareness and sensitivity

and curiosity. ... So for me, the next steps are to continue that on my own to get a better understanding. ... What that's done is really change my reading. And the other piece is going on a trip to Indonesia. So that's going to broaden my exposure. It's built up a whole new way of looking at things. As my learning deepens, I'm going to take it to the classroom. I'm not sure what that's going to look like yet but I'm going to take it to the classroom.

I think it's taking this information and sharing it with others to help them become aware of the influence of our culture on learning and that for myself it's to go deeper and go down these different avenues which I'm not sure any of those are yet.

For me, I find it hard to not think that the next thing for me is to travel some more and get reaffirmed in the particularities of cultures.

With regard to what's next with this project, if other people are going to follow, I hope there will be more for us. People often see it as a "one off." Don't toss us out of the Petri dish yet!

Conclusions

The intercultural and transformative focus of the faculty development program implemented at Malaspina University-College was intended to provide participants with the tools to undertake the complex task of integrating intercultural and international perspectives into the redesign and delivery of their curricula. Faculty play the central role in efforts to internationalize the curriculum, and it is important that they be given the resources and time to look deeply into the self that teaches and how it influences their approach to the overall design of their curriculum, their selection of teaching materials, their planning and, ultimately, their conduct of their lessons. The multi-phased structure of this faculty professional development design provides participants with time to reflect on, research and integrate the intercultural with the international in their curricula and instruction. Following transformative learning principles, faculty investigate the self that teaches and also look at how this self plays out in their instruction. Faculty have time to investigate their assumptions and those of their students, the curriculum, and the materials they use as part of their course.

Intercultural learning can be challenging, but the new perspectives and possibilities it provides can have a tremendous impact on student outcomes. This was made clear in the statements shared by participants. In the increasingly complex, diverse, yet integrated world we live in, the kinds of new approaches to curriculum and teaching this design is intended to promote seem timely and responsible if we are to prepare our students for success. Intercultural development is important for the perspective it provides and the skills it can impart.

Focus group results and discussions with faculty members through the course of the year-long development process have shown the researchers that this model can be very useful for other institutions embarking upon initiatives to internationalize their curriculum that go beyond infusion and add-on approaches.

The design and implementation of our development program will continue to be refined as we gather additional input from faculty on its effectiveness. Further exploration of the long-term impacts on faculty's ability to successfully deliver an internationalized curriculum is required to gain a better understanding of the transformative effect of our proposed approach at the individual level and at the wider institutional level.

12

Internationalizing Canada's Universities: Where Do International Faculty Fit in? [1]

Julia Richardson, Ken McBey and Steve McKenna,
York University[2]

Introduction

The increasing internationalization of higher education is the focus
of widespread political, economic and academic attention.[3] Much
of the existent Canadian research centres on education systems,
institutions, pedagogical issues and the student body;[4] key themes
in this research relate to the increasing number of international students, ethnic and cultural diversity, and the need for more
internationally focused course content and pedagogy. By comparison, there is a gap in our understanding of the internationalization
of faculty and the contribution of faculty with international experience.[5] This gap is of particular concern given that, in 2001, of the
43,765 faculty in Canadian universities, a full 40 percent were
immigrants.[6] It may be, for example, that faculty with international experience are especially well placed to meet the specific needs of
the increasingly international student body. At a national policy
level, examining the potential contribution of international faculty

in Canada is important in the context of a move towards a more international profile for Canadian higher education. It is also important for developing Canada's position as a preferred destination for international faculty in an increasingly competitive academic marketplace. Finally, little is known about the extent to which current management practices support the specific needs of international faculty with respect to research and teaching, tenure and promotion.

Drawing on a qualitative study of forty-four international faculty currently employed in six Canadian universities, this chapter explores the extent to which they have utilized their international experience in research and teaching. It especially explores the role of international faculty in the internationalization of curricula, pedagogy and research practice. The chapter also reports participants' perceptions of whether their international experience is recognized and/or rewarded by their host institution. This theme is important for understanding whether current management policies encourage the use of international experience as a mechanism for internationalization. First, however, we begin by exploring some of the challenges faced by institutions of higher education in Canada in the context of increasing faculty shortages.

Contemporary Challenges Facing Canadian Universities

Canadian universities are facing a number of challenges, not least of which is the growth in student enrolment and concomitant demand for improved facilities and resources including appropriately qualified and experienced faculty. They are also under pressure to reconcile tighter budgets while ensuring maximum teaching and research output. The increase in international students from East Asia, including South Korea, China, Japan and Hong Kong[7] represents a fruitful source of income. Yet it also demands that institutions address the specific needs of international students by providing English as a second language support and incorporating cross-cultural diversity in pedagogy and curricula. The need to expand and improve current postgraduate programs has been widely recognized by both federal and provincial governments. Canadian universities award around 4,100 doctoral degrees each year. However, roughly 25 percent of these are to foreign students,[8] who may take their qualifications overseas. Indeed, a recent post-secondary review conducted in Ontario reported an urgent need to increase the quality and quantity of graduate education at all levels, including Ph.D.s. The paucity of Ph.D.s also connects to concerns about ensuring an appropriate supply of faculty; the main concern is to augment numbers of completed Ph.D.s in order to address the predicted shortfall of qualified faculty. It is to that shortfall that we now turn.

Recruiting Faculty for Canadian Universities: Competing in an International Marketplace

The move from élite to mass higher education in Canada has widened opportunities for higher education. Yet successive governments have paid insufficient attention to ensuring an appropriately qualified and experienced supply of faculty to fill the newly created positions. Thus, for example, reduced funding resulted in a 7.8 percent decline in the number of faculty between 1996 and 2001. Moreover, large numbers of faculty are now nearing retirement. Ontario universities, for example, will have to hire eleven thousand faculty in the coming decade in order to replace retirees, improve student-faculty ratios and cater to increasing student enrolment.[9] The alleged flight of home-grown faculty to the United States in search of more lucrative salaries and research funding is also another cause for concern,[10] though there are also reports that some US faculty are seeking positions in Canada in order to escape what they believe is a change in higher education policy and dissatisfaction with political trends.[11] The challenges of recruitment and retention of international faculty are also important because institutions such as the *Financial Times* use the number of international faculty at an institution as a criterion for ranking.

From the discussion so far, it is clear that faculty recruitment is an urgent and complex challenge for Canadian universities. Indeed, it is a growing concern for many universities throughout the world.[12] In order to counter the shortage of "home-grown" faculty, some Canadian universities are recruiting internationally. They are not alone. With the expansion of higher education in Asia, the Middle East and South America, the international market for faculty is increasingly competitive and diverse.[13] Entering the international marketplace may be the only option, however, if Canadian universities are serious about developing an international profile. International recruitment might also encourage the "new blood" and corresponding vitality that Mwenifumbo and Renner[14] suggest is missing as a result of historically limited hiring agendas.

Internationalization of Higher Education and Academic Careers

International activity is a regular occurrence in academic careers[15] and campus life more generally. Kaulisch and Enders[16] suggest that faculty operate in several social contexts: the science context, the national context and the institutional context. The science context is the context of academia that is characterized by, amongst other things, disciplinary divisions, rules for conducting research and the production of knowledge. Faculty must also operate within a given national context, in this case within Canada, and within the institutional context of their employer. Drawing on these three contexts provides a framework within which to examine the contribution of international faculty to the internationalization of higher education in Canada. It especially allows exploration of the synergy among the international dimensions of academia, the Canadian national context and particular institutional contexts.

As Canadian universities seek to develop a more international profile, we might assume that having international experience would be advantageous for career development because faculty with such experience may be better equipped to manage an international student body and research agenda.[17] We might also assume that, in electing to take a position in a Canadian university, international faculty are demonstrating significant confidence in the portability and transferability of their knowledge and experience. Likewise, Canadian universities are demonstrating similar confidence in the transferability of that knowledge and experience. The confidence displayed by both parties is embedded in widely accepted assumptions of academia as a global enterprise.[18] Yet the link between international experience and a more internationally informed pedagogy and research agenda is unclear. Moreover, little is known about whether international experience supports career development. Studies in Canada and the US, for example, suggest that international experience receives only minimal recognition and reward.[19] The corporate arena reflects similar contradictions: although corporate rhetoric suggests that international experience is essential for promotion to senior management, it is inconsistently rewarded. Indeed, managers frequently complain about lack of recognition and/or reward for their international experience.[20]

Although there is little research on international faculty in Canada, a study of international faculty in New Zealand, Singapore, Turkey and the United Arab Emirates[21] suggests that they are explicitly aware of the internationalization of higher education and connect it very closely with their own mobility. A particularly dominant view was that international experience provides an advantage in the context of an increasingly international student body and calls for more internationally informed research agendas.[22] The study also suggests that international faculty are well placed to facilitate internationalization through expanded research agendas, international collaboration and strategic international alliances between universities. Where specific management processes were concerned, the study also suggested that (at least in the respective host institutions) international experience was recognized and rewarded in recruitment, tenure and promotion decisions and/or equivalent procedures,[23] a perception somewhat at odds with the findings in Canada and the US, noted above.

Addressing faculty careers in more detail, the study of international faculty, noted above, drew a strong connection between international experience and career development.[24] However, a caveat of "where" was introduced. Thus, it was not international experience *per se* that facilitated promotion but where the experience was gained. Experience in certain countries (notably North America, China, Singapore and Australia) and in specific institutions within those countries was understood to convey more advantage than experience in others. This finding suggests that the internationalization of higher education may not be international at all, but rather characterized by regional preferences.

Methodology
Data Collection
This study used in-depth semi-structured interviews in order to allow faculty to use their own words in answering the specific research questions about whether they were contributing to the internationalization of higher education in Canada and the extent to which their international experience was recognized and/or rewarded. Each interview lasted between one and one-and-a-half hours. All interviews, except one, were tape-recorded and transcribed verbatim. In the instance where the interviewee preferred not to be recorded, notes were taken and included in the data analysis.

Sampling

A letter describing the objectives of the study was sent to the academic vice-president in each of the host institutions. It requested that an invitation to participate in the study be circulated to all international faculty in the respective institution. All vice-presidents agreed to the request and sent the invitation either directly to all faculty or through respective deans. The faculty who volunteered to take part and who met the criteria set out below were contacted directly to schedule an interview. Of the fifty-two volunteers, forty-four were scheduled for interview; problems with scheduling prevented the remaining eight from being interviewed.

The final sample comprised forty-four international faculty in six Canadian universities. The universities were chosen for two reasons. First, they represent different geographical areas of Canada. Two were included because they are located in smaller communities whereas the remainder are located in or near large and more densely populated cities. This criterion reflects the findings in other studies[25] suggesting that proximity to large centres of population influence faculty experiences and willingness to relocate. Another university was included to capture experiences in smaller universities more focused on teaching than research.

For the purposes of this study, international faculty were defined as "teachers, researchers and senior academic staff"[26] not originating from Canada with appointments in a Canadian university. Faculty on sabbatical were excluded from the sample. All faculty had held a position in a university in another country before coming to Canada. This criterion allowed exploration of the perceived differences between Canada and other countries. It also allowed exploration of whether connections with overseas universities and their respective faculty are maintained and, if so, whether they are used to support the internationalization of higher education in Canada.

The majority of the sample was male (70 percent). Moreover,

although faculty were spread across different academic disciplines, most were from the natural or medical sciences (29, or 65 percent). Eighty-eight percent of the sample were European/Caucasian. The age distribution was considerably more balanced, as was the number of years that the faculty had been in Canada.

Data Analysis

All interviews were transcribed in full and then analyzed via computer-assisted qualitative data analysis software. The analysis comprised identifying themes that emerged in response to the research questions and then incorporating those themes into models. The final models reflected the dominant and subsidiary themes relating to faculty experiences in Canada and their evaluations of those experiences (Figure 1).

Figure 1

Internationalization of Canadian Universities and International Faculty

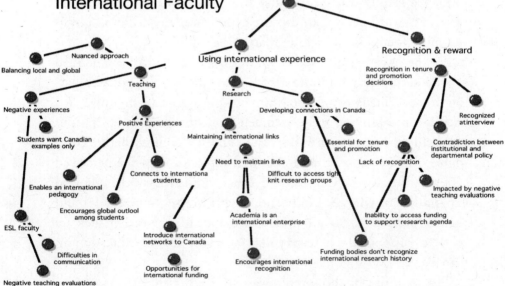

Results

The results of the study are presented below. Although the themes are discussed separately, the boundaries between them are blurred where, for example, some faculty drew on similar themes to explain different elements of their experience. The authors would also like to point out that, as with much empirical research, the findings presented here are only a portion of what might be discovered. It is expected that analysis will continue and may reveal further themes and concerns not reflected here.

Using International Experience to Support Research in Canada

Given the importance of research activity in academia, and particularly in places like Canada where tenure systems operate, it is unsurprising that most participants talked about the extent to which their international experience informed their research activity, including research networks and the ability to publish. On a positive note, twenty-one participants said they had established research networks in Canada while maintaining and extending existent international networks, as evidenced by the excerpts below:

> The collaborative [dimension of my work] is quite international … Some of my collaborators are in Europe, but the vast majority of them are in Canada or the US. (Bill)

> I've already established and maintained collaborations from when I was working in US universities and elsewhere which will continue for a few more years and now there's a kind of collaboration where we'll be exchanging students to do biology things here in my lab based on engineering platforms developed in their lab. (Evan)

> I'm collaborating with a former colleague [in the
> US] We worked together on a couple of teaching-
> related, pedagogy-related things and we're still in
> contact. I am on the executive board of the North
> American Catalan Society, I have now met three
> people in Canada who belong to it so it's primarily
> an American thing and I'm still very much
> involved with that and with their journal and all
> the professional associations. And I have another
> co-author at another university in the US I work
> with quite regularly. (Jane)

This finding suggests that international faculty are well placed to introduce international research networks in addition to the skills and knowledge they bring as individuals. Indeed, several faculty, such as Lucia and Noam, below, specifically identified the role of international faculty in the internationalization of higher education in Canada:

> I think in this world, our students have to be inter-
> national and they have to have an awareness of the
> world ... I think it's critical for us to recruit interna-
> tional faculty for our students to get that exposure.
> And international students, as well ... I know they
> make each other feel more at home. (Lucia)

> I think the fact that I have travelled widely ... and
> use examples when I'm talking to students from all
> around the world. I mean the book that I wrote
> was really a book of case studies from my previous
> experience. I think it's very important that when
> people study they understand the local geography
> and the local history; but also global geography and

global history. To really have it come to into the classroom by someone who has lived it. (Noam)

Establishing Research Networks in Canada

While the majority of participants maintained their international research networks and collaborations, they were also eager to develop networks and work with colleagues in Canada. Yet some said developing networks in Canada was problematic. The problem was particularly acute in the medical and natural sciences because of a lack of funding history and research connections in Canada, as suggested by Lily, below:

> I think that [my international experience] helps me tremendously but the downside, and there is a downside, is that the Canadian academic community is very small and they all know each other, especially in my field. I don't know any of them so I come here and I don't have a connection to all the biomedical researchers in Canada whereas they all pretty much were all in the same group. [During] my first couple of years I've sort of focused on looking at Canadian funding and that kind of thing but ultimately I think having international experience is important as I know of all the guys in the States who do this type of work and so eventually I'll be able to tap into that. (Lily)

Similarly Tony, who had also come from the US, talked about how his lack of funding and research history in Canada prevented him from getting access to funding for his research program. He was certain that this problem would ultimately have a negative impact on his overall research activity and productivity.

Using International Experience in the Classroom

The majority of participants said that they drew on their international experience in the classroom, as evidenced by the faculty below:

> So my students often say how much they enjoy hearing stories and seeing slides of the places in the world that I have worked in that give good examples of whether it's volcanoes or coral reefs or whatever it is. So I call upon that and I think that I'm the wiser teacher for it and certainly the richer person for it in terms of a global sense. I don't imagine a week goes by where I'm not summoning up something from Australia or South Africa or Nigeria. (Harry)

> I'll be able to talk about some of the interesting technologies that I worked on there [in Australia] and how some of them were uniquely Australian problems and talk about some of the blunders that Australians have made in their biological control. (Rudi)

> It was wonderful [having international experience] because I, being the new person on the block, when you come into a place, your approach has to be different from the residents' approach to things. So it's an advantage. (Liam)

The findings also suggested that most faculty in this study felt that their international experience promoted positive interactions with students seeking to pursue international careers themselves, as evidenced by Polina, below:

> Well, on teaching evaluations, they comment that
> they like to hear the anecdotal stuff. Many of
> them come and say, I would like to talk to you
> more about how you got to travel there, I would
> like to talk to you more about what you thought
> of it, and could you elaborate on it? (Polina)

What we observe here is the extent to which international faculty may be instrumental in encouraging international activity among students that extends beyond their undergraduate and postgraduate studies.

The Richardson study,[27] introduced above, suggested that faculty with international experience are well positioned to empathize with and support the needs of international students. This finding was substantiated by some of the faculty in this study, such as Harry:

> I often find that international students come and
> talk to me in my classes when they see that I've
> lived in their country or been outside of Canada
> because I think that they can relate to somebody
> because they are in this foreign environment and
> they realize that I've also been in a foreign envi-
> ronment. (Harry)

Like Harry, Glen also believed that being an international faculty member enabled him to empathize more readily with international students. However, he also introduced a cautionary note:

> Some students will see that I am not from here,
> but the ones from China will come and speak to
> me in Mandarin. I tell them you cannot go to the

> back door in this country and don't try it. You may
> think just because we look alike — I have to be fair
> to everyone you know, everybody gets marked just
> like that. What I can do is if you have problems
> understanding my English we work on that, I can
> help you with the library searches and all that but
> to try and get ahead in life just because you know
> someone is from your country or your ethnic
> group is not my idea of how it should be. (Glen)

Glen's comment also draws attention to the theme of faculty for whom English is a second language; we will return to this theme later.

Thus far we have reported predominantly positive accounts of how faculty used their international experience in the classroom. However, some participants no longer drew on their international experience as a result of negative reactions from students. Ashley and Mary, for example, felt that students do not accord any importance to international experience because they are more focused on the Canadian context. They felt that many students and colleagues see it as a sign that they lack experience and understanding of Canada. Similarly, Kerry believed that students didn't accept her because she was not Canadian:

> I told the students that I am from Germany and
> what my research areas are just to introduce
> myself, but I don't do that anymore, I don't say
> any more about Germany, because I think that is
> why they do not accept me. (Kerry)

From the accounts presented so far, the perceived value of international experience in the classroom emerges as either wholly positive or wholly negative. However, other participants believed that it is more a matter of how that experience is used. These participants recommended a more balanced approach drawing on both international and Canadian themes. Noam and Jane provide useful exemplars of this more nuanced approach:

> I used to be loath to make use of British examples because of the colonial thing. I tend to now as I am a little bit more relaxed about it but I also try to use examples from Canada. There are examples of particular things and uses of particular building material or whatever it may be. But, I also want them to realize what they see in [this city] is not the best they're going to see in the world. (Noam)

> [There is a] sort of uneasy, sometimes spoken and unspoken anti-Americanism, all over in Canada. I have a different perspective now having spent so much time there. They aren't completely evil but I think that there is respect for the experience. However, I have some caution about how it might be applied here because things are different in the States. (Jane)

This finding clearly encourages a more cautious approach to the use of international experience in the classroom and perhaps in Canadian universities more generally. Thus, it may be that while international experience is valuable, what will determine receptivity is the way in which it is implemented. Indeed, a more nuanced approach seems to embrace the notion of internationalization more fully.

Faculty for Whom English is a Second Language
Continuing with the theme of interaction with students, a key finding of this study relates to the challenges faced by faculty for whom

English is a second language. Except for Ben, all the participants in this study for whom English is a second language commented on the problems they faced as second-language speakers. Several reported complaints from students about their linguistic ability and subsequent low teaching evaluations:

> I think that the most important barrier is the language. It is very difficult to be in front of the class and speak in a clear way when you have a lot of complex thoughts. In Canada you should be able to endure this kind of psychological challenge — that is not being able to speak correctly in the first language. (Marta)

> I'm sure I made quite a fool of myself in the first two years language-wise. I know in my first year, a couple of students went to see the Dean to complain about my poor command of English and I know that at the end of the year in the course evaluations one of the complaints I got was I spoke too fast. So it was just about communication, which was a bit of a problem. (Enzo)

Other participants indicated a strong awareness of this problem when asked about their views about international faculty more generally. The particular point of concern was accent — where a hierarchy of accents emerged. Thus, whereas Tim reported that his students believed his British accent was "cute," colleagues from places such as India and China encountered more negative reactions. Rene also said that her language skills had presented a significant problem in the delivery of courses, which had, as with Enzo and Marta, resulted in poor teaching evaluations — a factor which she drew on to explain subsequent problems with tenure and promotion.

Faculty for whom English is a second language also said that students for whom English is also a second language were likely to be more critical than native speakers. This finding highlights the importance of communication skills for international faculty for whom English is a second language and, especially, the implications and challenges for teaching.

Recognizing and Rewarding International Experience

Thus far we have reported that the majority of faculty said that their international experience and research networks supported their research productivity and, for the most part, their teaching. Yet reports of whether international experience was explicitly recognized and rewarded by their host institution were mixed, particularly in recruitment and tenure and promotion decisions. Some faculty, like Bill and Rudi, reported that their international experience had been valued during their initial interview and subsequent experience in Canada:

> So, I think there's no question that foreign travel and my experience of living overseas has been good for my research career and that has been reflected in my promotions in Canada. (Bill)

> So having all of that [international] experience and the way they have treated me made me realize I'm not going to have any problem in the academic world here in that sense. I can come and teach comfortably here and I can present my ideas clearly to people and I come with a new perspective that the university is not fully versed in. (Rudi)

However, other participants reported that their international experience was neither recognized nor rewarded. One participant wondered how he had "made it through the interview." His subsequent difficulties during tenure and promotion applications supported this view even further:

> They didn't see it [international experience] as an accomplishment. They said "there's no continuity." I understood why but then this year I got it [tenure] from this institution so I'm hoping that it will be a smooth ride from now on. (Ashley)

By comparison, Evan — who had experience in industry and academia — felt that his international experience was explicitly recognized during his initial interview and subsequent recruitment. Yet, in later attempts to access funding and promotion, he felt that the same experience was undervalued:

> So I'm already ten years beyond my Ph.D. I came from academia in the US late, after industrial exposure. I justified that, for myself, [because I am in] an applied science area — biotechnology. I wanted to have that exposure to industry but now that is not being taken into account in my academic setting ... not with promotion or salary. (Evan)

James expressed similar confusion where his experience in Australia supported his initial recruitment but it was not recognized in his starting point on the tenure track system.

Discussion

The overall findings of this study suggest that international faculty have considerable potential to contribute to the internationalization of higher education in Canada. They are well placed to introduce international research networks and, indeed, are doing so — or at least attempting to do so. We have already noted that academic careers operate within different social contexts: first, within the context of the overall science system and the respective academic discipline; second, within the national context (in this case Canada); and third, within the institutional or respective university context. Contemporary academia is characterized by a global mindset where an individual faculty member's research activity is informed by what colleagues and peers elsewhere are doing.[28] Moreover, as members of a "global academy," faculty are encouraged to develop their research across international boundaries. A key issue here is that, when international faculty bring their international research and networks to Canada, they are adhering to the norms and values of the broader academic community. Yet, the extent to which those norms and values are accepted also depends on the synergy with the other two contexts, i.e., the national context and the institutional or university context. Although some were eager to utilize their international experience, they said that funding institutions and institutional policies on tenure and promotion are out of step with academia as an international enterprise. A key finding here, therefore, is that, if Canada is serious about developing a more international profile for its universities, then it must ensure that it does so at both a national and institutional level.

The majority of participants in this study said that they draw on their international experience to support their teaching and that, for the most part, students seem to be receptive to the alternative perspectives that they bring. Some participants also believed that their own international experience might encourage students to be more curious about developing their own careers internationally. Moreover, there was some evidence that international faculty are well placed to support the growing body of international students in Canada. Yet there was some concern that relationships between international faculty and international students need to be carefully managed. The findings especially point to the challenges faced by second-language speakers where linguistic ability may have a detrimental effect on teaching evaluations and overall competency in the classroom. It was also interesting to note that faculty who struggled with their linguistic ability were less inclined to draw on their international experience in the classroom. Overall, however, it appears that international experience can indeed contribute to the overall internationalization of higher education in terms of teaching but it should be used in conjunction with appropriate knowledge of and sensitivity to the Canadian context. Indeed, such an approach fits more fully with the notion of internationalization.

Further Research

The gap in our understanding of the potential contribution of international faculty to the internationalization of higher education in Canada presents an exciting opportunity for pioneering research into the broader theme of their role in higher education more generally. While this paper has addressed only a portion of the larger study, there are further themes that need to be explored. Clearly, it is not just international faculty who may play a role in the internationalization of higher education. "Home-grown" faculty have an equally important role to play. Further research might also explore whether "home-grown" faculty draw on international experience for research and teaching. Thus it may be international experience more generally (not simply that of international faculty) which can be used as a mechanism to internationalize higher education. Further research might also explore the experiences of university administrators and management with respect to recruitment, retention and performance of international faculty. Moreover, the student body and their experiences with international faculty might also be explored.

13

International Quality Provision in Cross-border Higher Education and the Internationalization of Canadian Degree-granting Institutions

Yves E. Beaudin, Council of Ministers of Education, Canada (CMEC)[1]

As we all know, governments, major educational associations and universities throughout the world are currently debating issues related to the internationalization of higher education. Quality assurance measures are being refined and implemented, degree programs are being scrutinized by governments and national qualification frameworks are redefining higher education in many countries. Universities are fine-tuning their international activities and reviewing many of their programs with a view to including an international component. The concerns raised by the General Agreement on Trade in Services (GATS) and the willingness of certain countries to accept education as a service are bringing many higher education institutions to reassess their marketing strategies. Quality has become an essential part of cross-border initiatives. All higher education officials now recognize that transnational education is becoming a worldwide phenomenon that must be dealt with.[2] Distance education and experiential learning initiatives are challenging the very nature of higher education. Recognition of credentials and qualifications is becoming a major issue.

Higher education institutions are concerned by these trends. Some are facing these challenges and responding by focusing on the internationalization of their activities. Provincial and territorial governments are also concerned. We may want to ask ourselves what measures are being discussed by the provinces and the territories. What impact will present and future changes in government policy have on the autonomy of Canadian institutions of higher learning? Will these changes continue to guarantee academic freedom and progressive research activities? What impact will globalization have on the liberalization of trade in goods and services? What does it mean for higher education in our country? While we all recognize that education must continue to be considered a public good, we should still ask ourselves if we are not exercising some sort of educational protectionism within and outside our borders out of fear that others may someday play an important role in our national environment. We may even want to ask ourselves if, in certain cases, we are not guilty of some type of modern-day educational colonialism.

Canadian Degree-granting Institutions

The vast majority of the 185 Canadian public or private higher education institutions, fully recognized or authorized to grant specific credentials at the university level and operating under a public or private bill, are interested in the internationalization of their activities. We believe that all higher education institutions should recognize one another and work collaboratively with governments to better internationalize and market their services, whether the institutions are traditional and well-known, are set up for distance learning or are new in the higher education environment. Examples of these distance and new degree-granting institutions are the Canadian Quest University, University Canada West and Lansbridge University as well as foreign institutions such as Charles Sturt University from Australia, Central Michigan University from the US and University of Abertay Dundee from Scotland, all now authorized to operate in Canada.

It is important to note that governments are also assessing the quality of and recognizing private distance education universities established in Canada and offering programs in Canada and worldwide. Good examples of these are Lansbridge and Yorkville Universities in New Brunswick. What relationships exist between these private institutions and the provincially recognized distance education institutions such as Athabasca University, UQAM (Téluq), and Thompson Rivers Open Learning Division?

Provincial Initiatives

If Canadian students are to benefit from the internationalization of curricula and of institutions in general within Canada or abroad and if they are encouraged to study abroad, we also need, as a country, to be more responsive to foreign students and foreign institutions. Shouldn't the internationalization of institutions and the internationalization of curricula be a two-way street? We believe so. More and more provincial and territorial governments are aware of the importance of internationalizing their educational systems. They encourage and support initiatives by all post-secondary institutions in Canada. They also understand that it is important to open their doors to international higher education institutions wishing to offer alternatives to Canadian students in a global market economy.

Recently, the provinces of Alberta, British Columbia, New Brunswick and Ontario legislated and implemented measures to permit foreign institutions to offer programs in their provinces. Does the arrival of foreign institutions on our territory not resemble the initiatives of certain Canadian universities that offer full programs in developed and emerging countries? Do these Canadian institutions go through a government validation or quality assessment process in the country in which the services are offered? We suspect that this is not always the case, whereas recognized foreign institutions wishing to establish themselves in our country must go through an assessment process; they simply will not be authorized to offer programs without due review. We are not referring here to joint arrangements between countries or recognized institutions.

In Canada, the four provinces that have opened their doors to foreign institutions did so by creating bodies that overview the quality of programs.   In Alberta, the Campus Alberta Quality Council reviews applications and assesses programs. In British Columbia, the Degree Quality Assessment Board assumes that responsibility, whereas in Ontario the government created the Post-secondary Education Quality Assessment Board. In New Brunswick, the Degree-Granting Act establishes a framework for evaluating the quality of programs leading to a degree.

Recommendation on Guidelines for Quality Provision in Cross-border Higher Education

We believe that these provincial initiatives are in perfect harmony with the Organisation for Economic Co-operation and Development (OECD) recommendation on "Guidelines for Quality Provision in Cross-border Higher Education" adopted in December 2005. These guidelines were developed in collaboration with UNESCO, which endorsed them in October 2005. The guidelines:

> provide an international framework to protect students and other stakeholders from low-quality provision and disreputable providers. They will sustain the development of quality cross-border higher education that meets human, social, eco-

nomic, and cultural needs. The guidelines set out
how governments, higher education
institutions/providers, student bodies, quality
assurance and accreditation bodies, academic and
professional recognition bodies of the sending
country and receiving country could share responsibilities, while respecting the diversity of higher
education systems.[3]

They also "recommend actions to six stakeholders: governments,
higher education institutions/providers including academic staff,
student bodies, quality assurance and accreditation bodies, academic recognition bodies, and professional bodies."[4]

According to the OECD/UNESCO guidelines, "external quality assurance and accreditation systems have been adopted in more
than 60 countries."[5] Should we also implement similar systems in
the provinces? The fact that Canada has no formal, independent,
national quality assurance processes in place for higher education
institutions may hinder recognition internationally for our lesser-
known universities and may be cause for concern for some
graduates who want to work outside of Canada.

The Role of Governments

Education being a public good, it is generally accepted that governments have a very important role in promoting quality assurance
measures that will guarantee not only the recognition of institutions within the country but also the quality of the programs
offered in countries throughout the world. I am sure that we are all
aware of substandard programs being offered in some foreign countries. Shouldn't we ask ourselves, as a country, whether a more
collaborative approach could be implemented to assess systemati-
cally the quality of institutions and programs within each
jurisdiction with the input of national and international experts

from the higher education community? Would that not give more credibility to our institutions internationally? Would it not be an ideal way to assess the quality of new and foreign institutions wishing to establish themselves in a particular province to offer specific programs? The contribution of existing higher education providers, academic staff and other professionals would only enhance the quality of programs offered to Canadian and foreign students. It would also enhance the quality of the internationalization processes in higher education institutions.

The Council of Ministers of Education, Canada (CMEC)

At their October 2005 meeting, the members of the Council of Ministers of Education were presented with a report they had commissioned on quality assurance of degree programming. In the months following its presentation to ministers, all provinces and territories formally adopted this report on a degree qualifications framework and quality assurance standards. Here again, this initiative is clearly in line with international goals promoted by international bodies such as UNESCO, OECD, the European Union, the Council of Europe, and the Southeast Asian Ministers of Education Organization (SEAMEO) as well as other national and international associations. It is also respectful of the expectations expressed by emerging countries in their search for quality programs and their desire also to offer programs and educational services in a country like Canada. We must ask ourselves whether we have the right to refuse their services if we promote ours in their countries. We should be acutely aware of the risk of protectionism and educational colonialism. Of course, we fully agree that foreign institutions must have their programs assessed for quality before offering them in Canada, as foreign countries should assess the quality of programs offered by Canadian higher education institutions within their borders.

Membership as a Criterion

One of the concerns raised while the report was being drafted was that some universities in Canada will not consider applications for further study from graduates of degree programs offered by Canadian non-members of the Association of Universities and Colleges of Canada (AUCC). What does this mean for students who graduate from fully recognized and government-sanctioned institutions that are not members of AUCC? Does it mean that foreign students have an advantage over Canadian students who perform very well in Canadian non-AUCC member universities? To our knowledge, foreign universities are not members of AUCC. It has always been our understanding that admission should not be based on membership.

An Objective and Independent Quality Assurance Mechanism

Would all Canadian students benefit from an objective and independent quality assurance mechanism that all institutions, whether members of associations or not, would have to submit to? Is self-regulated quality assurance really the best answer to national and global concerns about the quality of institutions and their programs? Should the eligibility of all Canadian students for admission not be based on performance rather than the membership of their university in a particular association? Does Canadian protectionism exist within an élite group of Canadian higher education institutions? The pan-Canadian committee's report "suggests that recognition of new degrees and new degree providers needs to be refocused on the level and quality of the academic credential itself rather than on other matters"[6] such as membership in an organization.

Degree (Diploma) Mills

The report also touches upon the "emergence of 'degree mills' offering unearned credentials and of 'accreditation mills' issuing meretricious badges of quality assurance." Many may think that these institutions do not exist in Canada. Well, they do exist, and they definitely have an impact upon the way Canada is viewed by the international community. In fact, in 2004, it was estimated that at least thirty-two degree mills existed or were in operation in Canada. At the time of writing, one had just been discovered in Toronto, called Solsbury University. If one checked out the location, it would probably be found to be just a drop-off point. Of course, these degree (diploma) mill providers are very active internationally. There are many medical schools offering dubious credentials in the Caribbean and elsewhere in the world. What is more alarming is that there is a school in Toronto that prepares students for the Medical Council of Canada (MCC) exams and the United States Medical Licensing Examination (USMLE). MCC exams are the first step leading to licensure in the provinces and territories. More troubling yet is the list that appears on Human Resources and Skills Development Canada's Web site of Caribbean schools that are acceptable destinations for Canadian students who want to obtain loans to study in those countries. We communicated with colleagues in the Netherlands to ask about the schools that are part of the Netherlands Antilles and were told that "a number of other unaccredited medical schools of the Netherlands Antilles likewise qualify for student loan purposes in Canada — something which is out of the question in the Netherlands."

Are we, in effect, encouraging our students to obtain "qualifications" from unaccredited institutions and degree (diploma) mills by not recognizing institutions and programs that are quality-assured by our legitimate governments? Are degree mills the real enemies? Are we shooting at the wrong target by not collaborating and recognizing all quality-assured institutions and programs in Canada?

This appears to be a very serious ethical issue, one that should be addressed by governments and all higher education institutions.

Qualification Frameworks

As other countries develop qualifications frameworks, we will, as a nation, have to better demonstrate how our educational systems operate. One of the difficult questions to answer will be how we assess quality in our higher education institutions and how we process our programs to guarantee quality. We will be challenged by other countries. We already are being challenged by such countries as Australia, New Zealand and South Africa, and soon will be challenged by the European countries that are members of the Bologna Process. The ministers of higher education of the forty-six countries that are part of the Bologna Process have agreed to the development of a European quality assurance framework that will be complemented by individual country qualification frameworks. We are not making a plea for a unique Canadian higher education framework, but we do believe that a concerted effort on the part of the provinces and territories could result in a national framework that could serve as a tool to better serve all students attending fully quality-assured higher education institutions.

Conclusion

The internationalization of Canadian universities is first and foremost for the benefit of Canadian students who pursue their ambitions at one of the 185 recognized higher education institutions in Canada. But while we know that internationalization is good for students, we also believe that it is essential for our country to continue to be a world leader in a global market economy. Our internationally minded graduates and leaders of tomorrow will be thankful to the universities, governments, associations and leaders of today for making internationalization a major preoccupation of our time for a better future.

Questioning the Emperor's New Clothes: Towards Ethical Practices in Internationalization

Kumari V. Beck, Simon Fraser University[1]

Entry Point

While international education has been eagerly embraced by most post-secondary institutions in Canada, there is a lack of agreement among theorists, practitioners and administrators about what it all means[2] as well as much ambiguity in interpreting terms, approaches and rationales.[3] This has resulted in an uneven practice of international education, a divide between theory and practice and even a disregard for research as a foundation for practice. It doesn't help when the literature about the field, as Mestenhauser asserts, "though rich and plentiful — remains ... accidental, occasional, and random."[4] As Knight herself notes, important questions about internationalization need to be raised: the purpose of internationalization, its benefits and outcomes, values underpinning it, its positive consequences, unintended results and negative implications, the sustainability, policy and funding implications of an increased emphasis on internationalization, and whether internationalization is a stimulus for or response to globalization.[5] While the questions have been identified, there have been few sustained efforts to research the conceptualization of internationalization itself in the context of those forces that give rise to it, such as globalization.

An Academic Rationale?

We are often lulled into complacency that an academic rationale drives internationalization in Canada. According to Knight's last national survey on internationalization, completed in 2000, a high percentage of post-secondary institutions in Canada stated that they espouse an academic rationale for internationalization, which is described as the preparation of graduates "who are internationally knowledgeable and inter-culturally competent."[6] Internationalization has been defined as a process that infuses an inter-cultural/international perspective into the teaching/learning, research and service functions of a university.[7] Thus, an academic rationale for internationalization should be represented by activity that promotes such outcomes. Issues related to intercultural understanding, difference and diversity, however, rank low in interest and/or activity.[8] In terms of teaching and learning, although curricular issues have been identified as high priorities in Canadian internationalization, 75 percent of the respondents in the last national survey reported very low levels of activity in internationalizing the curriculum.[9] Another expected contribution to an academic rationale for internationalization is the integration of domestic students and foreign students on the campus, leading to the international/intercultural competencies of graduates. Indeed, university administrators in the survey cited the integration of these two student groups as the main reason for enrolling international students. However, when asked to identify outcomes of enrolling international students, there was no mention of ways in which international students contributed towards bringing an intercultural or international dimension into the institution.

My reading around the data[10] led me to believe that internation-alization is less tied to an academic rationale than we may believe. In a later paper, Knight mentions several new emerging rationales from both the institutional and national sectors that would lend credence to the thesis that internationalization is more tied to eco-nomic and political rationales: at the national level, the trends include nation building, human resources development, commer-cial trade, strategic development and social cultural development; and at the institutional level, the trends include branding and pro-file, income generation, strategic alliance and research and knowledge production.[11]

This chapter focuses on developing an understanding of interna-tionalization, arguing that a comprehensive analysis of the process will support educators and scholars alike to discern and implement ethical practices. The desire for ethical practice comes out of a wish to avoid harm and promote well-being. In making a case for sound and deeper analysis and critique, my purpose is to equip us to be able to identify those approaches that reflect the values of higher education rather than, say, the market. An analysis of internation-alization that overlooks or excludes globalization, I contend, is incomplete and misleading, giving the impression that internation-alization is value-free and neutral. Internationalization seen in the context of globalization, however, recognizes its vulnerability to market-driven ideologies, acknowledges its complexity as a process and clarifies some of the confusion related to its practices. Hence I will briefly highlight the impact of globalization on higher educa-tion. Employing scholarship on globalization theory, I will explore alternative ways of theorizing internationalization. I will then briefly describe how other theoretical applications such as post-colonial theory will enrich the discussion. Using brief examples from my ongoing research, a qualitative study on the experiences of international students at a Canadian campus, I will illustrate how this framework has enabled an effective analysis of internationalization and deeper understanding of this process from a student perspective. This approach, I conclude, enables practitioners and scholars to develop a "grassroots" understanding of internationalization and a reconceptualization of what an academic rationale for internationalization means.

Part I: Developing a Conceptual Framework

An Alternative Analysis: Using the Discourses of Globalization

There is no area of human endeavour that does not seem to be connected to or impacted by globalization.[12] The controversies and debates on globalization take many forms. For example, globalization continues to be promoted as a means of progress and development through free trade, technology and a culture of efficiency.[13] Others have argued that globalization has driven the world towards greater divides of inequality[14] and that it is a means of recolonizing the world by industrialized countries.[15] There is much discussion on whether it homogenizes the world or encourages pluralism.[16] For the purposes of this chapter, I will first briefly consider some of the consequences of globalization in relation to higher education, recognizing that this is being addressed in detail by others in this volume (e.g. Marginson, Hanson, and Dwyer and Reed). I will then address how a sociological analysis of globalization — in particular, the cultural dimensions — enables us to resist its dominant assimilationist and consumer discourses and move into transformative strategies that are better aligned with the purposes of learning, teaching and research in higher education.

Globalization and Higher Education

The literature on the connections between globalization and

education supports the argument that economic globalization is making its mark on education.[17] The research alludes to common themes across several countries. Most educational reform is promoted through changes in governance, change is formulated in economic terms, institutions are encouraged to be run in business-oriented managerial styles, student outcomes are aligned to employment-related skills and competencies and there are attempts to control and initiate national curricula.[18] This trend has been noted in higher education as well. Universities are becoming more corporate and less collegial, more consumer-oriented and more concerned with accountability and excellence.[19]

Edwards and Usher,[20] citing Lyotard's analysis of knowledge production in postmodernity,[21] describe this in terms of "performativity,"[22] which they define as performing to external demands. Here, performativity of the institution is "located within wider discourses of economic globalization and competitiveness. Education becomes the means of attaining and maintaining the flexibility that is considered necessary in the face of the technological and socio-economic change required by these conditions."[23] It is seen as part of the economy and as an investment in human resource development that would maintain national competitiveness on the global stage.

This focus on performance has changed the whole notion of knowledge production: that is, the meaning and purposes of research, teaching and learning. Research itself, in general, is following technology and is becoming more oriented towards system efficiency and performance rather than to "free" inquiry. As knowledge is seen to be the most important resource, certainly in industrialized and developed countries, there is an increased emphasis on instrumental learning and more investment in scientific research than in other kinds of research.[24] "The instruments of international rivalry are no longer fleets and missiles but 'intellectual property,' in the shape of both basic science and commercial patents, and 'human capital,' in the form of highly skilled work-forces,"[25] and so higher education in general is viewed as an investment that will maintain comparative economic advantage.

Edwards and Usher[26] argue that performativity has led to a greater linkage between research and policy and a separation of ped-agogy from research. The prestige and "standing" of a university is assessed partly on the amount of research funding it attracts and partly on the standing of the researchers within it. In the West at least, this has led to the creation of élite groups of researchers, usu-ally attached to an élite group of institutions. In this regard, research is seen to be a higher priority than the pedagogical func-tion of the institution, which in turn affects the focus of faculty. The composition of the student body in higher education has changed as well, with learners of diverse backgrounds and purposes accessing post-secondary education.

Globalized conditions have created a tension in universities as they respond to the needs created by those conditions.[27] On the one hand, they are "local" institutions expected to take care of the needs of local communities, including providing access to marginalized people. This is the "inward-looking" orientation. On the other hand, competition, national pressures and opportunities created by globalization pull the university to look outwards to both enhance networks and widen the scope of the institution. This is the global/local tension of the times,[28] characterized as the tension between the "massification" of higher education and international-ization.[29]

It is a paradox that is consistent with globalization forces that, in an era when the significance of the nation-state is diminishing, it is seeking to tighten its connection with higher education. The univer-sity is linked to state power. It is dependent on the government for its budget, and in turn governments increasingly look to universities to fulfill a national purpose. Although competitiveness is not the sole reason for the funding of higher education, there is increased pressure for education to play a role in aligning with national policy in the "training" of graduates in specific competencies in order to maintain national competitiveness and national identity.

The irony is that, with increased pressure, government funding and resources to post-secondary institutions are declining, thus encouraging these institutions to develop a more entrepreneurial approach towards survival with strategies such as the marketing of educational products and services. Cambridge[30] compares international education to product branding:

> The espousal of the values of free-market capital-
> ism associated with the globalizing current of
> international education has led to the trans-
> formation of international education into a
> globally branded product. It has been proposed
> that international education "may be compared
> with other globally marketed goods and services
> such as soft drinks and hamburgers; a reliable
> product conforming to consistent quality stan-
> dards throughout the world."[31]

I suggest that agency — in other words, an ability to counter some of the harmful effects such as the commodification of higher education and the market orientation — is connected to having a deeper understanding of the complexity of the phenomenon. Thus, it is important to understand the forces of globalization and how they operate in order to think past the economic orientation.

Understanding the Nature of Globalization

The popular understanding of the term *globalization* refers to the perception that the globe is becoming a single space from the effects of communications and technology.[32] This has been attributed largely to technology, the increased levels of communication enabled by technology, fast travel and transport, and the vast movements or flows of goods, people, ideas and knowledge that accompany it.[33] It has been accelerated by global systems of trade, transnational networks and corporate empires.[34]

Globalization has been attributed by some to singular causes: for example, capitalism and a world systems theory, technological progress and the rapid development of communications technology in particular, and political factors.[35] Others view it as a complex process driven by a number of forces. Giddens sees it as a "dialectical process because it does not bring about a generalized set of changes acting in a uniform direction, but consists in mutually opposed tendencies."[36] Robertson characterizes these tendencies as a contradictory interplay between globalizing forces, "a massive two-fold process involving the interpenetration of the universalization of particularism and the particularization of universalism."[37]

Edwards and Usher argue that the heightened consciousness of "one place" produced by globalization results in an increased, intensified awareness of the "interconnectedness of local ecologies, economies and societies, of the significance of place and location."[38] Their work is particularly concerned with globalization as a conceptualization of space and its reconfiguration both physical and imagined.[39] Localization, accordingly, is not in opposition to globalization but must be understood as part of it.

Appadurai posits a process of indigenization which adapts and changes (indigenizes) a global idea, activity or object when assimilated into a local community. To understand these cultural flows, he proposes a framework of five perspectival constructs called "scapes." These are: ethnoscapes, the distribution of mobile individuals as tourists, refugees, migrants, etc.; technoscapes, the distribution of technology; finanscapes, the distribution of capital; mediascapes, the distribution of information through a variety of media; and ideoscapes, the distribution of political ideas and values.[40] The flows occur among these "scapes" in "increasingly non-isomorphic paths;"[41] in other words, the flows are unpredictable in the paths they take and their movements represented in a variety of forms. Appadurai provides many examples to illustrate the ways in which the "scapes" influence one another; the movement of money (finanscapes), people and work (ethnoscapes), culture and attitudes (mediascapes) impact one another in complex interaction, undermining the dominant view of centre-periphery relations.[42]

Appadurai's flow of "scapes" provides an appropriate metaphor to convey the fluidity, the irregularity and the variety of the globalization process and also serves to unravel the nature of those relationships. Consequently, globalization is uneven and has varied impacts, reconfiguring local cultures of the "periphery" as well as those of the "core." It is possible to see the simultaneity of convergence and fragmentation, of homogenization and heterogenization.

Implications: Internationalization as Eduscape?

How does this influence our understanding of internationalization? Thus far, what emerges from this picture of globalization is a very complex, and interwoven, set of forces and processes, often paradoxical, between local activities and interaction across distances, some intersecting with one another, some dialectical and contradictory. Themes of space and compression of space and tensions between global and local predominate. I am proposing that this analysis of globalization is useful in situating and understanding the issues relating to internationalization. They "crystallize" the social, political and economic conditions, both possibilities and constraints, that affect the "process" of internationalization. In this regard, I am particularly drawn to theorizing the internationalization of education (higher education, in this instance) as an *eduscape*, following Appadurai.

An eduscape could be conceptualized as the flow of educational theories, ideas, programs, activities and research in and across national boundaries. As with the other dimensions of this framework, the global relationships with the other "scapes" would be "deeply disjunctive" and "profoundly unpredictable" because "each is subject to its own constraints and incentives ... at the same time as each acts as a constraint and a parameter for movements in the others."[43] We cannot understand one in isolation without taking into consideration the influences of other "scapes." Hence, internationalization could be understood in a more complex manner than under the current definition, which limits internationalization to an infusion of intercultural and international dimensions into the various elements of the university. Such an infusion implies a one-way flow, and an assumption of stable categories of "intercultural" and "international," whereas the reconceptualization as eduscape reflects a multi-flow, a more nuanced and complex depiction of the evolution of these categories. I have introduced these ideas to show how and why I argue for a revisioning of internationalization as a necessary part of taking an ethical stance.

In the next section I briefly outline another aspect of my multidimensional framework before I provide illustrations from my study. I have found parallel ideas in post-colonial theory that support the particular focus and approach I used with globalization theory.

Lessons from the Past: Resisting the Colonial Condition

Why Post-colonial Theory?

Post-colonial theory draws upon a vast body of scholarship emerging from former colonies in Asia, Africa and South America and in a variety of disciplines such as literary theory, sociology, anthropology, history, geography, literature and philosophy, offering diverse perspectives on the condition and aftermath of colonization. Given the issues of dominance, power and inequity that surfaced from my foray into conditions of globalization, my interest in post-colonial theory is in the insights it might offer into the nature of such power relations: dominance, complicity, subordination and, most importantly, resistance in such conditions.

Parallels have been drawn between colonization and globalization.[44] The most obvious one noted is the extent of domination and control exerted. At the height of colonial power, 84.5 percent of the earth was in the hands of and controlled by the rest.[45] The escalation of globalization began about the time that decolonization was taking place, making way for an economic colonization, or "the new corporate colonialism," to take hold.[46]

Domination and empire building are nothing new in the history of civilization. What was new about western colonization, however, was the extent to which dependency was created on the West, and the pervasive domination of ideology and culture.[47] The forms of dependency that are continued by globalization[48] constitute a colonization of mind and culture that continues to exert influence long after the colonial masters have gone home.[49]

The "beginnings" of international education in its contemporary form can be traced to development aid offered soon after World War II to "underdeveloped" countries struggling to reestablish themselves. "Educated people were needed to build a country and to help others to build their nations abroad. Because in the minds of most Canadians the university defined what it means to be educated, education in general and universities in particular were at the heart of development."[50] It would appear that, unless recognized and named, international education may run the risk of reproducing and maintaining those power relations through the dependency noted by post-colonial scholars. In this context, as Leila Ghandi argues, post-colonial critique offers "the possibility of thinking our way through, and therefore, out of the historical imbalances and cultural inequalities produced by the colonial encounter."[51]

The market for international education has been mostly in the flow of international students to institutions in western/northern states, although there is a growing trend by these institutions towards establishing satellite campuses and offshore delivery.[52] Pengelly[53] cites various rationales for why "sending" nations choose the "receiving" countries they do: political alignment with the country, the need to catch up to the economic levels and trends of the countries they hope to learn from, the need to improve education systems and standards of the "sending" country, and a variety of other related reasons such as learning English, the dominant language of communication and business. "Receiving" nations are predominantly rich countries of the Organisation for Economic Co-operation and Development (OECD) who are all in the market to attract the larger share of the lucrative business of international students. One of the consequences of this is a brain drain for the poorer nations whose best students, their human resources, go overseas for their post-secondary education on aid-based scholarships and often remain there. The most difficult challenge to overcome, having implications for our topic at hand, is the desire that has been created for Western university education. If globalization creates the market for Western education, colonial dependency creates the desire. The widespread acceptance of this ideology as universal, and as part of the natural evolution of progress, establishes a hegemonic "world order."

Post-colonial theory also throws light on what Homi Bhabha has described as cultural creation and containment. On the one hand, we see the creation of cultural diversity; on the other hand, Bhabha finds a "containment" of cultural difference as dominant cultures "accommodate" others only within their own norms and frames.[54] This creation/containment theory is parallel to the paradoxes of globalization with its simultaneity of fragmentation, movement and convergence.

Power and Resistance

Colonial relationships are embedded in relations of power. Post-colonial scholar Nandy's[55] account of power in the colonial condition is generated from a Foucauldian analysis: power as being everywhere, invisible and pervasive, "employed and exercised through a net-like organization."[56] The conceptualization of power as complex movement and motion takes us out of the common assumption of imperial hegemony in which the act of domination is based on an interpretation of power as binary relations: colonizer/colonized, occidental/oriental, civilized/primitive, developed /underdeveloped and so on. Borrowing from a concept first suggested by Deleuze and Guattari,[57] Ashcroft posits colonial power as a rhizome. Described as a root system that has no main or central root, that "propagates itself in a fragmented, discontinuous, multidirectional way," [58] the metaphor aptly describes the ways in which power "inserts itself" into the multiple discourses of colonialism.

I would agree with Ashcroft[59] that, like power and ideology, resistance itself, in order to become tooled into an anti-colonial strategy, needs to be conceptualized as rhizomic. A rhizomic structure, because of its unpredictability and fragmentation, produces spaces and "fractures" that can be occupied. Bhabha[60] characterizes it as the "third space of enunciation" which enables new positions to emerge from the encounter between colonial and other. If discourse and counter-discourse then are both rhizomic, resistance is possible through interpolation: that is, to interrupt the dominant discourse with a counter-discourse that operates within it, borrows from it and yet turns its intention awry. A fundamental limitation of this kind of resistance, however, is the necessity to be knowledgeable about, well-trained and comfortable in the use of dominant discourse in order to initiate counter-discourse. This is ironic because agency is dependent on mastery of the very thing that is being resisted. This conceptualization moves resistance from simple opposition to a space of transformation.

These theories offer the possibility of examining contextualized power relations in the internationalization process. How are the discourses generated, by whom, and for what purpose? What are the ways in which dominant discourse might be reproduced, and how might that be experienced? How might counter-discourse be both recognized (so that it can be supported) and initiated? Another benefit of these theories is the concept of mutuality as ethical practice. By this I mean that the notion of "inter" or "between" expresses the idea that "international" is not one way, it is a two-way process. With post-colonial notions of "third space," and transformative resistance, it is possible to work towards ensuring that experiences are mutual, thus making it "inter-"national.

The framework described above has been developed in the context of a qualitative research study I am conducting to further explore these issues. Following are some highlights of that study, which is in the final stages of data analysis, to provide an illustration of how the framework serves to understand internationalization more comprehensively and, more importantly perhaps, to reconceptualize internationalization itself.

PART II: A Brief Illustration from the Field

The study investigates the experiences of international students in a post-secondary setting in order to better understand the process of internationalization from student perspectives and to inform the design of pedagogy and curriculum development. Two key values have guided the design of this research and its amenability to the overall goal of the study (that of bringing student experience to the fore): first, the notion of reciprocal participatory methods to elicit and build theory[61] and second, empowerment, interpreted both as mindfulness of the power relations between researcher and researched[62] and as " [providing] conditions under which subjects can enhance their capacity for self-determination."[63] This study was an experimental first step towards Patti Lather's notion of "research as praxis,"[64] where I hoped that students would be strengthened from their participation in this study to advocate for change as they defined it.

The literature that informs the main study includes globalization and post-colonial theory as highlighted above, as well as anti-racist frameworks, cultural studies, identity and recognition, diversity and higher education, curriculum as internationalized text, and pedagogy in higher education.

Method, Setting and Purpose

A mid-sized university in Western Canada, Good University,[65] was selected as a site primarily because of its familiarity to me and the access to international students made possible by my network of contacts. Good University (GU) had an enrolment of 19,979 undergraduate students and 3,666 graduate students in the 2005-06 academic year; of this number, 1,805 or 9.1 percent of the undergraduate and 505 or 15.4 percent of the graduate students were identified as international or visa students.

The students who responded to my invitation to participate were a mix of undergraduate and graduate students: 12 undergraduates (to date) and 14 graduate students (to date) from a variety of disciplines. The undergraduate students were from Engineering, Computing Science, Science, Business, Fine Arts and Linguistics departments, while the graduate students were from Physics, Mathematics, Engineering, Computing Science and Education. The undergraduate students hailed from Asian countries: China, Taiwan, Hong Kong, Japan and Bangladesh. There was a wider variety of backgrounds in the graduate student mix, although still they were predominantly from the Asian continent: China, Japan, Sri Lanka, Iran, Mauritius, the United Kingdom and the United States.

Guided by the main research question, — "What are the experiences of international students on the GU campus?" an ethnographic interview was the key method of data collection. The interviews were carried out in small groups, and some individually, according to the preferences of the participants; I characterize these as conversations[66] in order to indicate my role as "passionate participant."[67] The aspects of student experience we explored included why they came overseas to study, what their process of application was like, their first year of studies at GU, experiences of classes and courses favourable and/or negative, the barriers to learning, the factors that supported their learning, their social lives on and off campus and, overall, their assessment of whether and how internationalization was taking place, and how they rated their decision to study abroad.

The conversations among us were rich and generated a great variety of data on a number of different topics and themes. I will limit the presentation of these data, analyses and discussion to just three themes as illustrations of some of the issues raised earlier in this chapter: getting here, the factors that influence the cultural creation and containment on the campus, and the role of the students in internationalization.[68] This will enable an overview of whether and how students are caught up in the "scapes" of globalization, whether the concept of internationalization as an eduscape could be supported by the data, whether the goals of internationalization are being served by the presence of international students, and whether an academic rationale is the basis for internationalization, from the perspective of these students.

Student Experience

Getting Here: Why Canada, and Why Good University?

The wish to "study abroad" illustrates how the discourse of Western universality, strength and dominance is played out in the desires of students. While for the Iranian graduate students in particular, doing graduate study was dependent on studying abroad as studying in their home country was problematic, going abroad for most of the other students was something that completed family or personal dreams for personal and professional growth. Here are some of their stories. The students are identified by pseudonyms they chose for themselves.

As Long (China) describes:

> Now that there are more foreigners in China there is more influence from the Western world. There is a trend to study outside. ...There are many companies in China who need people who speak English fluently — when you study abroad and come back to do a job search it's easier .... I had a strong desire to go out. I had a one-year experience of university in China but I didn't feel like I learned a lot.

Long identifies Western influences, and therefore the knowledge about "outside," the fluency in English in commanding well-paying work, and the notion that learning "outside" must be better than in China. This was echoed by Krystal (China), who talked about how an imaginary of Western ideas, people and ways of doing things was created for her and her family. An aunt of hers had travelled in Canada and had given her family a *definition of North America* as *a really beautiful place, really rich, education is really high and people are high quality. ... from her mouth, North America was like heaven* (laughter*)*. Krystal's image of North Americans was one in which *white people .. do things better than us ... do things the right way, ... they are smarter than us and work harder*. She went on to say that academics was just 30 percent of the reason for her coming here. Her marks were not high enough to get into the best and most competitive universities in China and she wanted the chance to have an excellent education. Learning English was seen as being very useful; another reason for coming was *to make different coun-try's friends*. Having a future *net* of contacts was seen as an important consideration for living well. Krystal and many of the other students mentioned the economic benefits of having a degree from abroad to ensure better, higher paying and more secure jobs in their home countries as well as in the international job market (Chris, Long, Little Onion, David, Wayne).

In contrast, Sherry (Taiwan) and Sushant (India) did not want to leave their home countries at all; it was their mothers who insisted that an overseas university education would be good for them and for the family. The choice of city was made through the recommen-dation of friends and relatives; they would be able to live with a family friend or relative, which would reduce expenses as well as help them in becoming acclimatized to their new environment. In their opinion, many international students base their selection of country and city, and finally university, on this kind of networking and rationale.

Parental choice also played a role in how Wayne (Taiwan) and, to an extent, Samshul (Bangladesh) and Jay (China) arrived at GU. Wayne's parents decided to immigrate to Canada as part of a plan to get a good education for Wayne there. Samshul's parents are part of the South Asian expatriate professional community in the Gulf States, where they work to make it possible for them to finance their son's education in *a good place.* The original idea for Jay to study abroad came from the example set by her parents. They raised her to be a cosmopolitan world citizen, by travelling, having friends from a wide variety of backgrounds, and encouraging *a global view* so that learning in a foreign university came to be a natural selec-tion for her.

For some students, studying abroad was less of a long-time dream and more to do with personal circumstances. Peter (China), a graduate student, summarized the issue well: some countries are *having a heyday* (in reaping the benefits of increasing enrolments of international students) but he recognizes that he is very much caught up in fulfilling a childhood dream to study in an *advanced* country: *[P]eople need to have more in their life* and this is one way of attaining that dream. Andrew (US) wanted to live close to his brother who was studying nearby. Hiroki (Japan) was looking for a change. For Sonali (Mauritius), it was part of a wish to travel and to experience teaching in another country: *It was mostly for self development.* Lefty Blue (Hong Kong) was attracted to an international pre-university program, and he chose to get as far away from Hong Kong as possible. He studied in an International Baccalaureate (IB) program in Norway before he arrived at GU. He wanted to pursue a career in theatre at a university, and this would not have been possible to do in Hong Kong because of the lack of social status and recognition for theatre and the arts as a legitimate career: *You're not a doctor, or lawyer or something like this. "How are you going to make any money?" is what people say.*

For some students, getting here was a struggle. Parth (Iran), Shabnam (Iran), Peter, Shunfu (China) and Chris (China) learned some difficult lessons about access to opportunity. Shabnam and Parth went through immense difficulty; for example, going out of their country to sit for exams that would gain them entry to North American universities. The US was the preferred destination for Shabnam, Parth, Peter and Long, but the problem of getting visas for Shabnam and Parth, the lack of access and ranking information about US universities for Peter, and high fees in the case of Long, ruled out this choice. Global politics, the reinforcement of national boundaries and borders, and rules of access and denial are the first experiences of their learning journey. Paperwork was often cited as a normal but aggravating requirement. The processing of visas, transcripts and other documentation, while handled extremely well by GU, was time-consuming. Jay's processing took months, primarily because of the transcribing of transcripts. Hiroki had to travel to Seattle from Vancouver until his student visa was finalized.

The overseas and local reputation of GU as well as connections made with professors (in the case of graduate students) rated high as a reason for choosing GU. Polls and rankings in magazines such as *Maclean's* and on Web sites had influenced some students (Peter, Long). Amanda, from the US, reported that GU came highly recommended as *the Harvard of Canada*, which was part of the reason she chose it, together with her desire for a faculty or department that fit with her values for higher education and her own program of study. The recommendations of students, alumni, friends and relatives living nearby rated high in the selection of the university as well (Jay, Sherry, Sushant, David). Rojin's professor from her home university made connections and recommendations regarding her graduate study while visiting GU.

First Contact and Settling in

The initial contact and ongoing communications with GU were reported very positively, sometimes glowingly, and even with gratitude. Chris mentioned being happy to get a response from GU in twenty-four hours (although in Hiroki's case he didn't hear about his application until July). In the case of Peter, the university was the only one that offered him a place, and this opportunity still is associated with feelings of gratitude. When the students contacted faculty and staff at the university, they were proactive, welcoming and flexible. This is a *good, decent university* (Parth), *a really, really flexible university* (Shabnam). For Shabnam, when negotiations with other universities broke down for various reasons, *[a]t that hard time, [GU] was really kind to me.* Jay showed pride that, although the admission process took more than six months, she was admitted directly on her high-school marks with a requirement of a 3.8 grade point average (GPA), and she was impressed that GU had ways in which those marks could be understood across systems: *It's amazing that they understand and know everything because there are lots of cases to process.* Sushant made a point of saying how well the international office handled everything from inquiry to processing.

The students' experiences in their first semesters at GU were varied, depending on factors such as their exposure to Canada and prior educational experience. For those like Sherry and Wayne who had attended high school in Canada, the transition to university was much like that of all first-year students — getting used to a larger environment, independent study, new study expectations and so on. Some had attended other universities or private colleges to do a variety of courses ranging from regular first-year university courses (Samshul, Bowei) to discipline-related courses as a supplement (Jay), to prerequisites (Sushant, Chris) or intensive English for Academic Purposes (EAP) programs (Krystal, David, Long). Others, such as graduate students Peter (China), Parth, Shabnam, Rojin and Michelle (all from Iran), plunged right into programs without much orientation or assistance.

If students arrived at times outside the regular orientations that take place in late August and early September, it appears they did not receive the same level of assistance or information about how to settle in. Take Rojin, for example, who arrived in January from Iran:

> Those days were dark days. I was disoriented, didn't
> have access to anything. Nobody recommend[ed].
> No one told me anything, where to go even for
> information, no map to find my department.
> Nobody was available. I was like a ghost.

The move from a smaller institution to GU was another source of adjustment. David and Krystal moved from a smaller university where many students and staff had reached out to them in their English as a Second Language (ESL) program: *People want to help* (Krystal). At GU both noticed the absence of such personal attention. Sushant and Long commented on the smaller class sizes at a university college, and how these were conducive to better instructor-student relationships.

English or, rather, the lack of English skills, was a barrier for a number of students. As Shufan described it:

> Language has always been my headache, always been the obstacle. Social and academic success is prevented even now. I am dissatisfied with my spoken English ... I experienced much internal suffering because of this situation.

Getting the right score on the Test of English as a Foreign Language (TOEFL) was a recognition that students had a certain "knowledge" of English required to gain entrance to GU, but, as the students pointed out, this did not give them the fluency to function in an English language environment. In fact, it gave them a false sense of the linguistic expectations for study at GU. As Parth commented wryly:

> If you know English well, you are going to pass those exams with a good score no matter what. But if you don't know English, you can still pass those exams with a good score — just learn some tricks. ... I don't know which way they are looking at the problem — the ones who are giving the exams. ... just looking at people passing those exams or looking at people who know English.

Students discover they don't come equipped with the fluency they need. Some, as mentioned already, spent months in ESL preparation classes in private schools or colleges. Little Onion and Peter studied English for over a year in China, but it still was a shock to hear and practise the language in Canada. Exams and classes in their home country weren't enough, as Shabnam observed:

> I think I didn't change after studying for TOEFL.
> My English was the same. I just learned how to do
> those tests. ... I have to do English to write it and
> TOEFL was just something that stop you.

The topic of English and the topic of friends and socialization generated the greatest number of spontaneous stories and most animated engagement. Socialization was a topic on which we spent a great deal of time. The responses and the outcomes were varied. Many of the students echoed Long when he said strongly, *Campus isn't a good place to socialize.* Domestic students go back to their homes, families and established friendship networks and don't include newcomers in those networks. Sushant made many new friends while at a university college and he carried these skills over into the larger university environment, where he is the vice-president of a student club and seeks out social activity with students of the same discipline. For him, Lefty, Samshul and Jay, the secret was to join clubs or activities of people from the same discipline. Little Onion pointed out that, if you don't drink or find pub life attractive, there's not much you can do to socialize with domestic students.

A few of the students were successful in their residence life — Sherry, David, Lefty Blue — while others commented on a certain personality that was more helpful to socializing in residence: *You have to be brave* (Hiroki). Some students such as Long were living off campus because *you can get to know Canadians* and the life style. In a concerted effort to make the most of his time here, Long was volunteering at a seniors' care centre and as a Web designer for the local municipality. Sherry and David are interesting cases. Friends mean a lot to Sherry, and so she made a decision to move from her comfortable home-stay accommodation into residence to meet and make new friends. Similarly, David made a conscious decision to "hang out" with students who are not of the same cultural or ethnic background so he would broaden his circle of friends. These connections were all made mostly in residence and outside of classes. Residence wasn't all friendly and social for all the students I interviewed. Hiroki had a difficult time in his first year but was doing better in a residence that had a shared kitchen where he made some friends. Rojin, Michelle and Krystal found residence lonely and isolating, and, as Krystal concluded: *Maybe it is me — I don't know.*

Making Sense

An Eduscape?

The detail I have provided in the data on choice and decision-making in international study is meant to expand the sometimes simplistic representation of student mobility and the education market as a "recruit, cash and carry" operation. We are able to see how international students become part of the consumer culture created by the higher learning market as they research and make choices about their educational future. This market is driven by a demand for Western education in advanced countries that is created by the dominant world order. Students enter an institution whose interests are tied into nationalistic identifications and positioning. In bringing attention to these discourses, it becomes possible to uncover and question hidden narratives in these nation-building and competitive discourses that result in the difference-blind approach of assimilation.

Analyzing these stories through the lens of an eduscape reveals how the concept of "studying abroad" represents a complex relationship among mediascapes (the construct of information and perceptions about studying abroad), ideoscapes (political and social ideas about the value of studying abroad), finanscapes (the value ascribed to a foreign degree, and the ways in which money flows and influences the decisions to study abroad) and ethnoscapes (the role of mobile family members and friends who influence the students' decisions to change geographic locations). While offering a fascinating opportunity to examine just how educational programs and delivery might be influenced by these "scapes" to constitute an eduscape, internationalization-as-eduscape raises questions about the nature of educational programming in an international context. In educating to enhance intercultural and international skills and competencies, what are we trying to accomplish? The facilitated access to our universities feeds a larger desire for acquiring intercultural and international knowledge and skills, mostly from outsiders.

Looking at internationalization as an eduscape expands it from being simply an infusion of intercultural and international content into the learning, teaching, research and service areas of a university to being an understanding of the multiplicity of connections and flows that begin long before the student sets foot on the campus and are operational outside of the so-called "learning, teaching, research and service" areas of the university. Internationalization as eduscape situates the university in a larger flow of internationalizing forces and elements rather than as a focal point where activity begins and ends. The data point to international students as having a much larger role, as people who are already caught up in the process and who are actively seeking an internationalized identity through study abroad.

International Student Influence on Internationalization

As mentioned briefly in the introduction, university administrators and international program directors place high value on the presence of international students on the campus, citing it as the third highest influence on the internationalization of universities,[69] up there with organizational structures and mobility of Canadian students. Mestenhauser,[70] however, characterizes this interest as "utilitarian and instrumental":[71]

> It ... is ... the way that our pragmatic intellectual
> tradition does view the presence of foreign stu-
> dents. If in doubt that this is the case, just refer to
> the mission statements and publications and cata-
> logues of many of our "world class" universities
> that justify their "international ambience" on the
> ground that they have large numbers of foreign
> students from a specified number of countries who
> are great educational resources for our students.
> We usually do not hear more about how this
> ambience is accomplished, and what kind of learn-
> ing actually takes place. On the contrary, we hear
> with increasing frequency how they should be con-
> trolled, and how much of an economic value they
> represent to our countries.[72]

The participants in my study confirmed the premise that "their presence is undervalued, underappreciated, neglected and conceptually underdeveloped."[73] Mestenhauser reports that many studies about foreign students on North American campuses conclude that international students are often isolated, that interactions with domestic students are left to chance and are mostly superficial, and that they socialize for the most part with one another.[74]

Asked what impact they might be having on others, the students reported surface interactions where, for example, misconceptions about communism in China, or women in Iran were corrected, or office mates learned a few words of Farsi. Sushant was assertive about how he had to correct perceptions about his home city and India: *We are not backwards there. ... The lifestyle I led was way more lively than here — like in Mumbai the night life doesn't stop. It is much different than here, and it's hard for them to believe.* Lefty Blue was convinced that internationalization happens through the interaction of students, and acknowledged that his perceptions were influenced heavily by his international schooling experience in Norway, where students (all from different backgrounds) interacted intensively with one another, both in class and outside, rather than by his GU experience. He claimed that, by getting to know him, others in his classes could change their stereotypical views of Chinese students and what they do: *Wow! A Chinese student who talks and is in theatre. And doesn't like math!* He did conclude that this was happening *very slowly* and only with those with whom he was friends.

Do these interactions produce intercultural and international competence? While the jury is out on how this is for domestic students, my interest is in what was happening to the international students. From their accounts, they were becoming different persons in terms of the social relations and learning opportunities that were possible for them.[75] They gained enormous amounts of self-confidence and a sense of achievement in going through a rigorous process of preparation, test-taking and application. Contrast this with their first year after arriving at GU: an erosion of confidence for many of them, an intensification of the work required, isolation and an intense time of adjustment, away from familiar social and family networks of support. Their primary identification, what they wished to be known as, was as a math, physics or computing science student, a student of their discipline. Instead, they were often identified by staff, fellow students and faculty as "international students," marked by difference and, for many, by an overwhelming feeling of deficiency. In particular, for those who had difficulties with English, these reminders of deficiency were frequent as they were constantly positioned by their lack of facility in English in the classroom and outside. Although this experience varied among the students, some of the common themes were that they were limited in their choice of friends and in the time they had available to make new friends (except for the few who found residence life a success), limited by their vocabulary and comfort level in English, limited in their active participation in seminars and presentations, often essentialized as non-speakers of English, and constrained in their social relations.

Those who spoke of successful socialization were students such as Sushant, Jay, Samshul and Lefty Blue, who were fluent in English and outgoing in their personality.[76] David and Sherry also reported success with friends and school, but largely because of considerable efforts on their part. Others such as Chris, Little Onion, Long and Wayne were clear that their purpose was not socialization but academic goals.

A fairly common theme emerges across the narratives: the absence of consistent interaction and socialization with domestic students. Do international students contribute towards the internationalization of the university and, if so, in what ways? Without data from domestic students on their own perceptions of international students it is difficult to be definitive about the conclusion, but certainly from the perspectives of these students, few opportunities are presented to them to make that contribution: not in the classroom, not in regular interactions with fellow students, not with faculty members or staff. In fact, the culture of the campus encourages them to cluster in their own "international" groupings, thus reproducing the stereotyping of international students as being exclusive, not mixing with others and drawing boundaries around themselves.

It is interesting to see that students like Jay and Lefty Blue were constructing themselves consciously as being overtly non-international (*I don't feel international at all unless I am at an international event organized by the university* — Jay), or breaking the stereotypes, being *just* a student (Lefty Blue). This is in contrast with Long, for example, who said he feels *international all the time*. His explanation was of feeling *outside everything ... not really being part of it*. In other words, there appears to be a linkage between how "international" is experienced through difference, and when "international" is excluded from their self-identification.

An Academic Rationale?

I return now to the question I posed at the beginning of this chapter, regarding an academic rationale. I began by cautioning against the conviction that an academic rationale drives internationalization. From these student experiences, it does not appear that they are contributing towards the goals of internationalization or providing evidence of an academic rationale. However, the data are pointing to the conclusion that it was the international students *themselves* who were becoming internationally knowledgeable and interculturally competent. They have gone through application processes and endured protocols, selections and paperwork. They have moved to a new environment and dealt with challenges of housing, food and daily living. They have left established social networks and family and are learning to deal with new conditions not often supportive of their needs. They struggle through difficulty and, while some recognize their strength, some say it is learning to *ignore* the *hard things* (Long). They are meeting their goals, although in ways that are very different from what they envisioned when they first imagined themselves coming to Canada and to GU.

Was it worth it, then, to be in Canada at Good University? On the one hand, there was the feeling that there is *something lacking* (Parth), of a sense that the *image* of having a full and fulfilled life *hasn't come true* (Parth). As Shabnam reflected: *You can say I have all things I want like study, good program, good professor, good university and so maybe I should be happy.* So how do we and, more importantly, how do the students themselves, come to understand that, in spite of this lack of something, of not being completely happy, *[they] made a good decision to come* (Shabnam)?

The key perhaps lies in something that was common among all

the students: a strong belief that, in spite of the difficulty (where these difficulties were expressed), the loneliness and isolation in particular, and the *dark days*, the experience at GU was one of personal growth, change and increasing self-knowledge. Peter and Samshul were so grateful for the opportunity that GU gave them that they were spending their extra time in the department working with new students on projects to *give something back* to the university. The academic program has challenged Jay to stretch to the new heights of accomplishment of which she is so proud. A poignant description from Krystal even speaks to how she has created this as a place to which to belong:

> [On my first day] I walked [all] over the university. I walked up the stairs to the [Main Square], and up to the fourth stairs, and see the buildings and the view. I told my friends, you walked up all those stairs, one by one, and by the last one, you love this place.

GU, for all of them, was associated with opportunities that they never had before, of a chance to grow professionally, intellectually and personally, and this for them was the *goodness* to which they referred. The difficulty, hardship, the *something lacking*, the *level of noise* in their lives, the *dark days* were all *normal* personal hardship that no one can do anything about — something to be endured and overcome. These are the paradoxes they have come to accept as being associated with good decisions.

In practical terms, it became apparent that no assumptions can be made about the great variability of international learners and their needs. We need to become aware of the responsibilities and roles of all levels of the university in the learning and socializing processes of the learning environments in which international students seek to participate and experience a sense of belonging.

Indeed, students need to be seen in the context of the social and academic conditions and relationships that bound them.

More significantly, this study has confirmed for me a clear direction and sound basis for research. The conceptual framework allows for a comprehensive analysis of the social conditions and relationships in which internationalization takes place, and provides possibilities for transformation. Student experience yields rich data, and my experiences with and connections to the students have deepened my commitment to pursue this line of research.

15

From Critique to Contribution: Investigating the Purposes of Universities in an Age of Globalization

John Dwyer and Darryl Reed, York University[1]

Introduction

In order to fully appreciate the challenge confronting the contemporary university in the age of information and internationalization, forces that are intertwined, it is useful to begin by separating its core goal and essential role from its various functions. In practice, goals and roles are often inseparable from functions. But the capacity for *theoretical* separation is an analytical skill that a good university education should always foster, and it will serve us well in this discussion.

The Intellectual Goal, Public Role and Specific Functions of the Universities

Goal of the University

The traditional **goal** and *raison d'être* of the university is the pursuit or exploration of truth. The search for knowledge that is truthful, and not narrowly functional, is the thread that unites the medieval university with its modern counterpart. Whatever the status of this thing called "truth" in our postmodern society may be, and despite the contingencies between structures of knowledge and power, its *pursuit* is the overarching goal that makes sense of the university. The concept of truth, however, is not without its problems. The critical, postmodern and deconstructive undermining of the presumptions of reason, universality and foundationalism that the West has inherited from the Enlightenment suggests that we must: 1)speak of *truths* as partial and plural, 2)detach truth from the problematic concept cluster that is *modernity*, 3)replace instrumental rationality with participative deliberation, and 4)not only recognize but affirm *differences* within the human community.

truth-seeking must always be indeterminate and can never be completely neutral. It always needs to be able to interrogate or deconstruct itself. The appropriate stance of the professional seeker of truth, therefore, has to be **reflexive**. That stance requires three foundational propositions: 1)the cultivation of a self-reflection as an account of one's own presuppositions, 2)a critical edge that provides alternative possibilities, and 3)an openness to other viewpoints. In other words, truth-seeking has to consider its own origins, purposes, relations of means to ends and position with respect to other discourses. truth-seeking requires intellectual freedom and implies an interrogative or questioning stance to *whatever* is given as knowledge, including the *canonical* beliefs and artifacts of the academy and its disciplines.

Role of the University

The essential **role** of the university is to provide a legitimate space for the discussion and questioning of *everything*. It is imperative to underline that this questioning "without condition and without presupposition" is a public role and that the university itself, therefore, should be understood as an idealized public space for the unconditional discussion of *everything* that could be classified as *knowledge*.[2] There are three significant consequences that flow from this role: 1)the university should not become a corporation or the tool of corporations, 2)the university must seriously interrogate all questions but especially those that have to do with the question of humanity itself and 3)academic freedom is inseparable from civic responsibility in the broadest sense. The university represents an idealized *polis* that is coterminous with human flourishing.

To be sure, the university without restrictions or pressures has never existed, but that is not necessarily a bad thing. Relative powerlessness is part of the formula that allows universities to engage in reflexive learning and seek less tainted truths that can be communicated to various publics. While our vulnerability makes us an "exposed citadel," it also ensures that we do not fossilize into an "ivory tower." By their very nature, truth-seeking and perpetual questioning act as barriers to the assimilation of the university to the needs of the state or the marketplace. While the early modern state and the modern marketplace are dynamic forces that have had, and continue to have, an enormous impact on the evolution of university education, the university as an apex body has a different mandate and a unique agenda in terms of searching out new "truths" and making audible different and often critical viewpoints.[3] Our postmodern age may be witnessing the decline of the golden age of the intellectual but it cannot so easily jettison the intellectual's dialogic and critical functions. Despite all their internal tensions, universities have always proved themselves capable of astonishing bursts of intellectual energy and creativity. Even at their most vulnerable and tormented, universities continue to provide the tools for resistance, rethinking and reconstructing our internal and external worlds.

Functions of the University

Claims that the traditional university is in "ruins" typically focus on its "functions" rather than on the core meaning and role of the institution. There currently exists considerable confusion and conflict about what the primary function/functions of the university should be in this age of information and internationalization. Internal disputes and *turf wars* related to functionality have led some to suggest that the modern university should be understood as a *multiversity*. Internal confusions and conflicts are less troubling to us, however, than the external pressures pushing the university to: 1) focus on some functions at the expense of others and, what is much more dangerous, 2) subsume the university's goals and roles within a narrow band of functionality. The external *occupation* of the modern university is assisted and accelerated by administrative agendas that focus on functional efficiency. Perhaps the best argument for academic self-governance is the damage done to our common confession of faith — i.e., truth-seeking and the generation and sharing of new ideas — under the ruse of this kind of *restructuring*.

It makes sense to reiterate the complex *functions* of the university in order to appreciate why there must always be internal disagreements and to separate those from the more dangerous forces of commodification and corporatization that often lurk behind the banner of internationalization. The primary functions of the university are research, teaching, professional development and character formation. The functions of research and teaching would appear to be self-evident, but it is worth reminding ourselves that these are carried out by *professors* or a group that "professes" through their written and spoken discourse a belief in truth-seeking, questioning and communicating. Although they are not just professors and not so naive as to think that the university is an ideal discursive environment, they attempt to act *as if* such an ideal situation exists. Thus, their research and teaching is *responsible* and *responsive* to the extent that it contributes to a discursive community. For the same reason, the fabrication of research and the plagiarism of materials are considered to be the most serious internal challenges to communal integrity.

Developments in professional education have had the greatest impact on the character of the universities in the modern era. Whereas professional development once took place in diverse environments ranging from shops and offices to other institutions, since the late twentieth century, engineers, lawyers, teachers, nurses and managers of all kinds have found a more suitable access to expertise and resources within university communities. Professional training is obviously more applied and more closely related to the permutations of the occupational marketplace than the traditional liberal arts curriculum or the academic disciplines that emerged in the nineteenth century. Teachers and researchers in professional schools and faculties certainly face greater challenges in terms of truth-seeking and questioning professional assumptions or challenging conventional practices. Typically, professional development takes the form of learning expert systems, generating case studies, or imitating "best practices." We should not exaggerate the market dependence of these fields, however. They co-habit with the university for a reason and, to the extent that they merely mirror existing markets, they lose all credibility to providing creative leadership, even for those same markets. The real problem with the co-existence of disciplinary and applied programs is that it provides external forces, and internal administrative collaborators, with opportunities to move universities in more narrow and functionalist directions.

The spread of the disciplines in the nineteenth century and the professions in the twentieth century has obscured one of the traditional functions of universities — character formation and, especially, the virtues of active citizenship. Moral philosophy was a curriculum unto itself in eighteenth-century universities, one that related ethics to socio-political action. The roles of friend, family member, citizen and professional were, if not always perfectly united, at least connected. The twin forces of specialization and bureaucratization have artificially detached ethics from social responsibility, with clearly problematic effects for the professions. One of the exciting opportunities resulting from the recent *crises* in the professions is an "ethics boom" that shows no signs of diminishing.[4] It would be a shame if the interest in professional ethics does not stimulate a more general discussion of academic ethics and ethical agency. The unconditional pursuit of truth is only legitimate to the extent that it is balanced by a clear sense of responsibility to the public. Academic ethics needs to be more than "academic freedom in other words."[5]

The University in an Age of Globalization

The moral shallowness of our modern universities makes them suitable objects for hostile integration within a new global system engineered by transnational corporations and neo-liberal governments. This global economic agenda, typically articulated either as the transition from a Fordist to post-Fordist labour marketplace or from a fixed capital to a flexible information-driven economy, has to be conceptually separated from a broader process of internationalization that has been taking place at least since 1945. The neo-utilitarian definition of globalization transforms politics and culture into dependent variables of economics.[6] But internationalization is a complex process that cannot and should not be subsumed within a simple macro framework. It involves migration between countries; the development of cities that are connected as much to other parts of the world as to their own region; global cultural trends in fashion, cuisine and music; new class identifications based on international values; a developing cosmopolitanism of civil society and law; and a complex dialectic between de-territori-alization and regionalism that does not follow traditional geographical or national boundaries. Among the most striking new developments in this sphere of internationalization are: 1)the construction of virtual communities through the Internet, 2)the identification of the state and government with economic prosperity, 3)the "universalization of consumerism as an ideology," 4)the "carnivalization of culture," and 5)the increasing emphasis on "human rights" since 1948 when the Universal Declaration of Human Rights was created.[7]

Any serious academic assessment even of economic globalization needs to take into account its impact on a number of constituencies including socio-economic classes, unequal genders, increasingly disadvantaged and disempowered local communities, targeted racial groups, and exploited migrant workers. In its neo-liberal and corporate forms, what passes for *globalization* and is assumed to be immutable often conveniently ignores the following facts: 1)that women provide the low-waged workforce of the products sold by multinational corporations, 2)that migrant workers have been ghettoized by a Eurocentrism that is really market-driven neo-colonialism, 3)that the family structure in many cultures is being undermined by global imperatives and 4)that the new consumerism replaces cultural values with the kinds of psychic masturbation that may dull dissent but that offer no increase in happiness. Even by utilitarian standards, neo-utilitarianism would appear to be theoretically deficient.

University scholars who deal explicitly with international issues have a responsibility to resist the rhetoric of *globalization* and to expose the corporate cum neo-liberal agenda of world commodification. To the extent that they have a civic conscience, university researchers have an additional challenge of balancing their search for truth with an involvement in progressive causes, knowing full well that the current academic reward system does not typically favour engagement, even when confined to the classroom. Our focus here, however, is on the goal, role and function of the university *per se* rather than individual researchers or even those fields that confront globalization directly. Our concern is with the possible occupation of the university by a unilateral global corporate agenda. Our hope, however, lies in the opportunities that the broader processes of internationalization present for a richer and more imaginative dialogue that offers new modalities of action.

At present, universities are adopting a reactive posture rather than a principle or a "force of resistance."[8] There are two main ways in which contemporary universities are being co-opted into a global agenda that is imposed rather than freely chosen. The first relates to the pressures of globalization generally and involves the commodification of knowledge and the corporatization of the university. Information has become a prized commodity in the global age. Those organizations that have knowledge, especially technical and expert knowledge, are considered to have an enormous advantage in world markets. The extent to which the "information economy" is or may be a projection of bureaucratic normalization rather than a realistic description of today's economic system does not make it any less urgent as an external agenda. Universities are being pressured not only to produce and communicate "state of the art" information but also graduate students who are vessels of latest information.

The process of commodifying everything, including knowledge, is a corporate agenda. Corporations are not so much interested in the sharing or even exchange of information as they are in controlling and channelling information in ways that enhance profitability and power. As such, corporations privilege the information that is deemed most obviously usable by its systems, i.e., technical and managerial expertise. The new darling and favoured corporate model of university teaching and learning is the business school, historically an orphan in the university but now the new model of educational efficiency. But this special relationship is secondary to the broader corporate agenda for post-secondary education: the corporatization of the university. Despite the rhetoric of efficiency and accountability, it is difficult to see this process as anything other than an attempt to bring intellectual resources to heel, to limit the palate for teaching and learning, to apply the production formula to knowledge, and to measure knowledge in terms of system utility. The language of occupation projects the logic of the bureaucratic corporation on the university. Unfortunately, the ubiquity of this utilitarian and narrowly functionalist discourse dovetails with the "empire building" of ambitious university administrators and lends the corporatization of the university its air of inevitability and irreversibility.

The increasing convergence of corporations and universities is greatly assisted by the institutional embracement of *globalization*. Let's be absolutely clear about what is involved in this potentially fatal embrace. To the extent that any contemporary university or its faculty is relevant and progressive, internationalization will be part of its intellectual agenda. Therefore, it cannot be internationalization looked at critically and in the spirit of reflexive truth-seeking and public discussion that is being embraced. The internationalization of the university is an attempt to jump on a specifically corporate bandwagon of globalization, whether or not this bandwagon is being pushed by government funding agencies or pulled by senior university executives. The corporate connection and its terms of agreement are signed, sealed and delivered when chronically underfunded institutions or ambitious faculties attempt to brand themselves as "open" for global business.

An Alternative Vision of Internationalization

Leaving aside the question of whether or not the branding as an international or internationalizing university is a winning long-term strategy (bandwagon-hopping is notoriously unpredictable, and globalization could become passé), we would like to offer an alternative vision of internationalization based upon critical theory. Critical theory is an interdisciplinary framework that blends objectivist and subjectivist approaches or perspectives by: 1)illuminating the ways that "structures shape and constrain the actions of individuals and organizations," and 2)exploring new intersubjective fields of actions upon which more democratic alternatives can be built. Critical theorists point out that the current paradigm driving globalization not only privileges but also uncritically presumes a decidedly Eurocentric set of beliefs and institutional practices. While illuminating the ways that the evolution and interrelation of capital, technological and managerial structures have produced a version of globalization that is culturally biased, hegemonic and humanly limiting, discourse theorists such as Jürgen Habermas advocate approaches that organize and tap into the democratic resources of nonfoundational thinking. Foundational thinking is highly functionalist and privileges hegemonic political and economic systems. Nonfoundational thinking is not only human and democratic but also opens up many more discursive avenues for solving the difficult modern problems that we all face.

Critical theory challenges all of the "neo-utilitarian paradigms" that have contributed to the "orthodoxy of international theory."[9] It offers a reinvigoration of the democratic *polis* and its re-identification as a global arena for communicative action.[10] It reintegrates the connection between purposeful rationality and the human condition in terms of the quality of life rather than the quantity of production. It redirects the theme of human agency and emancipation, inherited from the Enlightenment, towards non-deterministic and non-universalistic outcomes. Whereas the nation-state was the locus of human improvement and civic freedom in the Enlightenment project, critical theorists imagine the international political arena as a more liberating domain for community building. That communal discussion depends entirely on mutual persuasion rather than the more rigid and reductionist requirements of raison d'état: "power, security, and deterrence."[11] In order to be legitimate, norms need to be based on an inclusive "dialogue" within and between communities that gives rise to consensual agreements.

Critical theory outlines a *possibility* for international relations and democratic communication that is far from being a reality. Conflict within communities was one of the problems that the nation-state was designed to solve, while the international state system was an attempt to balance power relations between national actors. While neither structure was able to achieve more than the maintenance of an uneasy and unequal status quo, nation-states legitimized their institutional and normative structures with reference to issues of practical significance. Admittedly, critical theorists have done a better job of exposing the power relations embedded in these structures than in providing more democratic alternatives. But Jürgen Habermas partially addressed the practical deficit by constructing the procedural steps though which "purposeful communicative action" should be legitimized. Essentially, Habermas presents a model of communicative rationality that: 1)is always public, 2)is continually open to reinterpretation, 3)never excludes or pre-empts discussion but builds in sophisticated publicity and public opinion measurements and mechanisms to ensure inclusiveness and 4)demands and depends on the systematic probing and challenging of evidence and arguments.

It is hardly surprising that many commentators on international politics find Habermas's account of the democratic potential of the public sphere *utopian*. In operational terms, the challenges are daunting, primarily because the most recognizably "open" forums for discussion (i.e., the United Nations or the European Economic Community) lack the public or accountability requirements that Habermas regards as essential. But, in their search for functional equivalents, what these and most other commentators have failed to appreciate is the way that real-life examples of "communicative engagement" and alternative models of "argumentative rationality" are developing in the new international arena. The activities of many NGOs, the renewed dynamism of civic society, and the spread of transnational issue networks would suggest that the Habermasian ideal type has considerable analytical significance for understanding alternative and epistemic communities. In any case, at present Habermas's emphasis on deliberation and communication is the most coherent and promising theory of international engagement for a new political order in which decisions based on exclusion and domination merely lead to the spiral of even greater coercion and inevitable resistance. While some of Habermas's universalist claims about procedural legitimacy have been criticized by postmodern theorists, the practical core of his theory is that everyone in society must be encouraged to enter into a dialogue that will restore the *lifeworld* and by implication revitalize civil society.

What is often overlooked is the unique position of the university in all this cogitation. The university is a public institution without an excess of the power that corrupts. It already embodies many of the discursive elements of the Habermasian ideal speech situation. It entertains a quite remarkable capacity for difference, and its characteristic productions are persuasive arguments that are required to be submitted for consensus. The university already has several of the normative characteristics of a genuine dialogic community, including freedom of speech, at least for tenured professors. The relationship between professors and students is one of mutual respect and communal endeavour, when not prostituted by the commodification of teaching and learning. The movement towards greater interdisciplinarity at York University, for example, reflects a more general and essentially Habermasian concern to problematize and process knowledge more inclusively than academic disciplinarity generally permits. What is perhaps most interesting is that, internally, the university is already re-imagining itself as a more internationally relevant institution by engaging in a reflexive critique of many of its own assumptions and practices. It is in the process of moving towards a less ethnocentric cosmopolitanism that nevertheless incorporates an appreciation for the identities and loyalties of particular communities.

Self-reflexive truth-seeking is well underway in the current university community and should be encouraged. It goes without saying that any attempt to hijack this dialogue within a neo-utilitarian version of globalization should be resisted. To the extent that university administrators are foisting this agenda on their institutions, they might want to consider that they are selling the university's birthright for a bowl of pottage. With respect to the role of the university as a "public" institution, most of our criticism should be directed at ourselves. Especially during periods characterized by complex change, it is incumbent upon all members of the academy to at least educate themselves and engage with global issues. To counter the power and oligopolistic tendencies of transnational corporations, those with international expertise need to communicate with the various relevant publics. Administrators at all levels can assist the communication process by readjusting the definition of productive knowledge in order to render the academic reward system more responsive to human needs (broadly defined). One measure of the failure of the university community to provide public leadership is the absence of connections with NGOs or other transnational networks.

To be a bona fide international university means much more than attracting foreign students, proclaiming diversity or even funding globally relevant projects. It must certainly go beyond a branding that has little to do with the product. It should offer a broader and less ethnocentric understanding of international processes than neo-utilitarianism. It will have absolutely no legitimacy if the university is seen to be an agent for the current corporate understanding of globalization. It cannot simply be a reactive critique of corporatization but must contribute to international dialogue and offer opportunities for change. While it cannot ignore the existing structures of economic cum bureaucratic power, it must attempt to break through the limitations of systemic models of agency — i.e., political, economic, technocratic — that transform flesh and blood human beings into predictable automata. In other words, it needs to provide the kind of knowledge that allows traditional and emerging communities to envision a wider variety of choices.

The university community should not change its functions. But its members might want to engage in a dialogue and collaborations that could recalibrate those functions in order to meet the challenges of internationalization. Without pre-empting that dialogue or those collaborations, here are some of the ways that critical theory could inform them:

1. Research needs to be **inclusive** of all possible discourses related to internationalization. Researchers with specialized expertise in uncovering public opinion have a responsibility to develop and refine those tools to put all possible discourses on the table of international dialogue, in particular the discourses of those communities who heretofore have been marginalized by globalization. In order to stimulate that dialogue, researchers need to develop and exploit all possible avenues for delivering information to the wider public, including the new communication tools such as the Internet. In order to play its public role, the contemporary university community must confront the issue of **publicity**. Control over the production and dissemination of information is the not so hidden agenda of those who want to restrict discourse within narrowly functionalist paradigms.

2. University teaching obviously needs to respond to the
   new challenges posed by migration and diversity in the
   classroom. But if university teachers want to be proactive
   in terms of promoting international discourse, they need
   to explore with their students the past and present experiences "not just of the opportunities posed by a globally
   interconnected world, but of the dangers and threats."[12]
   Students need to be provided with the critical and creative skills, in a safe learning environment, not only to
   interrogate their own presuppositions but to enter into
   dialogue with real or imagined others. Students need to
   suspend the limited but hegemonic values of commercial
   and consumerist communications, in order to navigate
   the multiplicity of discourses through which communities
   make sense of their own experiences. The discursive experiences of the vulnerable in the developing and
   underdeveloped world, and in our own society, need to
   be articulated and explored. Most important, the agency
   and engagement of our students needs to be affirmed in
   ways that support compromise and consensus but challenge all forms of coercion. Obviously, none of these
   objectives can be achieved if university teachers present
   themselves as authority figures or treat students as passive
   receptacles for information.

3. Academic specialization and professional education have
   obscured the character-building function of universities.
   Internationalization provides a welcome opportunity for
   reversing that trend, and it does so in an environment
   that militates against the ethnocentrism, institutional limitations and dogmatic excesses of the historical past. If
   our students are going to become global citizens, higher
   education has to develop competencies within a more

holistic framework.[13] In order for our students to play more complex roles in the international arena, we need to begin building the integrity or integrated character that can manage international diversity. It is important to reiterate that character is built through action, and especially through interaction, with other cultures. However, action and agency require a normative foundation. Internationalization has too often been conceived in terms of structures and strategies, whereas its core is cultural sensitivity. Critical theory can play a valuable role in developing the normative structure for inclusiveness and supporting the agency of global actors.

4. Global citizenship should be a function of all university education. It is crucial that those who are going to occupy professional positions of responsibility demonstrate good global stewardship. Today's doctors, lawyers, nurses, engineers, architects and artists interact with a variety of publics and serve as community role models. As members, they have input into the way their professions develop in terms of inclusiveness and hospitability to difference. The instructors and graduates of our business schools have a huge challenge and a particular responsibility to make the activities of transnational corporations more transparent, reflexive and sensitive to community building in the new global order. Here, more critical approaches have a valuable role to play in challenging the overly positivist and neo-utilitarian business strategies that tend to overlook the structural inequalities that are actually being exacerbated by globalization and which are all the more dangerous because they render the traditional fabric or national safeguards of communities obsolete. It is characteristic of the strategies of transnational corpora-

tions that they typically: 1)have little sense of the broader structural implications of their actions, 2)are unable to internalize adverse externalities in their business models and 3)unilaterally impose a reductionist, not to mention ethnocentric, interpretation of globalization that marginalizes a great deal of the discursive potential of internationalization.[14]

A number of possibilities exist for the inclusion of more broadly international perspectives in professional programs: 1)specific courses can be developed and offered in professional fields and disciplines, 2)units on internationalization can be built into core programs and 3) rofessionally relevant international courses incorporating sophisticated critical perspectives can be developed by scholars in other faculties/departments. The latter would be our preferred choice since it would: 1)alleviate the pressure on instructors in professional programs to adhere to so-called market realities, 2)encourage greater internal dialogue and consensus building between professional and liberal arts educators and 3)offset some of the financial inequities and corporatizing agendas associated with restructuring.

Conclusion

This paper has argued that *internationalization* is a much more complex process than most of what is discussed under the rubric of *globalization*. Dealing with internationalization at home and abroad requires more broadly based strategies and approaches than are offered by neo-utilitarian, neo-liberal or neo-realist approaches that are rooted in a more static state environment and a specific tradition of political economy. The authors have argued that a critical theoretical approach to internationalization could provide a valuable contribution. The self-reflective critical theories used to deconstruct the limited interpretation of globalization have a positive contribution to make in terms of a more inclusive international discourse and an open dialogue. Such a dialogue could allow traditional communities and their postmodern tribal counterparts[15] to reach outside themselves in order to develop the cultural sensitivities and inevitable compromises that, in turn, could lead to the creation of a legitimate global community. That global community or collaboration across boundaries would be one that not only tolerates but welcomes difference as a stimulus to exchange (in the broad sense) and change (in the dynamic sense).

We have explored the goal, role and functions of the university in ways that underline purposeful communicative action. We have found it necessary to remind administrators, and increasingly specialized and segregated scholars and professionals, that the traditional university, far from being irrelevant, is absolutely indispensable in an age when public discourse is impoverished, creative alterity reduced, and a more broadly human agency stifled, because of globalization's inability to generate meaningful evaluative norms or genuinely inclusive strategies. We have made a few suggestions about the way that the goal, role and functions of the university could be revitalized. Specifically, we have amended the search for truth to the search for "truths" that must always be open to negotiation. We have pointed out that the public role of the university needs to be more effectively managed and exploited to communicate a broader range of discursive choices than presently exists. We have tried to illuminate the ways in which the traditional functions of the university could be recast to provide our internal and external constituencies with the conceptual tools to build a more genuinely international community.

Internationalization and Higher Education Policy in Canada: Three Challenges

Glen A. Jones, Ontario Institute for Studies in
Education/University of Toronto

Introduction

Internationalization has become an important theme in national higher education policy in many jurisdictions.[2] The objectives of facilitating student mobility and providing new international opportunities for students underscore many of the major reforms currently taking place in Europe. Other European public policy initiatives have directly encouraged the internationalization of the curriculum through the support of joint degrees and have provided major support for new international research initiatives. American mechanisms for supporting research continue to provide the infrastructure associated with attracting and funding a significant number of international graduate students, and the Simon Study Abroad Act represents a strategic national approach to facilitating study abroad opportunities for undergraduate students.[3] Australia has devoted considerable attention to increasing its share of the international student market, and higher education has now become one of that country's leading industries. China has made substantive investments designed to increase the international experience of faculty, support the development of international partnerships and fund strategic research initiatives.

Some Canadian governments have also taken steps to facilitate or encourage international activity within the higher education sector. Several provinces provide support for international student mobility,[4] and different departments of the Government of Canada operate international scholarship and mobility programs.[5] The plethora of arrangements and initiatives emerging within individual universities includes major curriculum reform projects, funding development initiatives, encouraging international research partnerships and marketing international programs.[6]

Nonetheless, it is difficult to argue that internationalization has been anything like the driving force or major theme within Canadian higher education policy that it has within many other jurisdictions. My objective in this paper is to explain why internationalization has received so little attention within higher education policy in this country.[7] I will argue that the discussion of internationalization and higher education policy in Canada has faced three basic challenges during the last three decades: the challenge associated with the Canadianization movement of the 1970s; the challenge associated with Canada's federal structures and our decentralized approach to higher education policy; and the fear that international activities and initiatives will displace national activities and initiatives. I will conclude by offering a number of modest suggestions for change.

The Challenge of Canadianization

The first step towards understanding the strange intersection between internationalization and higher education policy in Canada is to recall that forty years ago the great debate was on the

"Canadianization" of Canadian universities. The centennial cele-
brations and Expo '67 in Montreal had awakened a new sense of
nationalism within Canadian society, but a series of reports and
polemics raised serious questions about whether the Canadian education system was teaching Canadians about Canada. A 1968
report of the National History Project, based on observations at
over 900 schools, revealed that there was surprisingly little Canadian content in our elementary and secondary schools.[8] In their 1969
book *The Struggle for Canadian Universities*, Mathews and Steele
argued that the mammoth expansion of higher education enrolment during the prior decade had largely been accomplished by
hiring foreign (most frequently American) professors.[9] How could
these institutions fulfill their social and cultural role when they were
staffed by individuals who knew little about Canadian history, politics or culture?

Within a few years the issue was taken up by the Association of
Universities and Colleges of Canada when it appointed Thomas
Symons, the founding president of Trent University, to review the
state of Canadian studies. In his detailed report, *To Know Ourselves*,
Symons concluded that there was much work to be done to increase
the coverage of Canadian topics and perspectives within the university curriculum and to strengthen Canadian scholarship on
Canadian studies.[10] As in any academic discussion, there were differences of opinion over how best to solve the problem, and there
continues to be a debate over the origins and influences associated
with what some have called the Canadianization movement.[11]

There was, however, little disagreement over the two components of the problem. The need for new professors by the rapidly
expanding Canadian higher education system far outpaced the
domestic output of graduates from doctoral programs, and in some
cases graduates with credentials from élite American institutions
were viewed as more qualified than their Canadian counterparts.
Claude Bissell, the president of the University of Toronto, wrote:

In our colonial heart of hearts, we believed that
advanced degrees from Harvard, Stanford, Michigan, and California, glowed more brightly than
advanced degrees from McGill, Toronto, Alberta,
and British Columbia. I think that attitude is
changing and we now have confidence in what we
can do ourselves.[12]

The second component of the problem, obviously related to the
first, was that not enough emphasis was being placed on the study
of Canada in Canadian schools and universities. More attention
needed to be paid to the study of Canada and those things Canadian within the humanities (including the study of Canadian
literature, art and history) and in the rapidly expanding social
sciences.

In many respects the Canadianization movement within higher
education was in tune with, and occasionally intersected, the nationalist public policy direction of the Trudeau era. Canada's foreign
policy was recast as an extension of domestic interests.[13] Canada's
cultural, social and economic interests needed to be protected. The
federal government moved to provide financial support for Canadian studies, the protection of cultural industries including the arts
and publishing, and, eventually, to create employment policies that
strongly affirmed the importance of employing Canadians except in
situations where no Canadian was qualified for the position.

I believe that the quite limited discussion of internationalization
within higher education policy during the 1970s and most of the
1980s, and the ways in which this discussion were taken up, can
largely be explained by the emphasis on Canadianization that
emerged in the late 1960s and continued until the Mulroney government shifted the policy discussion in the direction of free trade
in the context of global economic markets. The arguments for

Canadianization were not anti-internationalist, they were based on the assumption that it was extremely important for Canadians to understand who they were in relation to the rest of the world; the notion was to ensure that there was a clear focus on Canadian studies to complement the other perspectives, albeit largely American and British, that were already well represented in the curriculum.

With the recession of the 1970s the academic labour market shifted dramatically; the expansion of graduate programs and enrolment in the 1960s was now producing more doctoral graduates than the higher education system could absorb. There was little public sympathy for employing the best of the world's academic talent in Canada if it meant that the best Canadian talent would be underemployed or unemployed. There was nothing wrong with introducing Canadian students to concepts and ideas from other nations and cultures as long as it was Canadian citizens who were studying and teaching these concepts and ideas.

This is not to suggest that the Government of Canada had become isolationist and introverted. With its new emphasis on serving domestic interests, Canadian foreign policy under Trudeau was striking out in quite new directions. Canada strengthened its membership in francophone international organizations, developed new ties with Southeast Asia, and was one of the first Western countries to open relations with communist China. New international relationships frequently involved higher education sector components such as bilateral scholarship agreements or development initiatives. As Trilokekar notes, the biggest international academic relations initiative to emerge during this period was the development of the Canadian Studies Program Abroad which, in many important respects, linked the domestic Canadianization and international agendas to support the study of Canada in foreign countries.[14]

Given this context, there was little Canadian government interest in supporting major new initiatives that would further the international dimensions of Canadian higher education. The social/cultural rationale for internationalization[15] was simply over-shadowed by a nationalist agenda that favoured investments in Canadian studies, bilingual programs, and the development of a Canadian academic publishing infrastructure.

The Challenge of Federalism

Canada is a federation operating under a constitution that assigns authority over certain matters to a federal government and over others to provincial governments. As in other federations, constitutional responsibility for education is assigned to the provincial governments on the assumption that issues of curriculum and educational standards should respond to local needs.

In most other federations, higher education has come to be viewed as an issue of national importance, and steps have been taken to strengthen the role of the federal government in regulating a sector that now plays a key role in national economic development. In other words, while education continues to be viewed as a sector that should be regulated at the local level, higher education has been increasingly viewed as a distinct policy area that should be either governed centrally/nationally or should be governed through some form of shared authority relationship between the central and local governments.

The Canadian approach to higher education policy, in contrast, is the most decentralized of any nation in the developed world. There has never been a federal ministry of education or higher education, and there has never been a federal higher education policy framework.[16]

This does not mean that the federal government is not involved in higher education policy. In fact, it was the Government of Canada that initiated and largely funded the massification of the university sector in the post-war period. The veterans' benefit program provided a mechanism for a substantial expansion of access to post-secondary education funded under a system of direct federal grants to universities. In response to provincial concerns over federal interference in an area of provincial responsibility, the direct grants to universities were initially replaced by conditional, and later unconditional, transfer grants to the provinces.

In addition to providing core support for higher education through transfer programs, the federal government is also involved in wide range of policy areas that are directly related to higher education, including student financial assistance, research and development, cultural and language policy initiatives and human resource development. Since there is no ministry with explicit responsibility for higher education, federal involvement in the sector can be defined as the sum of the policy initiatives associated with a range of federal government departments.

The current Canadian reality of federalism has two very important implications for the discussion of internationalization in the context of Canadian higher education policy. The first, and perhaps the most obvious, is that there is no Canadian higher education policy and there is no clear mechanism to develop Canadian higher education policy. In its recent analysis of post-secondary education in Canada, the Canadian Council on Learning (CCL) concluded:

> Canada currently has no means to establish the national PSE objectives to which it aspires. It has not even reached the first step — the ongoing evaluation of national progress — that would indicate our seriousness about this pan-Canadian priority. If Canada is serious about improving educational outcomes for Canadians to stimulate economic growth, increase Canada's international competiveness and enhance social cohesion, it must develop and utilize appropriate tools to expedite this task.[17]

The CCL report identifies an important problem in the development of higher education policy, but it also serves to illustrate the dynamic tension between the federal government and the provinces that underscores this problem. In 1966 the Government of Canada began to develop an education support branch within the Department of the Secretary of State. As Cameron notes, "the prospect of a federal office of education was, of course, anathema to the provinces, and they were finally galvanized into taking defensive action."[18] The provinces moved quickly to establish the Council of Ministers of Education of Canada (CMEC) as a forum for interprovincial communication and coordination. The conclusion articulated in the above quotation from the CCL report can, therefore, be viewed as a not-so-subtle critique of the CMEC's failure to move towards pan-Canadian objectives and its work to develop national performance indicators. At the same time, it is important to remember that the Canadian Council on Learning is a somewhat controversial creation of the federal government that is supported by Human Resources and Skills Development Canada (HRSDC). It is, in other words, a federally supported body that is arguing for a much stronger national policy perspective in an area of provincial responsibility.

The second implication is that in the absence of a federal ministry of higher education and since the provincial governments are responsible for regulating and providing direct operating support for higher education, the federal government approach has been fragmented, with authority for a range of policy areas that directly intersect with the post-secondary sector dispersed to different departments and units.[19] A range of federal government departments support internationalization initiatives. The Department of Foreign Affairs and International Trade supports international scholarship programs, international marketing initiatives and the Canadian Studies abroad initiatives. HRSDC supports academic mobility programs. Other relevant departments and agencies include Industry Canada, Citizenship and Immigration Canada, and the Canadian International Development Agency. Under this fragmented approach the coordination of federal government initiatives in the area of internationalization, like other areas of post-secondary policy, becomes enormously challenging.[20] It is difficult for any single government unit or department to advocate for a strong, coherent policy for internationalization given the realities of departmental territoriality and unit rivalries,[21] and because internationalization is an umbrella concept that captures a wider range of initiatives that transcend the operational boundaries of any single federal department.

The Canadian federal arrangements, therefore, are far from conducive to the development and emergence of something resembling a national strategy for internationalization. In reality, what one might term "Canadian" policy for internationalization is essentially the sum of initiatives emerging from the provinces and a range of federal government units.

The Fear of Displacement

In the mid-1980s when the Government of Australia was initiating a series of policy changes that were to reposition international student enrolment as a major form of revenue generation within the higher education system,[22] the Canadian provinces were considering the question of foreign student fees. The ways in which these policy issues were framed in each country could not have been more different. In Australia the objective was to create an environment where institutions could increase international enrolment as a market activity. In Canada the question was whether international students should continue to pay the domestic student tuition fee and receive an education subsidized by provincial taxpayers or whether they should be charged a tuition fee that more accurately reflected the real cost of their education. The Australian conversation was about revenue; the Canadian policy discussion was really about the level of subsidy.

The two dominant themes in provincial government policy for higher education during the 1970s, 1980s and 1990s were to increase accessibility while stabilizing or reducing operating grants to institutions. The Canadian approach to higher education that had emerged by the early 1970s was centred around a network of relatively homogeneous publicly supported universities serving local geographic areas.[23] The vast majority of undergraduate students attended a university that was close to home, and the universities generally treated Canadian degrees as equivalent in terms of quality. There was no formal stratification of institutions, and there was limited competition between institutions since provincial governments generally treated universities as equals and the provinces controlled the two largest sources of institutional revenue: operating grants and tuition. The common threads linking provincial policies across the country in this context were to increase access to post-secondary education while tightly controlling operating grant allocations. Generally speaking, participation rates increased, government grants stabilized or increased modestly, and universities across the country complained bitterly about underfunding. One provincial civil servant, interviewed for the Stuart Smith review of university education released in 1991, noted "Our approach is just to starve the buggers to death and hope they'll react as we'd like."[24]

The issue of international student fees became intertwined with these dual policy themes of access and funding. If international students paid the same level of fees as domestic students, then it meant that international students were being subsidized by provincial taxpayers at the same level as domestic students. If universities were underfunded and unable to admit every student who applied, then provincial governments might be subsidizing an international student who was taking the place of a domestic student. There was nothing wrong with international students, as long as their presence in the system did not come at the expense of the local, domestic agenda of the provincial higher education system. The answer was to charge international students a much higher fee than domestic students but also to control the level of this fee through provincial regulation so that institutions would not compete with each other for international students. One-by-one, provincial governments reviewed tuition fee regulations and introduced foreign student fees.

The concern that the international might displace the local did not go away with the introduction of differential fees. In one revision to its complicated funding formula, the Ontario government created a mechanism for pooling and sharing international fee revenues so that there would be no financial advantage to an institution if it were to admit a larger number of international students than its peers. This approach was later abandoned by the Harris government in its re-regulation of tuition policy, but in early 2003, with the domestic demands of the double cohort raising issues of access throughout the Ontario system, the message from the government was to increase domestic enrolment, even if it meant reducing the number of international students that would be admitted to the system.

While some other countries came to view international students as an opportunity to generate revenue that could be used to subsidize other university activities, the concern underscoring elements of Canadian public policy in the sector was that the international could potentially displace the local. There were fears that international students would take part-time jobs away from domestic students, so international student visas prevented students from being employed off-campus. Even as attitudes changed in the early years of the twenty-first century and both federal and provincial governments began to see the possibilities associated with the international market in higher education, the actual level of government support to the sector for internationalization has been extremely modest, with the exception of Québec, which has viewed international student mobility and the support of international research as components of a broader economic/cultural agenda.

The fear of displacement was never limited to the issue of international students. Domestic students who want to study abroad have never had access to the financial support mechanisms available to students who decide to study in Canada. Graduate students who win major national competitive scholarships are, with few exceptions, required to study at Canadian universities. Until quite recently, Canada's research granting councils have provided limited support for comparative research projects involving international teams of scholars. The emphasis has been to support Canadian scholarship of international quality rather than on the participation of Canadian scholars in international projects. There are signs that this may be changing, but there continue to be concerns that since the level of funding is finite, every dollar spent in the support of international research activity, or every dollar spent supporting a Canadian student studying abroad, means one dollar that has not been spent within the domestic higher education system.

Moving Forward

I believe that these three challenges help to explain why internationalization has received so little attention within higher education policy in Canada. The Canadianization movement, while far from oppositional to the internationalization of research and curriculum, began with the assumption that it was the Canadian, not the international, perspective that needed reinforcement as the nation moved into its second century. Canada's federal arrangements are not conducive to the development of the sorts of national policies and strategies that have emerged in many other jurisdictions, and there are even basic challenges associated with the notion of coordinating initiatives across federal government departments, let alone between federal and provincial levels of government. Until quite recently, in a number of policy areas there has been a fear that the international will somehow displace the national or local, a perception that can have political salience.

These three factors have clearly not prevented individual institutions from focusing attention on internationalization, or individual governments from taking important (though frequently small) steps towards supporting elements of internationalization. Universities have always had an international dimension, though this has frequently reflected the international activities and interests of individual faculty and students. Elements of internationalization have also been institutionalized at the level of the academic unit with the support of area/international studies, inclusive/international curricula and international partnerships and exchange programs. Some Canadian universities have come to view internationalization as a strategic institutional objective.[25] However, there are clearly limitations to what can be done without some degree of coordinated effort or policy coherence. Individual universities cannot afford to open international offices to promote communications and partnerships and so they need to coordinate with the Government of Canada, which already maintains an infrastructure of embassies and consulates. They can facilitate exchange and mobility programs, and the Association of Universities and Colleges of Canada can provide some degree of coordination across the sector, but not to a level that might be possible if there were a national framework or if this were a federal government priority.

Moving forward begins with the understanding that internationalization should be an objective within Canadian policy for higher education because it is in the national interest. Underscoring the major investments in the internationalization of higher education in other jurisdictions is the recognition that this is an issue of domestic policy, though different countries have pursued quite different strategies and approaches. In contrast, the Canadian discussion of internationalization seems to take place at the margins rather than at the centre. The recent review of post-secondary education by the Canadian Council on Learning has very little to say about internationalization, and the goals for post-secondary education set out in the report have few points of intersection with the objectives of internationalization.[26] Reports at the provincial level — including recent reviews in both Ontario and British Columbia[27] — go much, much farther, but there is no evidence of anything approaching a national discussion, let alone a national policy objective. The discussion and debate on internationalization seems to be primarily local (issues of curriculum within departments and faculties, student mobility initiatives at the institutional level) or, at best, provincial.

In my opinion, moving forward means positioning the discussion of internationalization as a major issue of domestic higher education policy. The discussion of internationalization needs to be linked to domestic policy goals in the context of a diverse, multicultural Canadian population participating in an increasingly global economy. Internationalization can be regarded as a means of significantly contributing to, rather than displacing, the local. We need to recognize that our domestic objectives for higher education would be furthered by greater pan-Canadian coordination. It is only by recognizing the national potential of internationalization as a means of addressing domestic objectives that it will become a central, rather than marginal, area of higher education policy.

Of course, a national discussion of internationalization means far more than simply talking about the Australian success in the international student market or about European accomplishments in second-language programming and student mobility. We need to study, understand and compare the national policy approaches that have emerged in other jurisdictions, not so that we can replicate them but rather so that we have a greater sense of the various possibilities. We need to find a Canadian approach that makes sense in the context of our decentralized higher education system and that addresses Canada's domestic objectives. We need to find an approach that builds on Canada's strengths and values, and moves us forward in terms of improving post-secondary education in Canada.

Notes

Chapter 1

[1] A. Luijten-Lub, M. van der Wende & J. Huisman, "On Cooperation and Competition: A Comparative Analysis of National Policies for Internationalization of Higher Education in Seven Western European Countries," *Journal of Studies in Higher Education* 9, no. 2 (2005), 147-63.

[2] The notion that the *international* is about politics and the *global* is about economics is widespread in popular usage. Arguably, this reflects the fact that cross-border economic relationships, and the ideologies and other cultural forms supporting global markets, appear to be "thicker" and more extensive than do cross-border political relations. Unlike, say, the financial system, global politics appears not as one system but as pre-global jostling between separated nation-states premised on autarkic sovereignty.

[3] J-C. Smeby & J. Trondal, "Globalization or Europeanization? International Contact Among University Staff," *Higher Education* 49 (2005), 449-66.

[4] A. Welch, "Going Global? Internationalizing Australian Universities in a Time of Global Crisis," *Comparative Education Review* 46, no. 4 (2002), 433-71.

[5] J. Knight, "Internationalisation Remodeled: Definition, Approaches, and Rationales," *Journal of Studies in Higher Education* 8, no. 1 (2004), 11.

[6] U. Teichler, "The Changing Debate on Internationalization of Higher Education," *Higher Education* 48 (2004), 5-26.

[7] D. Held, A. McGrew, D. Goldblatt & J. Perraton, *Global Transformations: Politics, Economics and Culture* (Stanford: Stanford University Press, 1999).

[8] M. Castells, *The Rise of the Network Society* (Oxford: Blackwell, 2000).

[9] See also N. Fligstein & F. Merand, "Globalization or Europeanization? Evidence on the European Economy Since 1980," *Acta Sociologica* 45 (2002), 7-25.

[10] I. Kaul, I. Grunberg & M. Stern, eds., *Global Public Goods: International Cooperation in the 21st Century* (New York: Oxford University Press, 1999); I. Kaul, P. Conceicao, K. le Goulven & R. Mendoza, eds., *Providing Global Public Goods: Managing Globalisation* (New York: Oxford University Press, 2003).

[11] S. Marginson, "The Public/Private Divide in Higher Education: A Global Revision," *Higher Education* 53, no. 3 (2007), 307-33.

[12] M. Kaulisch & J. Enders, "Careers in Overlapping Institutional Contexts: The Case of Academe," *Career Development International* 10, no. 2 (2005).

[13] P. Scott, "Massification, Internationalization and Globalization," in *The Globalization of Higher Education,* ed. P. Scott (Buckingham: The Society for Research into Higher Education/Open University Press, 1998), 108-29.

[14] J. Enders & E. de Weert, "Science, Training and Career: Changing Modes of Knowledge Produc-

tion and Labour Markets," *Higher Education Policy* 17 (2004), 145.

[15]H.J.J.G. Beerkens, *Global Opportunities and Institutional Embeddedness: Higher Education Consortia in Europe and Southeast Asia* (Center for Higher Education Policy Studies, University of Twente, 2004). Retrieved February 10, 2006 from http://www.utwente.nl/cheps/documenten/thesis-beerkens.pdf.

[16]S. Marginson & E. Sawir, "University Leaders' Strategies in the Global Environment: A Comparative Study of Universitas Indonesia and the Australian National University," *Higher Education* 52, no. 2 (2006), 343-73.

[17]Kaulisch & Enders, "Careers in Overlapping Institutional Contexts."

[18]M. Van der Wende, "The International Dimension in National Higher Education Policies: What Has Changed in Europe in the Last Five Years?" *European Journal of Education* 36, no. 4 (2001), 432.

[19]Held et al., *Global Transformations*, 2.

[20]A. Appadurai, *Modernity at Large* (Minneapolis: University of Minnesota Press, 1996); Marginson & Sawir, "University Leaders' Strategies."

[21]S. Marginson & G. Rhoades, "Beyond National States, Markets, and Systems of Higher Education: A Glonacal Agency Heuristic," *Higher Education* 43 (2002), 281-309.

[22]G. Neave, "Editorial: Academic Freedom in an Age of Globalization," *Higher Education Policy* 15 (2002), 332.

[23]Of the major social theorists of the nineteenth century, only Marx in the *Grundrisse* anticipated contemporary globalization. At the beginning of the 1850s, he correctly linked the formation of an ever-expanding world market with the process of reduction in the turnover time of economic capital, tending towards zero, via the automation of production and circulation. Anticipating instantaneous screen-based global markets, this was extraordinarily prescient. K. Marx, *Grundrisse*, trans. M. Nicolaus (Harmondsworth: Penguin, 1973).

[24]Marginson, "The Public/Private Divide in Higher Education."

[25]P. Samuelson, "The Pure Theory of Public Expenditure," *Review of Economics and Statistics* 36, no. 4 (1954), 387–89; J. Stiglitz, "Knowledge as a Global Public Good," in *Global Public Goods: International Cooperation in the 21st Century*, eds. I. Kaul, I. Grunberg & M. Stern (New York: Oxford University Press, 1999), 308-25.

[26]S. Marginson & M. Considine, *The Enterprise University: Power, Governance and Reinvention in Australia* (Cambridge: Cambridge University Press, 2000).

[27]Teichler, "The Changing Debate," 21.

[28]Marginson & Sawir, "University Leaders' Strategies."

[29]Teichler, "The Changing Debate."

[30]Ibid., 23. No doubt this reflects not just the ideological overload of market-speak in universities

as elsewhere, and the culture of economism in public life, but also a certain lacuna in cultural reflexivity. We are both saturated in signification and formed in continuous reflexivities (N. Rose, *Powers of Freedom,* Cambridge: Cambridge University Press, 1999); yet the tools of critical reflexivity have been largely turned inward into the self rather than outward into the intersubjective and public realms.

[31]Smeby & Trondal, "Globalization or Europeanization," 453.

[32]Van der Wende, "The International Dimension in National Higher Education Policies," 433; D. Teferra, "Brain Circulation: Unparalleled Opportunities, Underlying Challenges, and Outmoded Presumptions," *Journal of Studies in International Education* 9, no. 3 (2005), 234-35. Arguably the universalizing potential of e-learning is as yet little realized because of inflated ideologies, poor business plans and the pedagogical inadequacy of the early mono-cultural prototypes. S. Marginson, "Don't Leave Me Hanging on the Anglophone: The Potential for Online Distance Education in the Asia-Pacific Region," *Higher Education Quarterly* 58, no. 2 & 3 (2004), 74-113.

[33]M. Castells, *The Internet Galaxy: Reflections on the Internet, Business and Society* (Oxford: Oxford University Press, 2001).

[34]Though there is some debate in the literature about whether the Internet functions as a stimulus to face-to-face relations or a substitute for them (for example, Scott, "Massification," 118), the weight of evidence suggests that electronic networking increases the necessity for meetings, conferencing and exchange visits. For example, as Smeby & Trondal state in relation to Norway: "Despite the advent and rapid development of electronic publishing facilities and computer-mediated communication, personal contact seems to have become increasingly important. One reason may be that these types of contact are mutually reinforcing." ("Globalization or Europeanization," 456). Between 1991 and 2000 in Norway, while research project collaboration increased by 18 percent, *journeys* related to research collaboration increased by 67 percent (Smeby & Trondal, "Globalization or Europeanization," 457).

[35]Teferra, "Brain Circulation," 232.

[36]For example, Smeby & Trondal remark that, between 1991 and 2000, the proportion of Norwegian scientific publications in English or another foreign language rose from 62 to 71 percent, and the proportion of faculty members publishing at least one publication in a foreign language rose from 65 to 80 percent, while noting that there remained some variation in language use between fields. In the hard sciences and medicine, the use of English is dominant. In the social sciences in 2000, only about half of all publications were written in a foreign language, though between 1991 and 2000, the proportion of faculty with at least one publication in a foreign language rose from 49 to 73 percent (Smeby & Trondal, "Globalization or Europeanization," 459).

[37]C. Musselin, "Towards a European Academic Labour Market? Some Lessons Drawn from Empirical Studies on Academic Mobility," *Higher Education* 48 (2004), 55-78; C. Musselin, "European Academic Labour Markets in Transition," *Higher Education* 49 (2005), 135-54.

[38]J. Valimaa, "Nationalisation, Localization and Globalization in Finnish Higher Education," *Higher Education* 48 (2004), 29.

[39]P. Altbach, "Centers and Peripheries in the Academic Profession: The Special Challenges of Developing Countries," in *The Decline of the Guru: The Academic Profession in Developing and Middle-Income Countries,* ed. P. Altbach (Chestnut Hill: Boston College, 2002), 1-22; A. Toakley,

"Globalization, Sustainable Development and Universities," *Higher Education Policy* 17 (2004), 311-24.

[40]However, higher education policy in the developing world is shaped by the World Bank; arguably, the Washington-based bank is a de facto American agency. The US government controls the appointment of its president.

[41]It could also be argued that Europeanization (though like Americanization premised on a sectional, in this case regional, global strategy, not a worldwide interest) is less aggressively sectional than is Anglo-Americanization. Western European nations more consistently support multilateralism, donate much more foreign aid as a share of GDP than does the US, and tend to focus on aid projects designed to build local agency in developing nations.

[42]Fligstein and Merand remark that, if trade is the measure, "much of what people call 'globalization' is in fact 'Europeanization'…The main effect of the EU's political project has been to increase dramatically trade within Western Europe." The nations of Western Europe are responsible for almost half of all world trade and almost 70 percent of their exports end up in other West European nations. Fligstein and Merand argue that economic globalization should be understood not as a single worldwide process but as a set of different processes of interaction, including regional integration. The formation of singular regional markets is facilitated by collaboration between states (Fligstein & Merand, "Globalization or Europeanization?" 8-10, 13, 21).

[43]Luijten-Lub et al., "On Cooperation and Competition."

[44]J. Enders & E. de Weert, eds., "The International Attractiveness of the Academic Workplace in Europe – Synopsis Report," in *The International Attractiveness of the Academic Workplace in Europe*, eds. J. Enders & E. de Weert (Frankfurt: Herausgeber und Bestelladresse, 2004), 27.

[45]Teichler, "The Changing Debate," 18-19.

[46]Enders & de Weert, "The International Attractiveness of the Academic Workplace," 27.

[47]Enders & de Weert, "The International Attractiveness of the Academic Workplace," 146.

[48]S. Avveduto, "International Mobility of PhDs," in *Innovative People: Mobility of Skilled Personnel in National Innovation Systems* (Paris: OECD, 2001), 243-60. See more discussion in S. Marginson, "Dynamics of National and Global Competition in Higher Education," *Higher Education* 52, no. 1 (2006), 1-39.

[49]*The Economist*, "The Brains Business," September 8, 2005.

[50]Shanghai Jiao Tong University Institute of Higher Education (SJTUIHE), *Academic Ranking of World Universities* (2005). Retrieved February 1, 2006 from http://ed.sjtu.edu.cn/ranking.htm.

[51]Note that the Jiao Tong data tend to favour large comprehensive universities that are strong in the science-based disciplines. These are mainly found in the US, UK, Canada, Japan and parts of Western Europe. SJTUIHE, *Academic Ranking of World Universities* (2005).

[52]Organisation for Economic Co-operation and Development (OECD), *Internationalization and Trade in Higher Education: Opportunities and Challenges* (Paris: OECD, 2004); OECD, *Education at a Glance* (Paris: OECD, 2005).

[53]D. Gupta, M. Nerad & J. Cerny, "International PhDs: Exploring the Decision to Stay or

Return," *International Higher Education* 31, no. 8 (2003). Retrieved February 10, 2006 from http://www.bc.edu/bc_org/avp/soe/cihe/newsletter/News31/text008.htm.

[54]OECD, *Dynamizing National Innovation Systems* (Paris: OECD, 2002), 49.

[55]K. Tremblay, "Academic Mobility and Immigration," *Journal of Studies in International Education* 9, no. 3 (2005), 208-09. Also see the more detailed breakdown by field of study for 1997 in M. Regets, "Research and Policy Issues in High-skilled International Migration: A Perspective with Data from the United States," in *Innovative People: Mobility of Skilled Personnel in National Innovation Systems* (OECD: Paris, 2001), 253.

[56]Gupta et al., "International PhDs."

[57]S. Vincent-Lancrin, "Building Capacity Through Cross-Border Tertiary Education," paper prepared for the UNESCO/OECD Australia Forum on Trade in Educational Services, October 11-12, 2004, 32. Accessed on February 10, 2006 at http://www.oecd.org/dataoecd/43/25/33784331.pdf.

[58]Tremblay, "Academic Mobility and Immigration," 208.

[59]D. Guellec & M. Cervantes (2002), "International Mobility of Highly Skilled Workers: From Statistical Analysis to Policy Formulation," in OECD, *International Mobility of the Highly Skilled* (OECD: Paris, 2002), 92.

[60]Guellec & Cervantes, "International Mobility of Highly Skilled Workers," 82. According to the Open Doors data for 2004-05, 43.6 percent of foreign graduate students, in all categories, not just doctoral students, are supported by the US college or university with another 10.5 percent supported by the home country university or by government or private sponsors. Institute for International Education, *Data on U.S. International Education* (2006). Retrieved February 1, 2006 from http://www.iie.org/.

[61]*Academe, Annual Report on the Economic Status of the Profession, 2003-2004*. Retrieved February 10, 2006 from http://www.aaup.org/surveys/04z/alltabs.pdf.

[62]Enders & de Weert, "The International Attractiveness of the Academic Workplace," 18.

[63]M. Lee, "The Academic Profession in Malaysia and Singapore: Between Bureaucratic and Corporate Cultures," in *The Decline of the Guru*, 156-58.

[64]S. H. Lee, "The Changing Academic Workplace in Korea," in *The Decline of the Guru* 182.

[65]C. Marquis, "Universities and Professors in Argentina: Changes and Challenges," in *The Decline of the Guru*, 69.

[66]Altbach, "Centers and Peripheries," 18-19.

[67]Musselin, "Towards a European Academic Labour Market," 58.

[68]Tenure also is by no means the only element in play: there is no evidence that countries with a fixed contract system have higher mobility than those with tenure (Enders & de Weert, "The International Attractiveness of the Academic Workplace," 29).

[69]However, it is shorter than in Germany, where the average age of tenure is 42 compared to 35-37

in the US; and faculty are required to complete a second Ph.D. (the Habilitation) to qualify for a professorial position (Kaulisch & Enders, "Careers in Overlapping Institutional Contexts," 135). Further, between initial appointment and tenure, Germany faculty have less control over the directions of their research than do their counterparts in the US. C. Musselin, "Internal Versus External Labour Markets," *Higher Education Management and Policy* 15, no. 3 (2003), 13. The introduction of junior professorships and merit pay in Germany (Musselin, "Internal Versus External Labour Markets," 19) are designed to compensate for the existing incentives to leave German faculty employment for universities abroad or for non-faculty employment.

[70]M. Kweik, "The Academic Workplace: Country Report Poland," in *The International Attractiveness of the Academic Workplace in Europe*, 342, 346.

[71]Guellec & Cervantes, "International Mobility," 91.

[72]Guellec & Cervantes, "International Mobility," 88.

[73]E. Berning, "Petrified Structures and Still Little Autonomy and Flexibility: Country Report Germany," in *The International Attractiveness of the Academic Workplace in Europe*, 177.

[74]Ibid. Berning also suggests that, to prospective German doctoral students, the non-university research institutes can be more attractive than the universities.

[75]Altbach, "Centers and Peripheries," 4-5.

[76]Altbach, "Centers and Peripheries," 10.

[77]R. Skeldon, "Introduction," in *Migration and the Labour Market in Asia: Recent Trends and Policies* (Paris: OECD, 2003), 12.

[78]Vincent-Lancrin, *Building Capacity*.

[79]Those policies have drawn much of their strength from the opportunity structures generated by national economic success. "Countries that have succeeded in fostering the return of skilled migrants have done so not just through specific return migration programs but through long-term and sustained efforts to build the national innovation infrastructure," including industrial policy and investments in public R&D capacity (Guellec & Cervantes, "International Mobility," 92). For Taiwan, see Y.-L. Luo & W.J. Wang, "High Skill Migration and Chinese Taipei's Industrial Development," in *International Mobility of the Highly Skilled* (Paris: OECD, 2002), 253ff.; S. H. Lee, "The Changing Academic Workplace in Korea, 233ff. A primary focus of government in both Taiwan and Korea was to create incentives to secure the return of expatriate faculty and the return of foreign-trained doctoral graduates (Skeldon, "Introduction," 12-13), including salary subsidies. However it should also be noted that the benefits of skilled diasporas can be exaggerated: there is no clear evidence they *necessarily* contribute to the economic development of the nation of origin (Vincent-Lancrin, *Building Capacity*, 32). Nations such as Mexico have also made some educational gains from mobility, including a rapid increase in the proportion of faculty with doctorates (Vincent-Lancrin, *Building Capacity*, 18). At present China is a clear net loser from brain drain (Z. Guochu & L. Wenjun, "International Mobility of China's Resources in Science and Technology and its Impact," in *International Mobility of the Highly Skilled*, Paris: OECD, 2002, 195-97), but it is hoped the strength of the economy and the development of the higher education sector will turn this around.

[80]One case in point is Nigeria; M. I. Barrow & F. E. Ukeje, "The Academic Workplace in a

Changing Environment: The Nigerian Scene," in *The Decline of the Guru*, 378.

[81]R. Adams, "International Migration, Remittances, and the Brain Drain: A Study of 24 Labour-Exporting Countries," *Policy Research Working Paper* 3069 (Washington: The World Bank, 2003); this is not the place to discuss the pros and cons of brain drain/brain circulation in detail, but see OECD, *Internationalization and Trade in Higher Education: Opportunities and Challenges* (Paris: OECD, 2004); Vincent-Lancrin, *Building Capacity*.

[82]Altbach, "Centers and Peripheries in the Academic Profession," 7-9.

[83]It was probably reached in the early 1990s, when the full impact of the Internet began to unfold in higher education at the same time as foreign graduate stay rates increased dramatically. This was the era of Clinton globalization characterized by a pronounced and simultaneous liberalization of culture and information, people movement and trade.

[84]G. Rhoades, *Managed Professionals* (New York: SUNY Press, 1998); *Academe, Annual Report on the Economic Status of the Profession, 2003-2004*.

[85]WTO/GATS, World Trade Organization Web site on *Negotiations on the General Agreement on Trade in Services (GATS) in Relation to Educational Services* (2005). Retrieved September 11, 2005 from http://www.wto.org/english/tratop_e/serv_e/education_e/education_e.htm.

[86]Enders & de Weert, "The International Attractiveness of the Academic Workplace," 26.

[87]OECD, *Internationalization and Trade in Higher Education*, 35.

[88]OECD, *Quality and Recognition in Higher Education*, 19.

[89]OECD, *Quality and Recognition in Higher Education*, 160.

[90]OECD, *Service Providers on the Move: A Closer Look at Labour Mobility and the GATS*, Working Party of the Trade Committee (TD/TC/WP 2001)26/FINAL (Paris: OECD, 2002), 28.

[91]OECD, *Education at a Glance*, 273.

[92]OECD, *Education at a Glance*, 257.

[93]OECD, *Internationalization and Trade in Higher Education*, 31-37.

[94]OECD, *Internationalization and Trade in Higher Education*, 266.

[95]However, more than one-quarter of Germany's "foreign students" are residents, mostly the children of migrant workers not granted citizenship. OECD, *Education at a Glance*, 254.

[96]OECD, *Education at a Glance*, 253.

[97]Institute for International Education, *Data on U.S. International Education*.

[98]OECD, *Education at a Glance*, 250-73.

[99]OECD, *Education at a Glance*, 267.

[100]Australian Education International (AEI), Statistical data. Accessed October 4, 2005 at http://aei.dest.gov.au/AEI/MIP/Statistics/StudentEnrolmentAndVisaStatistics/Default.htm.

[101]S. Hatekenaka, *Internationalism in Higher Education: A Review* (UK: Higher Education Policy Institute, 2004), 12. Accessed February 10, 2006 at http://www.hepi.ac.U.K./pubdetail.asp?ID=150&DOC=Reports.

[102]Department of Employment, Education and Training (DEST), *Selected Higher Education Statistics* (2005). Retrieved August 20, 2005 from http://www.dest.gov.au/sectors/higher_education/publications_resources/statistics/default.htm.

[103]Institute for International Education, IIE (2006), Data on US international education. Accessed February 1, 2006 at http://www.iie.org/.

[104]DEST, *Selected Higher Education Statistics.*

[105]Institute for International Education, IIE (2006), Data on US international education. Accessed February 1, 2006 at http://www.iie.org/.

[106]DEST, *Selected Higher Education Statistics;* Institute for International Education, IIE (2006), Data on US international education. Accessed February 1, 2006 at http://www.iie.org/.

[107]DEST, *Selected Higher Education Statistics.*

[108]A. Deumert, S. Marginson, C Nyland, G. Ramia & E. Sawir, "Global Migration and Social Protection: The Social and Economic Security of Foreign Students in Australia," *Global Social Policy* 5, no. 3 (2005), 329-52.

[109]T. Mazzarol & G. Soutar, "'Push-Pull' Factors Influencing Foreign Student Destination Choice," *The International Journal of Educational Management* 16, no. 2 & 3 (2002), 82-91.

[110]Market research available to the author, not in the public domain.

[111]See K. Tremblay, "Academic Mobility and Immigration," *Journal of Studies in International Education* 9, no. 3 (2005), 210-12.

[112]S. Marginson, "Higher Education Reform in Australia — An Evaluation," in *Globalisation and Reform in Higher Education,* ed. H. Eggins (Buckingham: SRHE/Open University Press, 2003), 133-63.

[113]Marginson & Considine, *The Enterprise University.*

[114]J. Dawkins, *Higher Education: A Policy Discussion Paper* (Australian Government Publishing Service: Canberra, 1997).

[115]DEST, *Higher Education: Report for the 2004 to 2006 Triennium* (2004). Retrieved May 24, 2005 from http://www.dest.gov.au/sectors/higher_education/publications_resources/profiles/higher_education_report_2004_2006_triennium.htm, 31.

[116]DEST, *Selected Higher Education Statistics.*

[117]S. Marginson, "Trends in the Funding of Australian Higher Education," *The Australian Economic Review* 34, no. 2 (2001), 205-15.

[118]DEST, *Selected Higher Education Statistics.*

[119]The UK and New Zealand also adopted a commercial approach to foreign students and have rapidly increased market revenues, but in both nations public expenditure on education institutions increased in 1995-2002. Public expenditure in 2002 was 72.0 percent of total expenditure in the UK, 62.5 percent in New Zealand and 48.7 percent in Australia (OECD, *Education at a Glance,* 198).

[120]OECD, *Education at a Glance,* 193.

[121]OECD, *Education at a Glance,* 175, 187.

[122]DEST, *Selected Higher Education Statistics.*

[123]Deumert et al., "Global Migration and Social Protection."

[124]Australian Universities Quality Agency (2006). Retrieved February 18, 2006 from http://www.auqa.edu.au/.

[125]SJTUIHE, *Academic Ranking of World Universities.*

[126]L. Butler, "Explaining Australia's Increased Share of ISI Publications — The Effects of a Funding Formula Based on Publication Counts," *Research Policy* 32, no. 1 (2003).

[127]According to Butler, between 1988 and 1998, Australia's share of publications in the *Science Citation Index* increased by 25 percent, but its share of citations declined from sixth in a ranking of eleven OECD countries in 1988 to tenth place by 1998, and there was a widening gap to ninth place. "Australia's increase in output appears to be at the expense of impact." (Butler, "Explaining Australia's Increased Share of ISI Publications," 147). One reason was that a growing proportion of Australian articles were published in lower status journals. These achieved the same public funding within Australia as high status journals and were easier to access.

[128]G. Davis, *Regulating Universities: An Assumption and Three Propositions* (paper for the Melbourne Institute/The Australian Conference on "Sustaining Prosperity," University of Melbourne, 2005), 1. Retrieved May 22, 2005 from http://www.unimelb.edu.au/speeches/glyndavis1april05.pdf.

[129]Marginson, "Higher Education Reform in Australia."

[130]DEST, *Higher Education: Report for the 2004 to 2006 Triennium,* 95.

[131]B. Nelson, *Our Universities: Backing Australia's Future* (Australian government: DEST, 2003). Retrieved December 18, 2004 from www.dest.gov.au/highered/index1.htm.

[132]Ibid.

[133]D. Kirp, *Shakespeare, Einstein and the Bottom-line: The Marketing of Higher Education* (Cambridge: Harvard University Press, 2004).

[134]World Bank comparison based on purchasing power parity across nations. See note accessed October 6, 2005 at http://www.worldbank.org/data/quickreference/quickref.html.

[135]M. Clyne, *Australia's Language Potential* (Sydney: UNSW Press, 2005).

[136] OECD, *Internationalization and Trade in Higher Education*, 215-20

[137]R. Naidoo & I. Jamieson, "Empowering Participants or Corroding Learning? Towards a Research Agenda on the Impact of Student Consumerism in Higher Education," *Journal of Education Policy* 20, no.3 (2005), 267-81.

Chapter 2

[1]J. Enders & U. Teichler, *Der Hochschullehrerberuf im internationalen Vergleich* (Bonn: Bundesministerium für Bildung, Wissenschaft, Forschung und Technologie, 1995).

[2]K. Hahn, "German Universities in the Process of Globalisation, Europeanisation and Internationalisation," in *On Cooperation and Competition II: Institutional Responses to Internationalisation, Europeanisation and Globalisation*, eds. J. Huisman & M. Van der Wende (Bonn: Lemmens, 2005), 19-38.

[3]See U. Teichler, "The Changing Debate on Internationalisation of Higher Education," *Higher Education* 48, no. 1 (2004), 5-26; K. Hahn & U. Teichler, "Internationalization Mainstreaming in German Higher Education," in *Globalization and Higher Education*, eds. Arimoto Akira, Huang Futao & Yokoyama Keiko (Hiroshima: Research Institute for Higher Education, Hiroshima University), 39-66.

[4]Cf. Bundesministerium für Bildung, Wissenschaft, Forschung und Technologie, *Die Attraktivität deutscher Hochschulen für ausländische Studenten* (Bonn: BMBF, 1997).

[5]U. Teichler, *ERASMUS in the SOCRATES Programme: Findings of an Evaluation Study* (Bonn: Lemmens, 2002).

[6]K. Hahn, *Die Internationalisierung der deutschen Hochschulen* (Wiesbaden: VS Verlag für Sozialwissenschaften, 2004).

[7]Cf. K. Hahn, "Germany," in *On Cooperation and Competition: National and European Policies for the Internationalisation of Higher Education*, eds. J. Huisman & M. Van der Wende (Bonn: Lemmens, 2004), 51-79; Hahn & Teichler, "Internationalization Mainstreaming."

[8]Deutscher Akademischer Austauschdienst (DAAD), "Auf dem Weg zur internationalen Hochschule: Drittes Aktionsprogramm des DAAD 2004-2010" (Bonn: DAAD, mimeo, 2004).

[9]Cf. B. Kehm & U. Teichler, "Introduction of Bachelor and Master Study Programmes in Germany: Considerations in the European Context," in *Bachelor and Master Courses in Selected European Countries Compared with Germany*, eds. Bettina Alesi et al. (Bonn and Berlin: BMBF, 2005), 23-36.

[10]DAAD, Auf dem Weg zur internationalen Hochschule.

[11]DAAD, *International Degree Programmes in Germany 2005/2006* (Bonn: DAAD, 2005).

[12]DAAD and HRK, eds., *Cross-Border Education and Development Co-operation* (CD-ROM), (Bonn, 2005).

[13]See DAAD, *Informationen zu den rechtlichen Rahmenbedingungen für Einreise und Aufenthalt von ausländischen Studierenden und Wissenschaftlern* (Bonn: DAAD, 2005).

[14]Federal Ministry of Education and Research, *Basic and Structural Data 2005* (Bonn and Berlin: BMBF, 2005), 89-92.

[15]M. Kelo, U. Teichler & B. Wächter, *EURODATA: Student Mobility in European Higher Education* (Bonn: Lemmens, 2006), 57.

[16]Deutsche Forschungsgemeinschaft, *Förder-Ranking 2003. Institutionen – Regionen – Netzwerke* (Bonn: DFG, 2003).

[17]Cf. DAAD, *Wissenschaft weltoffen 2005,* 64-65.

[18]DAAD, *Wissenschaft weltoffen 2005,* 66.

[19]W. Isserstedt & K. Schnitzer, *Internationalization of Higher Education. Foreign Students in Germany. German Students Abroad* (Bonn: Federal Ministry of Education and Research, 2005).

[20]Hochschul-Informations-System, *EUROSTUDENT Report 2005: Social and Economic Conditions of Student Life in Europe 2005* (Hannover: HIS, 2005).

[21]Hahn, "Germany," 61.

[22]DAAD, *International Degree Programmes in Germany 2005/2006,* 6.

[23]F. Maiworm & B. Wächter, *English-Language-Taught Degree Programmes in European Higher Education* (Bonn: Lemmens, 2002), 28.

[24]S. Schwarz-Hahn & M. Rehburg, *Bachelor and Master in Deutschland: Empirische Befunde zur Studienstrukturreform* (Münster: Waxmann, 2004), 82.

[25]Cf. DAAD and HRK, *Cross-Border Education;* Hahn, "Germany"; K. Hahn & U. Lanzendorf, eds., *Wegweiser Gloabilisierung – Hochschulsektoren in Bewegung: Länderanalysen aus vier Kontinenten zu Marktchancen für deutsche Studienangebote* (Kassel: Wissenschaftliches Zentrum für Berufs- und Hochschulforschung der Universität Kassel, 2005).

26 Deutsche Forschungsgemeinschaft, *Förder-Ranking 2003*

Chapter 3

[1]R. Farquhar, "Can Canada Get Its Act Together in International Education?" (paper presented at a Canadian Information Centre for International Credentials event, n.d.).

[2]R. Farquhar, *Advancing the Canadian Agenda for International Education* (Ottawa: CBIE, 2001),

[3]This paper will refer to the department with its former title, Department of Foreign Affairs and International Trade (DFAIT), although the department was split into two different departments, the Department of Foreign Affairs Canada (FAC) and the Department of International Trade

Canada (ITC) in 2004 through Bill C-32. As of 2006, the two departments have once again been merged. See Department of Foreign Affairs (March 2006). Retrieved in March 2006 from http://www.fac-aec.gc.ca/department/menu-en.asp.

[4]*Canada : At a Crossroads for International Education in the New Millennium,* briefing paper prepared by coalition group of the Association of Universities and Colleges in Canada (AUCC), the Association of Canadian Community Colleges (ACCC), the Canadian Bureau for International Education (CBIE), International Council for Canadian Studies (ICCS), World University Service of Canada (WUSC) and the Fulbright Foundation, for the Government of Canada (Ottawa, October 20, 1997); Conference Board of Canada, *The Economic Implications of International Education for Canada and Nine Comparator Countries: A Comparison of International Education Activities and Economic Performance,* report prepared for the International Cultural Relations Bureau, DFAIT (September 27, 1999). Retrieved from http://www.conferenceboard.ca/nbec/pdf/report3.pdf; Farquhar, *Advancing the Canadian Agenda*; Executive Summary, "Turning the Forces of Globalization to Our Advantage: An International Learning Strategy for Canada" (report prepared by coalition partners, AUCC, ACCC, CBIE, WUSC, ICCS and the Canada-US Fulbright Commission (Ottawa, October, 1998).

[5]See "Canada's International Cultural Relations" (Department of External Affairs, 1979); Public Works and Government Services Canada, "Report of the Special Joint Committee Reviewing Canadian Foreign Policy," *Canada's Foreign Policy: Principles and Priorities for the Future* (Ottawa, November 1994); S. Joyal, "International Cultural Affairs, Higher Education and Scientific Cooperation. Refocusing Canada's International Cultural Policy in the Nineties: Issues and Solutions," report to the Minister of Foreign Affairs, Department of Foreign Affairs and International Trade (Ottawa: DFAIT, 1994); Government of Canada, DFAIT Information Services, "Canada in the World" (Ottawa, 1995); Canada, "Government Response to the Recommendations of the Special Joint Parliamentary Committee Reviewing Canadian Foreign Policy" (Ottawa, 1995); Canada, Canada's International Policy Statement, *A Role of Pride and Influence in the World Commerce* (Ottawa, 2005).

[6]B. Kettner, *"Canadian Federalism and the International Activities of Three Provinces: Alberta, Ontario and Quebec"* (unpublished Master's thesis, Simon Fraser University, 1980); J.D. Allison, "Federalism, Diplomacy and Education: Canada's Role in Education-Related International Activities, 1960-1984" (unpublished Ph.D. dissertation, University of Toronto, 1999).

[7]M. Rudner, "Canada and International Education in the Asia Pacific Region," in *Canada Among Nations 1997, Asia Pacific Face-Off,* eds. F. Hampson, M. Molot & M. Rudner (Ottawa: Carleton University Press, 1997), 211-32; J. Graham, "Third Pillar or Fifth Wheel? International Education and Cultural Foreign Policy," in *Canada Among Nations, 1999. A Big League Player,* ed. F. O. Hampson, M.Hart & M. Rudner (Ontario: Oxford University Press, 1999), 137-54; J.R. Saul, "Culture and Foreign Policy" (n.p., n.d.).

[8] R. D. Trilokekar, "Federalism, Foreign Policy and the Internationalization of Higher Education: A Case Study of the International Academic Relations Division, Department of Foreign Affairs and International Trade, Canada" (unpublished Ph.D. dissertation, University of Toronto, 2007).

[9]DFAIT, "Brochure on International Academic Relations" (n.d.) Retrieved in March 2006 from http://www.dfait-maeci.gc.ca/culture/iear/contacts-en.asp.

[10]J. Nye, "Soft Power and Higher Education, Forum for the Future of Higher Education." Retrieved in November 2005 from http://www.educause.edu/ir/library/pdf/FFP0502S.pdf.

[11]Farquhar, *Advancing the Canadian Agenda*, 1. See also Stewart Fraser, ed., *Government Policy and International Education* (New York: John Wiley & Sons, 1965).

[12]J. Knight, "Internationalization Remodeled: Definition, Approaches and Rationales," *Journal of Studies in International Education* (Spring 2004), 11.

[13]In the late 1960s and early 1970s, the Bureau of Public Affairs within DEA had three divisions under it — the information, cultural and historical — the academic relations section being under the information bureau,and the cultural affairs bureau having responsibility for international exchange agreements.

[14]Department of Foreign Affairs, "The Department in History" (February 2, 2005). Retrieved in November 2005 from http://www.dfait-maeci.gc.ca/hist/menu-en.asp; G. Wright, "Mitchell Sharp: Legacy of a Foreign Policy Icon," *International Journal* (Summer 2004). Retrieved in November 2005 from http://proquest.umi.com/pqdweb?index=15&did=726710221&Srchmode=1&sid=3&Fmt=.

[15]National Archives of Canada, Government Archives Division, Records of the Department of External Affairs, RG 25, "Report on Visits To Ontario Universities To Discuss Academic Relations," vol. 10992, file 57-14-1, acc no. 205484 (September 1, 1967); National Archives of Canada, Government Archives Division, Records of the Department of External Affairs, RG 25, "Academic Relations in State Department" vol. 10992, file 57-14-2, acc no. 205485 (September 21, 1972); National Archives of Canada, Government Archives Division, Records of the Department of External Affairs, RG 25, "Academic Relations in FCO," vol. 10991, file 57-14-CAC-72, acc no. 216053 (January 17, 1973).

[16]National Archives of Canada, Government Archives Division, Records of the Department of External Affairs, RG 25, "Relations Between the Department And the Canadian Academic Community," vol. 10991, file 57-14-1, acc no. 205483 (March 1966-August 1967).

[17]Under Prime Minister Trudeau, a new foreign policy document titled "The Foreign Policy for Canadians" was published in 1974 and this document marked a radical change in foreign policy orientation making Canada's national interest paramount, and defining foreign policy as "the extension abroad of national policies." Trudeau emphasized a new rationale of cultural diplomacy as a mechanism to distance Canada from the overpowering influence of the US. He initiated the counterweight policy and promoted relations with the USSR, Europe and Asia.

[18]J. Graham, "Recent Growth of Interest in Canadian Studies Abroad," *International Perspectives: Journal of Foreign Policy* (Ottawa, 1976).

[19]Department of Foreign Affairs and International Trade, "About Canadian Studies History" (April 27, 2006). Retrieved in May 2006 from http://www.cdnstudies.ca/a_aboutCS/menu-en.html.

[20]National Archives of Canada, Government Archives Division, Records of the Department of External Affairs, RG 25, "Review of the Programme of International Cultural Relations" (November, 1982), 18.

[21]See Council of Ministers of Education, Canada Web site (March 17, 1986). Retrieved in August 2005 from http://www.cmec.ca/international/ententes.en.stm.

[22]Council of Ministers of Education, Canada, Federal-Provincial Consultative Committee on Education-Related International Activities (FPCCERIA), "Background Notes" (May 14, 1992), 1.

[23]For full description of reports, refer to National archives of Canada, Government Archives Division, Records of the Department of External Affairs, RG 25, "Evaluation of International Cultural Relations," vol. 18351, File 55-1, acc. no. 212731 (October 19, 1990); National Archives of Canada, Government Archives Division, Records of the Department of External Affairs, RG 25, "Discussion Paper ICR," vol. 18351, File 55-1, acc. no. 220132 (March 1991); National Archives of Canada, Government Archives Division, Records of the Department of External Affairs, RG 25, "Dysfunctions in the Cultural Sector," vol. 18351, File 55-1, acc. no. 224668 (n.d.).

[24]Canada, DFAIT Information Services, "Canada in the World" (Ottawa, 1995).

[25]The Government of Canada had made a commitment to the Prosperity/Learning Initiative and, in 1991, had released — under the auspices of the Departments of Employment and Immigration, Industry and Science and Technology — two green papers titled "Learning Well, Living Well" and "Prosperity Through Competitiveness." Both papers initiated "a national, consensus-building discussion on targets and priorities for learning in Canada," with the aim to strengthen and "increase national prosperity and create more employment opportunities for Canadians." See Canada, Parliament of Canada, *Green Papers* (June 30, 2005). Retrieved in April 2006 from http://www.parl.gc.ca/Information/about/related/Federal/papers/index.asp?

[26]Department of Foreign Affairs, "The International Dimensions of Higher Education in Canada Collaborative Policy Framework" (draft discussion paper, May 1994), ix.

[27]*Intermistic* is a term used by the division; see C. Greenshields, *Public Diplomacy, International Education and You* (March 2-3 2006). Retrieved April 2006 from http://international.yorku.ca/global/conference/canada/papers.htm.

[28]E. Potter, "Canada and the New Public Diplomacy," in *Discussion Papers in Diplomacy* (Netherlands: Institute of International Relations, n.d.). Retrieved March 2006 from http://www.clingendael.nl/publications/2002/20020700_cli_paper_dip_issue81.pdf.

[29]The geographization in 1983 further complicated matters as some of the ICR roles, such as the Canadian studies program, were transferred from the division to the program departments within the geographic bureaus. Although this was an attempt by the department to streamline policy coordination, since it did not completely dissolve the division it contributed towards further confusion in roles and responsibilities within the department. In the 1990s, the Asia-Pacific branch initiated the CEC network and became active in the marketing of Canadian higher education in that region, further complicating the roles and responsibilities of the different divisions within the department.

[30]E. Sheffield, "National Educational Planning in a Federal State: A Sketch of the Canadian Experience," *Educational Planning* 1, no. 3 (January 1975), 64-75.

[31]Joyal, "International Cultural Affairs;" Conference Board of Canada, *The Economic Implications*.

[32]A. Cohen, *While Canada Slept: How We Lost Our Place in the World* (Toronto: McClelland & Stewart Ltd., 2003).

[33]Ibid.

[34]Ibid.

[35]See A. Cooper, *Canadian Culture: International Dimensions* (Toronto: Canadian Institute of International Affairs, 1985), 19.

[36]As elaborated by J. Knight, "A Shared Vision? Stakeholders Perspectives on the Internationalization of Higher Education in Canada," *Journal of Studies in International Education* (Spring 1997), 27-45.

[37]For a comparative analysis of country approaches see Trilokekar, "Federalism, Foreign Policy and the Internationalization of Higher Education."

[38]J. Enders & O. Fulton, "Blurring Boundaries and Blistering Institutions: An Introduction," in *Higher Education in a Globalising World*, eds. J. Enders & O. Fulton (Netherlands: Klumer Academic Publishers, 2002), 4.

[39]DFAIT, "A Role of Pride and Influence in the World," Apparent contradiction of Canadian Education Centres program described in previous paragraph.

Chapter 4

[1]C. Savage, *The National Report on International Students in Canada 2001/2* (Ontario: Canadian Bureau for International Education, 2005).

[2]G. Tillman, *Internationalization of Advanced Learning: Toward a Planning Framework* (Ontario: Association of Canadian Community Colleges, Association of Universities and Colleges of Canada, Canadian Bureau for International Education, 1997); M. Bloom et al., *The Economic Implications of International Education for Canada and Nine Comparator Countries: A Comparison of International Education Activities and Economic Performance* (Ontario: The Conference Board of Canada, 1999); R. Farquhar, *Advancing the Canadian Agenda for International Education: Report of the Millennium Consultation on International Education* (Ontario: The Canadian Bureau for International Education, 2001).

[3]S. Trimble, *Manitoba's International Education Branch* (PowerPoint presentation at Canadian Education Centre Network Conference, November 2005).

[4]Government of Manitoba, *Mandate of International Education Branch*. Retrieved on December 14, 2005 from http://www.gov.mb.ca/ie/public/intl_branch.html.

[5]Trimble, *Manitoba's International Education Branch*.

[6]Ibid.

[7]Government of Manitoba, *Reaching Beyond our Borders* (2005). Retrieved on March 1, 2006 from http://www.gov.mb.ca/international/executive_summary.html.

[8]S. Trimble, *Manitoba's International Education Branch*.

[9]Alberta Learning, *Alberta's International Education Strategy* (Edmonton: Alberta Learning, 2001).

[10]Ibid., 3.

[11]Government of Alberta, *Today's Opportunities, Tomorrow's Promise* (2004). Retrieved on April, 2005 from http://www.gov.ab.ca/home/index.cfm?page=757.

[12]C. Savage, "Profile of Alberta's Post-Secondary International Education Sector" (unpublished report, Alberta Advanced Education).

[13] Alberta Advanced Education, *International Education Action Plan* (2005). Retrieved on December 14, 2005 from http://www.advancededucation.gov.ab.ca/IntlEd/ActionPlan.pdf.

[14]Ibid.

[15]"Internationalization is the process of integrating an international, intercultural, or global dimension into the purpose, functions or delivery of higher education." J. Knight, "Updating the Definition of Internationalization," *International Higher Education* 33, no. 1 (2003), 1.

[16]A. Francis, *Facing the Future: The Internationalization of the Post-Secondary Institutions in British Columbia* (British Columbia: British Columbia Centre for International Education, 1993); J. Knight, *Internationalization: Elements and Checkpoints* (Ontario: Canadian Bureau for International Education, CBIE Research Series No. 7, 1994); K. McKellin, *Anticipating the Future: Workshops and Resources for Internationalizing the Post-Secondary Campus*, 2nd ed. (British Columbia: British Columbia Centre for International Education, 1996); H. de Wit, *Internationalization of Higher Education in the United States of America and Europe: A Historical, Comparative and Conceptual Analysis* (Connecticut: Greenwood Press, 2002).

[17]Francis, *Facing the Future*; Knight, *Internationalization*; McKellin, *Anticipating the Future*; de Wit, *Internationalization of Highehr Education*.

Chapter 5

[1]The Conseil supérieur de l'éducation (CSE) is a government body whose mandate is to advise Québec's Minister of Education, Recreation and Sports on matters relating to the development of education in Québec, from preschool to the university level, including adult education. Briefs on university affairs are drafted with the assistance of its Commission on University Education and Research, most of whose members work in the Québec university system.

[2]All the data for this section were taken from a CSE brief published in Fall 2005, "*Internationalization: Supporting the Dynamism of Québec's Universities.*" The brief in French and its abridged version in English are available online at www.cse.gouv.qc.ca.

[3]H. de Wit, *Internationalization of Higher Education in the United States of America and Europe* (Westport: Greenwood Press, 2002), 10.

[4]M. Green & J. Knight, *Cross-Border Post-Secondary Education in North America* (Trondheim: Organisation for Economic Co-operation and Development, 2003), 5-6.

[5]S. Bond & J. Lemasson, eds., *A New World of Knowledge: Canadian Universities and Globalization* (Ottawa: International Development Research Centre, 1999).

[6]L. Ferretti, *L'université en réseau: les 25 ans de l'Université du Québec* (Sainte-Foy: Presses de l'Université du Québec, 1994).

[7]In February 2005, the Ministère de l'Éducation changed its name to Ministère de l'Éducation, du Loisir et du Sport (Ministry of Education, Recreation and Sports). In this paper, we refer to "the ministry."

[8]Ministère des Relations internationales, *Québec's International Policy: Working in Concert* (Québec: Ministère des Relations internationales, 2006), 29.

[9]Ministère des Relations internationales, *Québec's International Policy.*

[10]J. Leclerc, *L'aménagement linguistique dans le monde* (Québec: Université Laval, 2000). Retrieved June 2006 from www.tlfq.ulaval.ca/axl/index.shtml.

[11]Conseil supérieur de l'éducation, *L'internationalisation: nourrir le dynamisme des universités québécoises* (Sainte-Foy: Conseil supérieur de l'éducation, 2005), 35.

[12]Organisation for Economic Co-operation and Development (OECD), *Internationalisation and Trade in Higher Education: Opportunities and Challenge* (Paris: OECD, 2004), 150.

[13]The public policies concerned are as follows: Ministère de l'Éducation, *Politique québécoise à l'égard des universités: pour mieux assurer notre avenir collectif* (2000); Ministère de la recherche, de la Science et de la Technologie, *Politique québécoise de la science et de l'innovation: savoir changer le monde* (2001); Ministère de l'Éducation, *Pour réussir l'internationalisation de l'éducation…: une stratégie mutuellement avantageuse* (2002); Ministère des Relations internationales *La politique internationale du Québec: la force de l'action concertée* (2006).

[14]Ministère des Relations internationales, *Québec's International Policy*, 22.

[15]Ibid., 56.

[16]Ibid., 63.

[17]Conseil supérieur de l'éducation, *L'internationalisation*, 59.

[18]Ibid., 47.

[19]Statistics Canada, "University Enrolment," *The Daily* (2005). Retrieved October 11, 2005 from www.statcan.ca/Daily/English/051011/d051011b.htm.

[20]Conseil supérieur de l'éducation, *L'internationalisation*, 48.

[21]D. Bertrand, *Diversité, continuité et transformation du travail professoral dans les universités québécoises (1991 et 2003)* (Sainte-Foy: Conseil supérieur de l'éducation, 2004), 124-25.

[22]Conseil supérieur de l'éducation, *L'internationalisation*, 41.

[23]Conseil supérieur de l'éducation, *L'internationalisation*, 43 (based on the data of Benoît Godin, Professor at Institut national de recherche scientifique).

[24]J. Knight, "Assurance-qualité et reconnaissance des qualifications dans l'enseignement postsecondaire," in Organisation de coopération et de développement économiques (OCDE), *Qualité et reconnaissance des diplômes de l'enseignement supérieur: un défi international* (Paris: OCDE, 2004), 49-70.

[25]Conseil supérieur de l'éducation, *L'internationalisation*, 56.

[26]M. Byram, *Teaching and Assessing Intercultural Communicative Competence* (Clevedon: Multilingual Matters, 1997).

[27]D. Deardorff, "Introduction, The Role of International Education in Global Workforce Development" (NAFSA: Association of International Educators Webinar, December 8, 2005).

[28] G. Treverton & T. Bikson, "New Challenges for International Leadership" (Rand Issue Paper, 2003). Retrieved June 2006 from www.rand.org/publications/MR/MR1670?MR1670.pdf.

Chapter 6

[1]J. Liu, "Writing from Chinese to English: My Cultural Transformation," in *Reflections on Multiliterate Lives,* eds. D. Belcher & U. Connor (Clevedon, UK: Multilingual Matters, 2001), 131.

[2]N. Thiong'o, "Recovering the Original," in *The Genius of Language: Fifteen Writers Reflect on their Mother Tongues,* ed. W. Lesser (New York: Pantheon, 2004), 102-10.

[3]V. Zamel & R. Spack, eds., *Negotiating Academic Literacies* (Mahwah, NJ: Lawrence Erlbaum, 1998), xi.

[4]U. Connor, *Contrastive Rhetoric: Cross-cultural Aspects of Second Language Writing* (New York: Cambridge University Press, 1996), 5.

[5]V. Ramanathan & R. B. Kaplan, "Audience and Voice in Current L1 Composition Texts: Some Implications for ESL Student Writers," *Journal of Second Language Writing* 5, no. 1 (1996), 22.

[6]Lisle & Mano (1997), cited in K. Lovejoy, "Practical Pedagogy for Composition," in *Language Diversity in the Classroom,* eds. G. Smitherman & V. Villanueva (Carbondale, Illinois: Southern Illinois University Press, 2003), 90.

[7]D. Brand, *No Language is Neutral* (Toronto: Coach House Press, 1990).

[8]S. Canagarajah, "The Fortunate Traveler: Shuttling Between Communities and Literacies by Economy Class," in *Reflections on Multiliterate Lives,* eds. D. Belcher & U. Connor (Clevedon: Multilingual Matters, 2001), 35.

[9]R. B. Kaplan, "Cultural Thought Patterns in International Education," *Language Learning* 16 (1966), 1-20.

[10]K. Gilyard, Preface in *Rhetoric and Ethnicity,* eds. K. Gilyard & V. Nunley (Portsmouth, NH: Boynton/Cook, 2004), v.

[11]L. Mao, "Uniqueness or Borderlands? The Making of Asian-American Rhetorics," in *Rhetoric and Ethnicity,* eds. K. Gilyard & V. Nunley (Portsmouth, NH: Boynton/Cook, 2004), 46.

[12]C. Panetta, *Contrastive Rhetoric Revisited and Redefined* (Mahwah, NJ: Lawrence Erlbaum, 2001).

[13]M. Bakhtin, *The Dialogic Imagination: Four Essays by M.M. Bakhtin,* M. Holquist, ed., C. Emerson & M. Holquist, trans. (Austin: University of Texas Press, 1981).

[14]J. Wertsch, *Mind As Action* (New York: Oxford University Press, 1998), 25.

[15]Wertsch, *Mind As Action,* 43.

[16]J. Carson, "Becoming Biliterate: First Language Influence," *Journal of Second Language Writing* 1 (1992), 37-60.

[17]W. G. Eggington, "Written Academic Discourse in Korean: Implications for Effective Communication," in *Writing across Languages: Analysis of L2 text,* eds. U. Connor & R.B. Kaplan (Reading, MA: Addison-Wesley, 1987), 153-68.

[18]J. Hinds, "Inductive, Deductive, Quasi-Inductive: Expository Writing in Japanese, Korean, Chinese and Thai," in *Coherence in Writing: Research and Pedagogical Perspectives,* ed. U. Connor & A. Johns (Alexandria, VA: TESOL, 1990), 89-109.

[19]Connor, *Contrastive Rhetoric.*

[20]M. G. Clyne, "Linguistics and Written Discourse in Particular Languages: Contrastive Studies: English and German," in *Annual Review of Applied Linguistics 3,* ed. R. B. Kaplan (Rowley, MA: Newbury House, 1987), 38-49.

[21]Reppen & Grabe (1993), cited in Connor, *Contrastive Rhetoric.*

[22]J. Hinds, "Reader vs. Writer Responsibility: A New Typology," in *Writing across* Languages, 141-52; Hinds, "Inductive, Deductive, Quasi-Inductive."

[23]R. B. Kaplan, "Writing in a Multilingual/Multicultural Context: What's Contrastive About Contrastive Rhetoric?" *The Writing Instructor* (Fall 1990), 10.

[24]I. Leki, *Understanding ESL Writers* (Portsmouth, NH: Boynton/Cook, 1992), 68.

[25]Leki, *Understanding ESL Writers,* 92.

[26]D. Atkinson, "Reflections and Refractions on the JSLW Special Issue on Voice," *Journal of Second Language Writing* 10 (2001), 108.

[27]L. Steinman, "Cultural Collisions in L2 Academic Writing," *TESL Canada Journal* 20, no. 2 (2003), 80-91.

[28]F. Shen, "The Classroom and the Wider Culture: Identity as a Key to Learning English Composition," in *Negotiating Academic Literacies,* eds. V. Zamel & R. Spack (Mahwah, NJ: Erlbaum, 1998), 124.

[29]C. Casanave, *Controversies in Second Language Writing* (Ann Arbor: University of Michigan Press, 2003); A. Cumming, "Writing Expertise and Second Language Proficiency," *Language Learning* 29 (1989), 81-141; Connor, *Contrastive Rhetoric;* A. Friedlander, "Composing in English: Effects of First Language Writing in English as a Second Language," in *Second Language Writing,* ed. B. Kroll

(New York: Cambridge University Press, 1990).

30G. Kamani, "Code Switching," in *Becoming American,* ed. M. Danquah (New York: Hyperion, 2000), 100.

31B. Keiser, "Circus Biped," in *The Genius of Language: Fifteen Writers Reflect on Their Mother Tongues,* ed. W. Lesser (New York: Pantheon, 2004), 66.

32L. Brintrup, "Turbulent Times," in *Becoming American,* ed. M. Danquah (New York: Hyperion, 2000), 15.

33S. Canagarajah, *A Geopolitics of Academic Writing* (Pittsburgh: University of Pittsburgh Press, 2002).

34Canagarajah, *A Geopolitics of Academic Writing,* 32.

35Canagarajah, *A Geopolitics of Academic Writing,* 35.

36Canagarajah, *A Geopolitics of Academic Writing,* 36.

37Sommers (1992), cited in V. Zamel, "Questioning Academic Discourse," in *Negotiating Academic Literacies,* eds. V. Zamel & R. Spack (Mahwah, NJ: Lawrence Erlbaum, 1998), 188.

38J. P. Gee, "New People in New Worlds," in *Multiliteracies: Literacy Learning and Design of Social Futures,* ed. B. Cope & M. Kalantzis (New York: Routledge, 2003), 47.

39Canagarajah, *A Geopolitics of Academic Writing.*

40Mao, "Uniqueness or Borderlands?" 54.

41Steinman, "Cultural Collisions," 85.

42B. Cope & M. Kalantzis, eds., *Multiliteracies: Literacy Learning and the Design of Social Futures* (New York: Routledge, 2000), 7.

43Ibid.

44Cope & Kalantzis, *Multiliteracies,* 18.

45G. Dei, "Anti-Racism Teaching in Classrooms and Beyond!" (paper presented at the 29th TESL Ontario Annual Conference, Toronto, Ontario, November 2001).

46R. Kubota & A. Lehner, "Toward Critical Contrastive Rhetoric," *Journal of Second Language Writing* 13, no. 1 (2004), 7-28.

47A. Pennycook, *Critical Applied Linguistics: A Critical Introduction* (Mahwah, NJ: Lawrence Erlbaum Associates, 2001).

48V. Zamel, "Questioning Academic Discourse," 299.

49L. Shi, "Writing in Two Cultures: Chinese Professors Return from the West," *Canadian Modern Language Review* 5, no. 3 (2003), 369-91.

[50]P. Bourdieu, "The Economics of Linguistic Exchanges," *Social Science Information* 16 (1977), 645-68.

[51]Maya, a student, cited in J. Comfort, "African-American Women's Rhetorics and the Culture of Eurocentric Scholarly Discourse," in *Contrastive Rhetoric Revisited and Redefined,* ed. C. Panetta (Mahwah, NJ: Lawrence Erlbaum, 2001), 91.

[52]B. Ballard & J. Clanchy, "Assessment by Misconception," in *Assessing Second Language Writing in Academic Contexts,* ed. L. Hamp-Lyons (Norwood: Ablex, 1992), 20.

[53]Steinman, "Cultural Collisions," 88.

[54]Zamel & Spack, *Negotiating Academic Literacies,* xi.

[55]Lloyd (1954, 40) cited in G. Smitherman, "The Historical Struggle for Language Rights in the CCCC," in *Language Diversity in the Classroom,* eds. G. Smitherman & V. Villanueva (Carbondale, Illinois: Southern Illinois University Press, 2003), 13.

Chapter 7

[1]"I" in the paper is Ms. Hanson. A few sections of the paper include her reflections as course instructor and internationalization chair and hence use the first person. The title of the class was changed in 2005 to better reflect the content. It is now called Global Health and Local Communities: Issues and Approaches or GH-I for short.

[2]University of Saskatchewan International Activities Committee of Council, *Internationalization at the University of Saskatchewan Mission Statement* (2000). Retrieved January 30, 2006 from: http://www.usask.ca/university_council/reports/06-01-00.shtml.

[3]University of Saskatchewan Integrated Planning, *Globalism and the University of Saskatchewan: A Foundational Document for International Activities at the University of Saskatchewan* (2003). Retrieved January 30, 2006 from: http://www.usask.ca/vpacademic/integrated-planning/plandocs/docs/new_International_Plan_FINAL_ApprovedbyCouncil.pdf.

[4]R. Arnold, B. Burke, C. James, D. Martin & B. Thomas, *Educating for a Change* (Toronto: Between the Lines, 1991).

[5]S. Bond & J. Scott, "From Reluctant Acceptance to Modest Embrace: Internationalization of Higher Education," in *A New World of Knowledge: Canadian Universities and Globalization,* eds. S Bond & J-P. Lemasson (Ottawa: International Development Research Centre, 1999), 45-76.

[6]J. Knight, *A Time of Turbulence and Transformation for Internationalization* (Ottawa: Canadian Bureau for International Education: Research Monograph No. 14, 1999).

[7]G. Warner, "Internationalization Models and the Role of the University," *McMaster Courier* 10, no. 14 (1991), 4.

[8]M. Tjomsland, "Internationalization at Norwegian Universities and Colleges After the Quality Reform" (Working Paper 6, Stein Rokkan Centre for Social Studies UNIFOB AS, Bergen, 2004).

[9]Bond & Scott, "From Reluctant Acceptance to Modest Embrace;" Knight, *A Time of Turbulence*; M. Epprecht, "Work/Study Abroad Courses in International Development Studies: Some Ethical and Pedagogical Issues," *Canadian Journal of Development Studies* 25, no. 4 (2004), 709-28; Association of Universities and Colleges of Canada, *AUCC Statement on Internationalization and Canadian Universities* (Ottawa: Association of Universities and Colleges of Canada, 1995). Retrieved January 30, 2006 from http://www.aucc.ca/publications/statements/1995/intl_04_e.html.

[10]Warner, "Internationalization Models."

[11]AUCC, *AUCC Statement on Internationalization.*

[12]Warner, "Internationalization Models."

[13]University of Saskatchewan College of Medicine, *Integrated Plan 2003-2007* (2003). Retrieved January 30, 2006 from: http://www.usask.ca/medicine/dean/integrated_plan_updated_nov28.pdf.

[14]International Activities Committee of Council, *Internationalization at the University of Saskatchewan.*

[15]World Health Organization, *Defining and Measuring the Social Accountability of Medical Schools* (Geneva: Division of Development of Human Resources for Health, World Health Organization, 1995); Health Canada, *Social Accountability: A Vision for Canadian Medical Schools* (Ottawa: Publications Health Canada, 2001).

[16]College of Medicine, *Integrated Plan*, 152.

[17]AUCC, *AUCC Statement on Internationalization.*

[18]Bond & Scott, "From Reluctant Acceptance to Modest Embrace."

[19]M. Byers, "Are You a Global Citizen?" *The Tyee* (October 5, 2005). Retrieved January 30, 2006 from: http://thetyee.ca/Views/2005/10/05/globalcitizen/print.html.

[20]Global Health Watch, *Global Health Watch 2005-2006: An Alternative World Health Report* (London and New York: Zed Books, 2005).

[21]C. Victora, "How Successful are Pro-Poor Health Programs at Reaching the Poor?" in *Global Forum Update of Research for Health*, vol. 2, eds. Global Forum for Health Research (Geneva: Pro-Book Publishing, 2005), 20-24.

[22]M. Marmot, "Social Determinants of Health Inequalities," in *Global Forum Update of Research for Health*, vol. 2, 39.

[23]G.J.S. Dei, B.L. Hall & D.G. Rosenberg, eds., *Indigenous Knowledges in Global Contexts* (Toronto: University of Toronto Press, 2000); P. Farmer, *Pathologies of Power* (Berkeley: University of California Press, 2005).

[24]L. Daloz, C. Keen, J., Keen & S. Parks, *Common Fire: Leading Lives of Commitment in a Complex World* (Boston: Beacon Press, 1996).

[25]b. hooks, *Teaching Community: A Pedagogy of Hope* (New York: Routledge, 2003); Daloz et al.,

Common Fire.

[26]S-H.Toh, "Partnerships as Solidarity: Crossing North-South Boundaries," *The Alberta Journal of Educational Research* 42, no. 2 (1996), 185.

[27]S. Appiah-Padi, "How Study in North America Shapes the Global Perspectives of African Students," *Diversity Digest* (Spring 2001). Retrieved January 30, 2006 from http://www.diversityweb.org/Digest/Sp01/study.html.

[28]Byers, "Are You a Global Citizen?"

[29]M. Edwards & G. Sen, "NGO's, Social Change, and the Transformation of Human Relationships: A 21st Century Civic Agenda," *Third World Quarterly* 21, no. 4 (2000), 605-16.

[30]M. Bartell, "Internationalization of Universities: A University Culture-Based Framework," *Higher Education* 45 (2003), 66.

[31]P. Freire, *Pedagogy of the Oppressed* (New York: Herder & Herder, 1970).

[32]J. Mezirow, "Transformative Learning as Discourse", *Journal of Transformative Education* 1, no. 1 (2003), 58-63.

[33]L. Srinivasan, *Options for Educators: A Monograph for Decision Makers on Alternative Participatory Strategies* (New York: PACT/CDS Inc., 2001).

[34]E. Kasl & D. Elias, "Transformative Learning in Action: A Case Study," *Re-vision* 20, no. 1 (1997), 21.

[35] The East-side/West-side descriptors of Saskatoon point out within-city socioeconomic differences and inequalities that are both real and symbolic. The west side, as the more economically disadvantaged side, suffers the associated stigma.

[36]A. Shotwell, "Liminality, Radical Personal Transformation, and Conditions for Rational Deliberation: Susan Babbitt, María Lugones, and Toni Morrison's *Beloved*," *Limen* 2. Retrieved January 31, 2006 from: http://limen.mi2.hr/limen2-2001/shotwell.html; W. McWhinney & L. Markos, "Transformative Education Across the Threshold," *Journal of Transformative Education* 1, no. 1 (2003), 16-37.

[37]L.E. Swaner, *Linking Engaged Learning, Student Mental Health and Well-Being, and Civic Development: A Review of the Literature* (Washington: Bringing Theory to Practice & Association of American Colleges and Universities, 2005), 2. Retrieved January 31, 2006 from http://www.bringingtheorytopractice.org/pdfs/BTtP%202005%20Literature%20Review.pdf.

[38]Byers, "Are You a Global Citizen?"

[39]McWhinney & Markos, "Transformative Education."

[40]Ontario Institute for Studies in Education (OISE), Transformative Learning Center, *The TLC Approach to Transformative Learning: Grounded Hope* (Toronto: OISE, 2004). Retrieved January 31, 2006 from: http://tlc.oise.utoronto.ca/about.html.

[41]Freire, *Pedagogy of the Oppressed*, 34.

[42]P. Mayo, "A Rationale for a Transformative Approach to Education," *Journal of Transformative Education* Mezirow, "Transformative Learning," 63.

Chapter 8

[1]E. Said, quoted in P. Young, *Postcolonialism: A Very Short Introduction* (Oxford, UK: Oxford University Press, 2003), 59.

[2]A. Escobar, *Encountering Development: The Making and Unmaking of the Third World* (New Brunswick, New Jersey: Princeton University Press, 1994).

[3]The Canadian International Development Agency (CIDA) uses the French term 'cooperant' for people who work internationally as technical assistants on development projects.

[4]P. Young, *Postcolonialism*, 18.

[5]S. Strega, "The View from the Poststructural Margins: Epistemology and Methodology Reconsidered," in *Research as Resistance: Critical, Indigenous, and Anti-Oppressive Approaches*, eds. L. Brown and S. Strega (Toronto: Canadian Scholars' Press, 2005), 213.

[6]P. Young, *Postcolonialism*, 20.

[7]"Intersectional analysis based on class, race, gender, sexuality, religion and other social relations of power was introduced as an epistemology and as praxis by feminists of colour located in the United States. Patricia Hill Collins articulated intersectionality as an examination of gender, race, class and nationality as mutually constructed rather than as distinctive social hierarchies (156). The framework thus introduces fluidity, depth and integration to former race-, class-, and gender-only approaches (206). E. Martinez Salazar, "The Everyday Praxis of Guatemalan Mayan Women: Confronting Marginalization, Racism and Contested Citizenship." (unpublished Ph.D. thesis., York University, 2005), 128-29. See P. Hill Collins, *Black Feminist Thought: Knowledge, Consciousness, and the Politics of Empowerment*, Revised 10th Anniversary 2nd Edition (Boston: Unwin Hyman, 2000).

[8]*Cosmovision* is a term used by indigenous peoples to describe their world view that incorporates ecological as well as social dimensions.

[9]P. Cole, "Memorandum to FES Committee of Instruction," April 14, 2005.

[10]Faculty of Environmental Studies, Minutes of FES Faculty Council, May 26, 2005.

[11]A. Sandberg, "Memo to FES Committee of Instruction," April 14, 2005.

[12]Ibid.

[13]L. Tihiwai Smith, *Decolonizing Methodologies: Research and Indigenous Peoples* (New York: ZED Books, 1999); and M. Battiste, ed., *Reclaiming Indigenous Voice and Vision* (Vancouver: UBC Press, 2000).

[14]C. McNaughton & D. Rock, *Opportunities in Aboriginal Research: Results of SSHRC's Dialogue in*

Research and Aboriginal Peoples (Ottawa, 2003).

[15]A. Hua, "Diaspora and Cultural Memory," in *Diaspora, Memory, and Identity: A Search for Home*, ed. V. Agnew (Toronto: University of Toronto Press, 2005), 193.

[16]Ibid.

[17]Brah, quoted in Hua, "Diaspora and Cultural Memory," 189.

[18]Faculty of Environmental Studies and Centre for the Support of Teaching, York University, *Voices of Diversity and Equity: Transforming University Curriculum* (DVD and Users' Guide for Workshops and Classrooms, 2005). The kit also includes an extensive bibliography around various areas of equity.

Chapter 9

[1]See, for example, A. Immelman & P. Schneider, "Assessing Student Learning in Study Abroad Programs: A Conceptual Framework and Methodology for Assessing Student Learning in Study Abroad Programs," *Journal of Studies in International Education* 2, no. 2 (1998), 59-79; special issue of *Frontiers: The Interdisciplinary Journal of Study Abroad* (2004); T. Williams, "Exploring the Impact of Study Abroad on Students' Intercultural Communication Skills: Adaptability and Sensitivity," *Journal of Studies in International Education* 9, no. 4 (2005), 356-71.

[2]G. Honigsblum, "Internships Abroad: The View from Paris," *Frontiers: The Interdisciplinary Journal of Study Abroad* 8 (2002), 111. Available online: http://www.frontiersjournal.com/issues/vol8/vol8-06_honigsblum.pdf.

[3]E. Murphy-Lejeune, *Student Mobility and Narrative in Europe* (London and New York: Routledge, 2002), 51.

[4]D. McGray, "Lost in America," *Foreign Policy* (May-June 2006), 42.

[5]J. Geller, *The Ethnographic Participant/Observer in Study Abroad: Training the Eye* (2006). Retrieved April 12, 2006 from http://usp1.scholars.nus.edu.sg/~geconvnt/pdf/B3_Jeremy_U_of_Illinois.pdf.

[6]N. Razack, "A Critical Examination of International Student Exchanges," *International Social Work* 45, no. 2 (2002), 251-65; F. Rizvi, "Globalization and Education after September 11" (keynote speech at the Colloquium on Education and Globalization, York University, Toronto, Canada, March 6, 2003).

[7]M. Merryfield, "Why Aren't Teachers Being Prepared to Teach for Diversity, Equity, and Global Interconnectedness? A Study of Lived Experiences in the Making of Multicultural and Global Educators," *Teaching and Teacher Education* 16 (2000), 429-43.

[8]M. Singh, "Enabling Transnational Learning Communities: Policies, Pedagogies and Politics of Education Power," in *Internationalizing Higher Education: Critical Explorations of Pedagogy and Policy*, eds. P. Ninnes & M. Hellsten (CERC, University of Hong Kong: Springer), 9-37.

[9]Geller, *The Ethnographic Participant*; Singh, "Enabling Transnational Learning Communities."

[10]Geller, *The Ethnographic Participant.*

[11]Singh, "Enabling Transnational Learning Communities."

[12]Geller, *The Ethnographic Participant.*

[13]Ibid., 3

[14]Ibid., 4.

[15]S. Opper, U. Teichler & J. Carlson, *Impacts of Study Abroad Programmes on Students and Graduates* (London: Jessica Kingsley, 1990).

[16]Singh, "Enabling Transnational Learning Communities."

[17]E. Taylor, "Intercultural Competency: A Transformative Learning Process," *Adult Education Quarterly* 44, no. 3 (1994), 154-74.

[18]A.H. Wilson, "Cross-Cultural Experiential Learning for Teachers," *Theory into Practice* 26 (1987), 519-27.

[19]I. Kapoor, "Hyper-Self-Reflexive Development? Spivak on Representing the Third World 'Other'," *Third World Quarterly* 25 no.4 (2004), 627-47

Chapter 10

[1]Office of the Associate Vice-President International, York University, "A Strategic Plan for the Internationalization of York University" (unpublished document, January 27, 2004).

[2]Ibid., 6.

[3]N. Razack, "A Critical Examination of International Student Exchanges," *International Social Work* 45, no. 2 (2002), 257.

[4]Ibid., 260.

[5]Ibid., 257.

[6]A. Escobar, *Encountering Development: The Making and Unmaking of the Third World* (Princeton: Princeton University Press, 1995), 8.

[7]Ibid., 9.

Chapter 11

[1]A brief biographical statement for each author is presented in the concluding statement of this volume.

[2]R.M. Paige & J.A. Mestenhauser, "Internationalizing Educational Administration," *Educational Administration Quarterly* 35, no. 4 (1999), 500-17.

[3]S. Bond, *Untapped Resources, Internationalization of the Curriculum and Classroom Experience: A Selected Literature Review* (Ottawa: Canadian Bureau for International Education, 2003).

[4]J. Knight, "Internationalization Remodeled: Definition, Approaches, and Rationales," *Journal of Studies in International Education* 8, no. 1 (2004), 6.

[5]J. Knight, "Internationalization: Elements and Checkpoints," *Research Monograph* No. 7 (Ottawa: Canadian Bureau for International Education, 1994), 7.

[6]Knight, "Internationalization Remodeled," 49.

[7]J. Crichton, M. Paige, L. Papademetre, & A. Scarino, *Integrated Resources for Intercultural Training and Learning in the Context of Internationalization of Higher Education* (2004), 3. Retrieved May 17, 2005 from http://www.unisa.edu.au/staff/grants/archive/2003-integrated-report.doc.

[8]Ibid., 11.

[9] J.M. Bennett & M.J. Bennett, "Developing Intercultural Sensitivity: An Integrative Approach to Global and Domestic Diversity," in *Handbook of Intercultural Training*, eds. D. Landis, J. M. Bennett, & M. J. Bennett, 3rd ed. (Thousand Oaks, CA: Sage, 2004), 147-165.

[10]Crichton et al., *Integrated Resources.*

[11]Ibid, 149.

[12]Ibid.

[13] Bond, *Untapped Resources.*

[14] J. Knight & H. de Wit, "Strategies for Internationalization of Higher Education: Historical and Conceptual Perspectives," in *Strategies for Internationalization in Higher Education*, ed. H. de Wit (Amsterdam: European Association of International Education, 1995).

[15]P. Maidstone, *International Literacy: A Paradigm for Change: A Manual for Internationalizing the Curriculum* (Victoria, BC: Centre for Curriculum, Transfer and Technology, 1996), 7.

[16] R.M. Paige, "The American Case: The University of Minnesota," *Journal of Studies in International Education*, 7, no. 1 (2003), 56.

[17]T. Whalley, *Best Practice Guidelines for Internationalizing the Curriculum* (Victoria, BC: Ministry of Education, Skills, and Training and the Centre for Curriculum, Transfer, and Technology, Province of British Columbia, 1997).

[18]M. Bell, *Internationalizing the Higher Education Curriculum — Do You Agree?* (2004). Retrieved May 20, 2005 from http://herdsa2004.curtin.edu.my/Contributions/RPapers/ P036-jt.pdf.

[19]L. Bremer & M. van der Wende, *Internationalizing the Curriculum in Higher Education: Experiences in the Netherlands* (The Hague: The Netherlands Organization for International Cooperation in Higher Education, 1995).

[20]Whalley, *Best Practice Guidelines*, 10.

[21]B. Nilsson, "Internationalizing the Curriculum," in *Internationalisation at Home: A Position Paper*, eds. P. Crowther, M. Joris, M. Otten, B. Nilsson, H. Teekens, & B. Wachter (Amsterdam: European Association for International Education, 2000), 21.

[22]B. Wachter, "Internationalization at Home: The Context," in *Internationalisation at Home*, 10.

[23]J.A. Mestenhauser, "Portraits of an International Curriculum: An Uncommon Multidimensional Perspective," in *Reforming the Higher Education Curriculum: Internationalizing the Campus*, eds. J.A. Mestenhauser & B.J. Ellingboe (Phoenix: Oryx Press, 1998), 3-39.

[24]Paige & Mestenhauser, "Internationalizing Educational Administration."

[25]Paige, "The American Case."

[26]Y. Yershova, J. DeJaegere and J. Mestenhauser,"Thinking Not As Usual: Adding the Intercultural Perspective," *Journal of Studies in International Education* 4 (2000), 43-78.

[27]Mestenhauser, "Portraits of an International Curriculum," 31.

[28]Mestenhauser, "Portraits of an International Curriculum;" J.A. Mestenhauser, "Missing in Action: Leadership for International and Global Education for the Twenty-First Century," in *Internationalization of Higher Education: An Institutional Perspective. Papers on Higher Education*, eds. L.C. Barrows (United Nations Educational, Scientific, and Cultural Organization: Bucharest European Centre for Higher Education, 2000), 23-62; Paige & Mestenhauser, "Internationalizing Educational Administration."

[29]Paige & Mestenhauser, "Internationalizing Educational Administration;" Paige, "The American Case."

[30]Paige & Mestenhauser, "Internationalizing Educational Administration," 501.

[31]H. Teekens, "The Requirement to Develop Specific Skills for Teaching in an Intercultural Setting," *Journal of Studies in International Education* 7, no.1 (2003), 108-19.

[32]M. Otten, "Intercultural Learning and Diversity in Higher Education," *Journal of Studies in International Education* 7, no. 1 (2003), 12-26.

[33]G.W. Allport, *The Nature of Prejudice* (Reading, MA: Addison-Wesley, 1954).

[34]T.F. Pettigrew & L.R. Tropp, "Does Intergroup Contact Reduce Prejudice? Recent Meta-Analytic Findings," in *Reducing Prejudice and Discrimination. The Claremont Symposium on Applied Social Psychology*, ed. S. Oskamp (Mahwah, NJ: Laurence Erlbaum Associates, 2000), 111.

[35]B. Leask, "Internationalisation of the Curriculum: Key Challenges and Strategies" (paper presented at the IDP Education Australia 1999 Australian International Conference, Fremantle, Australia, October, 1999); B. Leask, "Bridging the Gap: Internationalizing University Curricula, *Journal of Studies in International Education* 5, no. 2 (2001), 100-15.

[36]A.J. Liddicoat, "Internationalisation as Education," in *Integrated Resources for Intercultural Training and Learning*, 71. Retrieved May 17, 2005 from http://www.unisa.edu.au/staff/grants/archive/2003-integrated-report.doc.

[37]Crichton et al., *Integrated Resources*.

[38]Bell, *Internationalizing the Higher Education Curriculum.*

[39]B.J. Ellingboe, "Divisional Strategies to Internationalize a Campus Portrait: Results, Resistance, and Recommendations From a Case Study at a U.S. University," in *Reforming the Higher Education Curriculum,* 198-228.

[40]M.J. Bennett, "Toward Ethnorelativism: A Developmental Model of Intercultural Sensitivity," in *Education for the Intercultural* Experience, ed. R. M. Paige (Yarmouth, ME: Intercultural Press, 1993), 21-71.

[41]Bell, *Internationalizing the Higher Education Curriculum.*

[42]A.I. Morey, "Changing Higher Education Curricula for a Global and Multicultural World," *Higher Education in Europe* XXV, no. 1 (2000), 26-39.

[43]M.K. Kitano, "What a Course Will Look Like After Multicultural Change," in *Multicultural Course Transformation in Higher Education: A Broader Truth,* eds. A.I. Morey & M. Kitano (Boston: Allyn and Bacon, 1997), 18-30.

[44]Morey, "Changing Higher Education Curricula," 28.

[45]Ibid., 30.

[46]Bond, *Untapped Resources,* 8.

[47]Mestenhauser, "Portraits of an International Curriculum."

[48]J. Banks, *An Introduction to Multicultural Education* (Boston: Allyn and Bacon, 1999).

[49]Ibid., 7.

[50]Ibid., 8.

[51]Bond, *Untapped Resources.*

[52]Teekens, "The Requirement to Develop Specific Skills," 30.

[53]Paige, "The American Case," 58.

[54]Ibid.

[55]Mestenhauser, "Missing in Action," 33.

[56]Paige & Mestenhauser, "Internationalizing Educational Administration."

[57]R.M. Paige, "The Intercultural in Teaching and Learning: A Developmental Perspective," in *Integrated Resources for Intercultural Teaching and Learning in the Context of Internationalization of Higher Education,* 79-90; Crichton et al., *Integrated Resources;* Bell, *Internationalizing the Higher Education Curriculum;* Teekens, "The Requirement to Develop Specific Skills;" Morey, "Changing Higher Education Curricula;" Maidstone, *International Literacy.*

[58]Teekens, "The Requirement to Develop Specific Skills."

[59]Nilsson, "Internationalizing the Curriculum."

[60]M. Otten, "Impacts of Cultural Diversity at Home," in *Internationalisation at Home: A Position Paper*, eds. P. Crowther, M. Joris, M. Otten, B. Nilsson, H. Teekens & B. Wachter (Amsterdam: European Association for International Education, 2000), 15-20.

[61]R.M. Paige, *Education for the Intercultural Experience* (Yarmouth, ME: Intercultural Press, 1993).

[62]Liddicoat, "Internationalisation as Education."

[63]Paige, *Education for the Intercultural Experience*; Paige, "The Intercultural in Teaching and Learning."

[64]Leask, "Internationalisation of the Curriculum."

[65]K. McKellin, *Maintaining the Momentum: The Internationalization of British Columbia's Post-Secondary Institutions* (Victoria, BC: British Columbia Centre for International Education, 1998).

[66]Paige, "The Intercultural in Teaching and Learning."

[67]Paige, *Education for the Intercultural Experience*.

[68]Bennett, "Toward Ethnorelativism."

[69]Morey, "Changing Higher Education Curricula."

[70]Maidstone, *International Literacy*, 37.

[71]Mestenhauser, "Portraits of an International Curriculum," 21.

[72]Paige, *Education for the Intercultural Experience*; R.M. Paige, "Intercultural Trainer Competencies," in *Handbook of Intercultural Training*, eds. D. Landis, J. M. Bennett, & M. J. Bennett, 2nd ed. (Thousand Oaks, CA: Sage, 1996), 148-64.

[73]R.M. Paige & J.N. Martin, "Ethics in Intercultural Training," in *Handbook of Intercultural Training*, 2nd ed., 35-60.

[74]Paige, *Education for the Intercultural Experience*; Paige, "Intercultural Trainer Competencies."

[75]Paige & Martin, "Ethics in Intercultural Training."

[76]Ibid., 46.

[77]Bennett & Bennett, "Developing Intercultural Sensitivity."

[78] J.M. Bennett, "Modes of Cross-Cultural Training: Conceptualizing Cross-Cultural Training as Education," *International Journal of Intercultural Relations* 102 (1993), 117-34.

[79]Bennett, "Toward Ethnorelativism."

[80]Crichton et al., *Integrated Resources.*

[81]D.P.S. Bhawuk & H.C. Triandis, "The Role of Culture Theory in the Study of Culture and Intercultural Training," in *Handbook of Intercultural Training,* 2nd ed., 17-34.

[82]R.M. Paige, "Instrumentation in Intercultural Training," in *Handbook of Intercultural Training,* 3rd ed., 85-128.

[83]J. Mezirow, "Learning to Think Like an Adult: Core Concepts of Transformation Theory," in *Learning as Transformation: Critical Perspectives on a Theory in Progress,* ed. J. Mezirow (San Francisco: Jossey-Bass, 2000), 3-33; P. Cranton, U*nderstanding and Promoting Transformative Learning: A Guide for Educators of Adults* (San Francisco: Jossey-Bass, 1994); P. Cranton, "Teaching for Transformation," *New Directions for Adult and Continuing Education* 9 (2002), 63-71.

[84]Mezirow, "Learning to Think Like an Adult," 7-8.

[85]Leask, "Internationalisation of the Curriculum," 2.

[86]Otten, "Intercultural Learning and Diversity in Higher Education," 20.

[87]D.A. Schon, *Educating the Reflective Practitioner: Toward a New Design for Teaching and Learning in the Professions* (San Francisco: Jossey-Bass, 1987).

[88]A. Saroyan & C. Amundsen, *Rethinking Teaching in Higher Education* (Sterling, VA: Stylus, 2004).

[89]Mestenhauser, "Portraits of an International Curriculum."

[90]G. Gaskell, "Individual and Group Interviewing," in *Qualitative Researching with Text, Image and Sound,* eds. M. Bauer & G. Gaskell (London: Sage Publications, 2000), 39.

Chapter 12

[1]Acknowledgements: This study was supported by a grant from a joint initiative (Initiative for the New Economy) between the Social Science and Humanities Research Council of Canada and the Human Resources Development Canada.

[2]A brief biographical statement for each author is presented in the concluding statement of this volume.

[3]P. G. Altbach, ed., *The International Academic Profession: Portraits of Fourteen Countries* (Princeton: Carnegie Foundation for the Advancement of Teaching, 1996); K. Barlett, *National Report on International Students in Canada (2000/2001)* (Ottawa: The Canadian Bureau for International Education, 2002); S. L. Bond & J. P. Lemasson, eds., *A New World of Knowledge: Canadian Universities and Globalization* (Ottawa: International Development Research Centre, 1999); W. H. Turnley & D. C. Feldman, "The Impact of Psychological Contract Violations on Exit, Loyalty and Neglect," *Human Relations* 52 (1999), 895-992.

[4]Bartlett, *National Report;* S. L. Bond, *Untapped Resources, Internationalization of the Curriculum and Classroom Experience: A Selected Literature Review* (Ottawa: Canadian Bureau for International Education Research Series, 2003); P. Grayson, "Does Race Matter? Outcomes of the First Year Experience in a Canadian University," *The Canadian Journal of Higher Education* 25, no. 2 (1995), 79-100.

[5]S. L. Bond & J. Thayer-Scott, "From Reluctant Acceptance to Modest Embrace: Internationalization of Undergraduate Education," in *A New World of Knowledge.*

[6]These international faculty can be further divided into those who had subsequently obtained citizenship or permanent residence and those who were nonpermanent residents or on work permits. CAUT, *CAUT Almanac of Post Secondary Education in Canada* (Canadian Association of University Teachers, 2005).

[7]Ibid.

[8]AUCC, *Trends in Higher Education* (2002). Retrieved on October 11, 2006 from http://www.aucc.ca/publications/media/2002/trendsback_e.html.

[9]M. Doucet, "A Window of Opportunity," *OCUFA Forum* (Spring 2005), 8-9.

[10]A. Holloway, "The Brain Game," *Canadian Business Magazine,* October 25, 2004.

[11]O. Ward, "Scholars Breathe 'Fresh Air'," *Toronto Star,* December 4, 2004, A35.

[12]S. Ambrose, T. Huston & M. Norman, "A Qualitative Method for Assessing Faculty Satisfaction," *Research in Higher Education* 46, no.7 (2005), 803-30.

[13]A. Kershaw, "Wanted: 11,000 New Professors," *Queen's Alumni Review* (2005), 18-24.

[14]L. Mwenifumbo & K. E. Renner, "Institutional Variations in Faculty Demographic Profiles," *The Canadian Journal of Higher Education* 28, no. 23 (1998), 21-46.

[15]Y. Baruch & D. T. Hall, "The Academic Career: A Model for Future Careers in Other Sectors?" *Journal of Vocational Behaviour* 64 (2004), 241-62; M. Kaulisch & J. Enders, "Careers in Overlapping Institutional Contexts," *Career Development International* 10, no. 2, (2005), 130-44.

[16]Kaulisch & Enders, "Careers in Overlapping Institutional Contexts."

[17]A. Bird, J. S. Osland, M. Mendenhall & S. C. Schneider, "Adapting and Adjusting to Other Cultures: What We Know But Don't Always Tell," *Journal of Management Inquiry* 8, no. 2 (1999), 152-65; N. K. Napier, D. A. Vu, M. H. Ngo, V. T. Nguyen & V. T. Vu, "Reflections on Building a Business School in Vietnam," *Journal of Management Inquiry* 6, no. 4 (1997), 341-54.

[18]Kaulisch & Enders, "Careers in Overlapping Institutional Contexts."

[19]J. Knight, *Internationalizing Higher Education: A Shared Vision?* (Ottawa: Canadian Bureau for International Education, 1996); J. A. Mestenhauser, "The Portraits of International Curriculum: An Uncommon Multidimensional Perspective" (unpublished manuscript, University of Minnesota, Minneapolis, 1996).

[20]M. Dickmann & H. Harris, "Developing Career Capital for Global Careers: The Role of International Assignments," *Journal of World Business* 40, no. 4 (2005), 399-408.

[21]J. Richardson, "Experiencing Expatriation: A Study of Expatriate Academics" (unpublished Ph.D. thesis, University of Otago, New Zealand, Dunedin, 2002).

[22]J. Richardson & M. Mallon, "Career Interrupted? The Case of the Self-Directed Expatriate," *Journal of World Business* 40 (2005), 409-20.

[23]Ibid.

[24]Ibid.

[25]S. Ambrose et al., "A Qualitative Method"; L.K. Johnsrud & V.J. Rosser, "Faculty Members' Morale and their Intention to Leave," *The Journal of Higher Education* 73, no. 4 (2003), 518-41.

[26]Mwenifumbo & Renner, "Institutional Variations."

[27]Richardson, "Experiencing Expatriation."

[28]Kaulisch & Enders, "Careers in Overlapping Institutional Contexts."

Chapter 13

[1]UNESCO/Council of Europe, "Code of Good Practice in the Provision of Transnational Education" (June 6, 2001). http://www.cicic.ca/docs/TNE-Code2001.en.pdf .

[2]Organisation for Economic Co-operation and Development, "Guidelines for Quality Provision in Cross-border Higher Education" (2005), 3. http://www.oecd.org/dataoecd/27/51/35779480.pdf).

[3]Ibid., 12.

[4]Ibid., 16.

[5]Canada, Council of Ministers of Education, "Report of the Pan-Canadian Committee on Quality Assurance of Degree Programming" (August 2005).

Chapter 14

[1]A brief biographical statement for each author is presented in the concluding statement of this volume.

[2]J. Knight, *Internationalization: Elements and Checkpoints* (Ottawa: Canadian Bureau of International Education, 1994); J. Knight, *Progress and Promise: The 2000 AUCC Report on Internationalization at Canadian Universities* (Ottawa: Association of Universities and Colleges of Canada, 2000); H. de Wit, *Strategies for Internationalization of Higher Education: A Comparative Study of Australia, Canada, Europe and the United States of America* (Amsterdam: European Association for International Education, 1995).

[3]See, for example, J. Knight, "Internationalization Remodeled: Definition, Approaches, and Rationales," *Journal of Studies in International Education* 8, no. 1 (2004), 5-31.

[4]J. Mestenhauser, "Introduction," in *Reforming the Higher Education Curriculum: Internationalizing the Campus*, eds. J. Mestenhauser & B. Ellingboe (Phoenix: American Council on Education & Oryx Press: Series on Higher Education, 1998), xviii.

[5]Knight, "Internationalization Remodeled," 5-31.

[6]T. Knight, *Progress and Promise*, 17.

[7]Knight, *Internationalization at Canadian Universities*, 28.

[8]Knight, *Progress and Promise*.

[9]Ibid.

[10]K. Beck, "An Ethic of Inclusion for International Education: A Response to Globalization" (unpublished M.A. thesis, Simon Fraser University).

[11]Knight, "Internationalization Remodeled," 22-28.

[12]F. Rizvi & B. Lingard, "Globalization and Education: Complexities and Contingencies," *Educational Theory* 50, no. 4 (2002), 419-26.

[13]T. Friedman, *The Lexus and the Olive Tree: Understanding Globalization* (New York: Anchor Books, 2000). This has also been documented by those who critique this view. See, for example, J. McMurtry, *Unequal Freedoms: The Global Market as an Ethical System* (Toronto: Garamond Press, 1998); D. Korten, *When Corporations Rule the World* (West Hartford: Kumarian Press & San Francisco: Berrett-Koehler Publishers, 1995); Z. Bauman, *Globalization: The Human Consequences* (New York: Columbia University Press, 1998); R. Ghosh, "Globalization in the North American Region: Towards Renegotiation of Cultural Space," *McGill Journal of Education* 39, no. 1 (2004), 87-102.

[14]Rizvi & Lingard, "Globalization and Education;" McMurtry, *Unequal Freedoms*.

[15]Korten, *When Corporations Rule the World*; Bauman, *Globalization: The Human Consequences*.

[16]For example, M. Waters, *Globalization* (London & New York: Routledge, 1995); A. King, *Culture, Globalization and the World System* (Minneapolis: University of Minnesota Press, 1997).

[17]S. Bond & J-P. Lemasson, eds., *A New World of Knowledge: Canadian Universities and Globalization* (Ottawa: International Development Research Centre, 1999); R. Edwards & R. Usher, *Globalization and Pedagogy: Space, Place and Identity* (London & New York: Routledge, 2000); Rizvi & Lingard, "Globalization and Education;" J. Cambridge, "Global Product Branding and International Education," *Journal of Research in International Education* 1, no. 2 (2002), 227-43; M. Bartell, "Internationalization of Universities: A University Culture-Based Framework," *Higher Education* 45, no. 1 (2003), 43-70; John S. Levin, "Two British Columbia University Colleges and the Process of Economic Globalization," *The Canadian Journal of Higher Education* 33, no. 1 (2003).

[18]Edwards & Usher, *Globalization and Pedagogy*; Bartell, "Internationalization of Universities."

[19]Edwards & Usher, *Globalization and Pedagogy*, 79; Bartell, "Internationalization of Universities."

[20]Edwards & Usher, *Globalization and Pedagogy*, chap. 4.

[21]Ibid., 76-81.

[22]The reference to "performativity" relates to knowledge production and institutional performance and not to the concept of "performativity" relating to identity.

[23]Edwards & Usher, *Globalization and Pedagogy*, 76.

[24] P. Scott, "Massification, Internationalization and Globalization," in *The Globalization of Higher Education*, ed. P. Scott (UK: The Society for Research into Higher Education & Open University Press, 1998); Edwards & Usher, *Globalization and Pedagogy*; R. Ghosh, "Globalization in the North American Region."

[25]Scott, "Massification," 110.

[26]Edwards & Usher, *Globalization and Pedagogy*.

[27]Scott, "Massification."

[28]Ibid.

[29]Ibid., 109.

[30]Cambridge, "Global Product Branding."

[31]Ibid., 230.

[32]A. McGrew, "A Global Society?" in *Modernity and Its Futures*, eds. S. Hall, D. Held & A. McGrew (Milton Keynes, UK: Open University Press, 1992).

[33]Ibid.; Waters, *Globalization*; A. Appadurai, *Modernity At Large: Cultural Dimensions of Globalization* (Minneapolis: University of Minnesota Press, 1995); T. Spybey, *Globalization and World Society* (Cambridge: Polity Press, 1996); R. Kilminster, "Globalization as an Emergent Concept," in *The Limits of Globalization: Cases and Arguments*, ed. Allan Scott (London & New York: Routledge, 1997); Edwards & Usher, *Globalization and Pedagogy*.

[34]McGrew, "A Global Society?"; Korten, *When Corporations Rule the World*; McMurtry, *Unequal Freedoms*.

[35]Ibid.

[36]A. Giddens, *The Consequences of Modernity* (Stanford: Stanford University Press, 1990), 64.

[37]R. Robertson, quoted in *The Limits of Globalization*, 7.

[38]Edwards & Usher, *Globalization and Pedagogy*, 10.

[39]Ibid., 15.

[40]A. Appadurai, "Disjuncture and Difference in the Global Cultural Economy," in *Global Culture: Nationalism, Globalization, and Modernity*, ed. M. Featherstone (London: Sage, 1990), 296-97.

[41]Ibid., 301.

[42]Appadurai, "Modernity at Large," 48-50.

[43]Appadurai, "Modernity at Large," 35.

[44]See, for example, W. Sachs, *The Development Dictionary: A Guide to Knowledge as Power* (London & New Jersey: Zed Books, 1992); A. Prasad, "The Gaze of the Other: Postcolonial Theory and Organizational Analysis," in *Postcolonial Theory and Organizational Analysis: A Critical Engagement* (New York & Hampshire: Palgrave MacMillan, 2003); R. Young, *Postcolonialism: An Historical Introduction* (Oxford: Blackwell, 2001); McMurtry, *Unequal Freedoms.*

[45]Prasad, "The Gaze of the Other"; G. Castle, ed., *Postcolonial Discourses: An Anthology* (Oxford & Malden, MA: Blackwell Publishers, 2001).

[46]Mander & Goldsmith as quoted in D. Smith, "Economic Fundamentalism, Globalization and the Public Remains of Education, *Interchange* 30, no. 1 (1999), 97.

[47]Castle, *Postcolonial Discourses.*

[48]Rizvi & Lingard, "Globalization and Education."

[49]A. Nandy, *The Intimate Enemy: Loss and Recovery of Self Under Colonialism* (New Delhi: Oxford University Press, 1983); D. Smith, "Economic Fundamentalism, Globalization and the Public Remains of Education, *Interchange* 30, no. 1 (1999).

[50]S. Bond & J. Scott, "From Reluctant Acceptance to Modest Embrace: Internationalization of Undergraduate Education," in *A New World of Knowledge: Canadian Universities and Globalization*, eds. S. Bond & J-P Lemasson (Ottawa: International Development Research Centre, 1999), 77-98.

[51]L. Gandhi, *Postcolonial Theory: A Critical Introduction* (New York: Columbia University Press, 1998).

[52]J. Knight, "Internationalization: New Realities, Challenges and Opportunities," (presentation, Trent University, September 28, 2006).

[53]B. Pengelly, "The Development of International Education Activities in British Columbia Colleges 1978-1988" (unpublished Master's thesis, University of British Columbia, 1989).

[54]As discussed in J. Rutherford, "Interview with Homi Bhabha," in *Identity: Community, Culture, Difference*, ed. J. Rutherford (London: Lawrence & Wishart, 1990).

[55]Nandy, *The Intimate Enemy.*

[56]M. Foucault, "Prison Talk," in *Power/Knowledge: Selected Interviews and Other Writings by Michel Foucault, 1972-1977*, ed. and trans. C. Gordon (New York: Pantheon, 1980), 98.

[57]G. Deleuze & F. Guattari, *A Thousand Plateaus: Capitalism and Schizophrenia*, trans. B. Massumi (London: Athlone Press, 1987).

[58]B. Ashcroft, *Postcolonial Transformations* (London & New York: Routledge, 2001), 50.

[59]Ashcroft, *Postcolonial Transformations*.

[60]H. Bhabha, *The Location of Culture* (London: Routledge, 1994); Rutherford, "Interview with Homi Bhabha."

[61]F. Ibanez, "From Confession to Dialogue," in *Radical Interventions*, eds. S. de Castell & M. Bryson (Albany: SUNY Press, 1997); P. Lather, "Research as Praxis," *Harvard Educational Review* 53 (1986), 257-77; S. Te Hennepe, "Respectful Research: That Is What My People Say, You Learn It From the Story," in *Radical Interventions*.

[62]S. Te Hennepe, "Respectful Research"; L. Jayamane & A. Rutherford, "Why a Fishpond? Fiction at the Heart of Documentation," *Filmnews* 20, no. 10 (1990), 162-78.

[63]J. Heron as quoted in P. Lather, "Research as Praxis," *Harvard Educational Review* 56, no. 3 (1986), 262.

[64]Lather, "Research as Praxis."

[65]This is a pseudonym.

[66]Ibanez, "From Confession to Dialogue."

[67]E. Guba & Y. Lincoln, "Competing Paradigms in Qualitative Research," in *Handbook of Qualitative Research*, 2nd eds. N. Denzin & Y. Lincoln (Thousand Oaks, CA: Sage Publications, 2000), 115.

[68]In the larger study, I examine, among others, issues of identity, language, socialization, learning, student services, losses and gains, and a more in-depth examination of internationalization.

[69]Knight, *Progress and Promise*, 19.

[70]J. Mestenhauser, "The Utilization of Foreign Students in Internationalization of Universities," in *Connections and Complexities: The Internationalization of Higher Education in Canada*, eds. S. Bond & C. Bowry (Winnipeg: Occasional Papers in Higher Education 11, The Centre for Higher Education Research and Development, The University of Manitoba, 2002),13-28.

[71]Ibid., 15.

[72]Ibid., 15.

[73]Ibid., 15.

[74]Ibid., 16.

[75]This will be documented and discussed at length in my dissertation.

[76]It should be noted that fluency in English did not necessarily lead to successful social relations, as in the case of Sonali, who is fluent in English and whose analysis was that "everyone has their own life to lead, and their families and friends" so there was no room and no time for newcomers.

Chapter 15

[1]A brief biographical statement for each author is presented in the concluding statement of this volume.

[2]J. Derrida, "The Future of the Profession or the University without Condition (Thanks to the 'Humanities,' What Could Take Place Tomorrow)," in *Jacques Derrida and the Humanities: A Critical Reader*, ed. T. Cohen (Cambridge: Cambridge University Press, 2001), 25-26.

[3]Z. Bauman, *Life in Fragments: Essays in Postmodern Morality* (Oxford: Blackwell, 1995), 240-41.

[4]M. Davis, *Ethics and the University* (London: Routledge, 1999), 8ff.

[5]Davis, *Ethics and the University,* 39.

[6]It is telling how many authors, even those who are critical of certain aspects of globalization, fall into the econometric neo-utilitarian paradigm. See, for example, N. Burbules & C. Torres, eds., *Globalization and Education: Critical Perspectives* (New York: Routledge, 2000), 5ff.

[7]R. Appelbaum and W. Robinson, eds., *Critical Globalization Studies* (New York: Routledge, 2005), xxii-xxvii.

[8]Derrida, "The Future of the Profession," 28.

[9]R. Payne and N. Samhat, *Democratizing Global Politics: Discourse Norms, International Regimes, and Political Community* (Albany: SUNY Press, 2004), 12.

[10]M. Neufeld, *The Restructuring of International Relations Theory* (Cambridge: Cambridge University Press, 1995).

[11]Payne and Samhat, *Democratizing Global Politics,* 19.

[12]D. Held, *Global Covenant: The Social Democratic Alternative to the Washington Consensus* (Cambridge: Polity Press, 2004), 3.

[13]J. Knight, "An International Model: Responding to New Realities and Challenges," in *Higher Education in Latin America: The International Dimension*, eds. Hans de Wit et al. (Washington: The World Bank, 2005), 1-38.

[14]D. Reed, "Management Education in an Age of Globalization: The Need for Critical Perspectives," in *Rethinking Management Education for the 21st Century*, eds. C. Wankel & R. DeFillippi (Greenwich, Connecticut: Information Age Publishing, 2002), 209-36.

[15]Bauman, *Life in Fragments*

Chapter 16

[1]A brief biographical statement for each author is presented in the concluding statement of this volume.

[2]For example, see the papers in this volume by Marginson and Teichler.

[3]In June of 2007 the American Congress approved an Act "To establish the Senator Paul Simon Study Abroad Foundation under the authorities of the Mutual Educational and Cultural Exchange Act of 1961." At the time of writing, this Act was being considered by the Senate.

[4]For example, see the papers by Savage, and Picard and Mills in this volume.

[5]See the paper by Trilokekar in this volume.

[6]See, for example, the papers by Taraban, Trilokekar, and Fynbo; Odgers and Giroux; Brandt; and Dwyer and Reed in this volume.

[7]I would like to acknowledge the comments and suggests provided by Roopa Desai Trilokekar on an earlier version of this paper. Many of the ideas that I discuss in this paper emerged from our conversations while she was conducting her doctoral research.

[8]A. B. Hodgets, *What Culture? What Heritage? A Study of Civic Education in Canada* (Toronto: Ontario Institute for Studies in Education, 1968).

[9]R. Mathews & J. Steele, *The Struggle for Canadian Universities* (Toronto: New Press, 1969).

[10]T. H. B. Symons, *To Know Ourselves. The Report of the Commission on Canadian Studies, Volumes I and II* (Ottawa: Association of Universities and Colleges of Canada, 1975).

[11]J. D. Bercuson, R. Bothwell, & J. L. Granatstein, *The Great Brain Robbery: Canada's Universities on the Road to Ruin* (Toronto: McClelland and Steward, 1984); J.J. Cormier, *The Canadianization Movement: Emergence, Survival and Success* (Toronto: University of Toronto Press, 2004); H.H. Hiller, "The Canadian Sociology Movement: Analysis and Assessment," *Canadian Journal of Sociology*, 4 no.2 (1979), 125-150; J. Steele & R. Mathews, "Canadianization Revisited: A Comment on Cormier's 'The Canadianization Movement in Context'," *Canadian Journal of Sociology*. 31 no. 4 (2006), 491-508.

[12]C. T. Bissell, "The Recovery of the Canadian Tradition in Higher Education," *Canadian Journal of Higher Education*, 7 no.2 (1977), 1-10.

[13]B. Thordarson, *Trudeau and Foreign Policy: A Study in Decision-Making*, (Toronto: Oxford University Press, 1972).

[14]R. D. Trilokekar, "Federalism, Foreign Policy and the Internationalization of Higher Education: A Case Study of the International Academic Relations Division, Department of Foreign Affairs and International Trade, Canada" (unpublished Ph.D. dissertation, University of Toronto, 2007).

[15]J. Knight, "Internationalization: Concepts, Complexities and Challenges," in *International Handbook of Higher Education*, eds. J. J. F. Forest and P. G. Altbach (Dordrecht: Springer, 2006), 207-227.

[16]G. A. Jones, "Canada," In *International Handbook of Higher Education*, eds. J.K. Forest & P. G. Altbach (Dordrecht: Springer. 2006) 627-646; T. Shanahan & G. A. Jones, "Shifting roles and approaches: Government coordination of post-secondary education in Canada, 1995-2006," *Higher Education Research and Development*, 26 no. 1 (2007), 31-43; D. M. Cameron, *More Than an Academic Question: Universities, Government, and Public Policy in Canada*, (Halifax: Institute for Research on Public Policy, 1991); G. A. Jones (ed), *Higher Education in Canada: Different Systems, Different Perspectives* (New York: Garland, 1997).

[17]Canadian Council on Learning, *Report on Learning in Canada 2006, Canadian Post-secondary Education: A Positive Record — An Uncertain Future* (Ottawa: Canadian Council on Learning, 2006) vi.

[18]Cameron, *More Than an Academic Question*, 130.

[19]D. Fisher, K. Rubenson, J. Bernatchez, R. Clift, G. Jones, J. Lee, M. MacIvor, J. Meredith, T. Shanahan, & C. Trottier. *Canadian Federal Policy and Post-secondary Education*, (Vancouver: Centre for Policy Studies in Higher Education and Training, Faculty of Education, University of British Columbia, 2006).

[20]R. D. Trilokekar & G. A. Jones, "Internationalizing Canada's Universities," *International Higher Education*, 46 (2007), 12-14.

[21]See the paper by Trilokekar in this volume.

[22]See the paper by Marginson in this volume.

[23]G. A. Jones, "Governments, Governance, and Canadian Universities," in *Higher Education: Handbook of Theory and Research, Volume XI*, ed. J. Smart (New York: Agathon, 1996) 337-371.

[24]R. J. Baker, "Review of S. Smith (1991), *Report on the Commission of Inquiry on Canadian University Education* (Ottawa: AUCC, 1991)," *Canadian Journal of Higher Education*, 22 no. 2 (1992), 106.

[25]J. Knight, *Internationalization at Canadian Universities: The Changing Landscape* (Ottawa: Association of Universities and Colleges of Canada, 1995); J. Knight, *Progress and Promise: The 2000 AUCC Report on Internationalization at Canadian Universities* (Ottawa: Association of Universities and Colleges of Canada, 2000).

[26]Canadian Council on Learning, *Report on Learning in Canada 2006.*

[27]B. Rae, *Ontario A Leader in Learning. Report and Recommendations* (Toronto: Ministry of Training, Colleges and Universities, 2005); G. Plant, *Access and Excellence: The Campus 2020 Plan for British Columbia's Post-Secondary Education System*, (Victoria: Ministry of Advanced Education, 2007).

Contributors

Deborah Barndt

Deborah Barndt is a professor and coordinator of the Community Arts Program in the Faculty of Environmental Studies at York University. For thirty years, she has engaged in international research on educational practices in both Latin America and North America, resulting in numerous publications on popular education methodologies; food, globalization, and women workers; and community arts. As a faculty associate of York's Centre for the Support of Teaching, she coordinated the Curriculum Diversity and Equity Project, resulting in a kit, "Voice of Diversity and Equity: Transforming University Curriculum." Since 2004, she has coordinated the VIVA! Project, a transnational collaborative research project on community arts and popular education in the Panama, Nicaragua, Mexico, the US and Canada.

Yves E. Beaudin

Yves E. Beaudin is the National Coordinator of the Canadian Information Centre for International Credentials (CICIC), at the Council of Ministers of Education, Canada (CMEC). From June 2005 to June 2007 he was President of the ENIC Bureau of the European Network of National Information Centres on Academic Recognition and Mobility. Throughout his career, Mr. Beaudin was involved in all aspects of Education as a teacher, high school principal, school administrator, director general of school divisions and of a post-secondary higher education college.

Kumari Beck

Kumari Beck is an assistant professor in the Faculty of Education at Simon Fraser University, specializing in social education and global/international education. Her work experience includes teaching English as a second language to immigrants, race relations and diversity in a variety of community and educational settings, and community/international development. Her research interests include international education, globalization, race, diversity and critical multiculturalism, identity, pedagogy and curriculum in higher education, postcolonial theory, and the ethics of care.

John Dwyer

John Dwyer hails from British Columbia and has taught at York University off and on since 1985. Dwyer obtained his doctorate in the history of ideas at the University of British Columbia in 1985 and has held teaching or administrative positions at the University of British Columbia, Simon Fraser University, McMaster University and North Island College on Vancouver Island. He is the author of numerous articles; edited collections; textbooks; and two monographs that focus on the economist/philosopher Adam Smith, sentimental literature and the Scottish Enlightenment of the eighteenth century. He has held many positions in university administration, including several years as associate director of York's Centre for the Support of Teaching. Dwyer currently teaches undergraduate courses on modernity and on love and a graduate course on the Enlightenment for York's Division of Humanities.

Tove Fynbo

Tove Fynbo is the international education coordinator for the Faculty of Education at York University. Currently the faculty is involved in a variety of international programs and projects ranging from exchanges, study abroad programs and internships, to custom designed programs for teacher candidates, teachers and administrators from Hong Kong, China, Sri Lanka, Kuwait, Germany and the US. She also teaches in the Bachelor of Education Program at York.

Isabelle Giroux

Isabelle Giroux currently teaches in the Faculty of Business at Brock University in Ontario and has previously taught in the MBA and Business programs at Malaspina University-College in British Colombia. Dr. Giroux completed her Ph.D. at the University of Hertfordshire in England where her research focused on utilizing interpretive approaches to study the unique aspects of problem-solving practices in small firms. Her research on internation- alization examines the results of a multi-phased faculty development initiative on how to internationalize course development and delivery at Malaspina University-College.

Lori Hanson

Lori Hanson specializes in community-based and participatory approaches to development, research, education and action and has worked both locally and internationally for CBOs, NGOs and government agencies in health promotion and community development. Currently she is an assistant professor in the Department of Community Health and Epidemiology at the University of Saskatchewan, teaching in the area of global health. She was chair of the College of Medicine's internationalization initiative from 2002 to 2007.

Glen A. Jones

Glen A. Jones is the Ontario Research Chair in Post-secondary Education Policy and Measurement and associate dean, academic at the Ontario Institute for Studies in Education of the University of Toronto. His research focuses on higher education systems, policy and governance and he is a frequent contributor to the Canadian and international higher education research literature. In 2001 he received the Distinguished Research Award from the Canadian Society for the Study of Higher Education.

Nicole MacMillan

Nikki MacMillan is a recent graduate of the International Development Studies Program at York University in Toronto. Her academic focus on Latin American politics and political economy led her to pursue an international internship in rural Peru in 2005. Her research interests include new social movements, the politics of place and identity, and popular education. After finishing her degree, Nikki worked for the Children's Peace Theatre, a Toronto organization dedicated to social change through the arts. She currently lives in Montreal and can be reached at nikki. macmillan@gmail.com.

Simon Marginson

Simon Marginson is a professor of higher education in the Centre for the Study of Higher Education at the University of Melbourne, Australia. He is also a government-funded Australian Professorial Fellow (APF), one of a small number of leading Australian social scientists so designated. His books include *Markets in Education* (1997) and *The Enterprise University* (with Mark Considine, 2000), which won the 2001 American Educational Research Association publications award for publications on post-secondary education. His edited collection, *Prospects of Higher Education: Globalization, Market Competition, Public Goods and the Future of the University* (Sense Publishers), was released late in 2007. Marginson is also a frequent public commentator on education policy and has worked on three reports for the OECD, including an analysis of the globalization of higher education and review of tertiary education in the Netherlands.

Kenneth McBey

Kenneth McBey is director of the Graduate Program in Human Resources Management, and an associate professor of HRM at York University. He has extensive teaching and research experience in Canadian universities as well as in Europe and, most recently, Australia and New Zealand.

Steve McKenna

Steve McKenna is an associate professor of Human Resource Management in the School of Administrative Studies at York University. Dr. McKenna came to York University in 2003 from Singapore and has experience in both the corporate and academic worlds in Asia, Europe and North America.

Diane Mills

Diane Mills holds a BA from Bishop's University in Sociology and Criminology, and an Intercultural Studies Certificate from the University of British Columbia, and is currently completing a master's program in Intercultural Studies at the Université de Sherbrooke. She is assistant to the vice-principal, whose office is responsible for international relations, at Bishop's University. From 1996 to 2000, she was the international student and exchange coordinator at Bishop's University. Since 2003, she has been a member of the Bishop's-Champlain International Centre Advisory Committee. She has played an active role as a member and/or officer of several international education committees and organizations, including the Student Exchange and International Relations Committees of the Conference of Rectors and Principals of the Universities of Québec (CREPUQ) in Montreal, the Canadian Special Interest Group of NAFSA: Association of International Educators (co-chair), the Local Arrangements Team for the 58th Annual NAFSA Conference held in Montreal in 2006, the Canadian Bureau of International Education, the National Education Marketing Roundtable of the Canadian Department of Foreign Affairs and International Trade, and, currently, the Canadian International Education Week Steering Committee, Council of Ministers of Education (CMEC), Canada.

Todd Odgers

Todd Odgers is an international student advisor at Malaspina University-College, British Colombia, balancing advising with designing and delivering intercultural awareness and skill-building workshops for students, faculty and staff. Odgers was once a Malaspina student, and is now completing an MA in Intercultural Relations at Antioch University in adult learning and organizational development. His career includes ten years in Japan, teaching and facilitating work skills and intercultural communication programs for language instructors, post-secondary students and staff of international and Japanese corporations.

France Picard

France Picard graduated from Laval University with a doctorate in guidance counselling. She is currently a professor in the Faculty of Education at Laval University. From 1996 to 2007, she coordinated the work of the university teaching and research committee at the Conseil supérieur de l'éducation (Québec Advisory Council on Education), and has produced five briefs for submission to the Minister of Education on university internationalization, faculty renewal, student success, the teaching-research balance and university-community partnerships. She has worked previously as a researcher, focusing in particular on university funding in Québec.

Julia Richardson

Julia Richardson's research interests centre on international human resources management and careers. Her most recent research project examined the experiences of corporate executives and academics who have chosen to pursue an international career. This project also explored the implications of international mobility for family members and career development. She has also conducted research examining flexible work practices where individuals take responsibility for managing both their own work schedules and their careers more generally. This project has given rise to further research on flexible work practices and work/life balance. Dr. Richardson was awarded a Ph.D. in Expatriate Management from the University of Otago in New Zealand and has extensive professional experience in the UK, Japan, Indonesia, New Zealand and Singapore.

Christine Savage

Christine Savage has been involved in the planning, management and delivery of international education for more than nineteen years, with seven years' experience in the BC Ministry of Advanced Education, nine years as the executive director of the British Columbia Centre for International Education (BCCIE), and three years as an international education consultant; she is currently with Alberta Advanced Education and Technology. Christine is an Ed.D. candidate at Simon Fraser University and working on her dissertation in the area of provincial post-secondary internationalization. In 2001, Christine received the Canadian Bureau for International Education (CBIE) Award for Internationalization Leadership.

Adrian Shubert

Adrian Shubert holds degrees from the University of Toronto (BA), the University of New Mexico (MA), the University of Warwick (MA), and the University of London (PhD). He has been at York since 1985, and is a full professor in the Department of History. He has extensive experience in administration and governance, having served as the history department's director of the Undergraduate Program from 1991 to 1993 and its chair from

1994 to 2000. In 2000-01, he was the interim associate director of the Canadian Centre for German and European Studies and coordinator of the newly-established European Studies Program. Professor Shubert's teaching and research interests focus on European social history, in particular the history of Spain. He became York University's first associate vice-president international in July 2002.

Linda Steinman

Linda Steinman joined the Department of Languages, Literatures and Linguistics at York University as an assistant professor in July 2005. Steinman teaches in the undergraduate credit English-as-a-second-language (ESL) program and in the theoretical and applied linguistics graduate program. She has worked in the field of ESL for decades as a teacher, teacher educator and program administrator. Her research interests include second language acquisition, contrastive rhetoric, diasporic autobiography; and teacher education.

Svitlana Taraban

Svitlana Taraban has completed a BA in linguistics at Zaporozhye University, Ukraine, and a master's degree in education at the University at Buffalo, USA. She holds a Ph.D. from the Faculty of Education at York University, where she also worked as a research assistant in the area of international education. Throughout her studies at York University, Taraban participated in various academic mobility programs, including extended research stays in Germany and Denmark. She is now an instructional developer at the University of Waterloo. She can be contacted at: staraban@admmail.uwaterloo.ca.

Ulrich Teichler

Ulrich Teichler is a professor at the International Centre for Higher Education Research (INCHER-Kassel) and the Department for Social Sciences, University of Kassel, Germany. His expert and consultancy activities include those for UNESCO, OECD, the World Bank, the Council of Europe, the

European Commission, and national governments, as well as for various international and national university organizations. He has also held several research fellowships and guest professorships in Argentina, Austria, Belgium, Japan, the Netherlands, and the US. He has been awarded the Research Prize of the Council on International Educational Exchange (1997), the Comenius Prize of UNESCO (1998) and the Dr. h.c. of the University of Turku, Finland. He has published more than 900 academic publications in the following research areas: higher education and the world of work, international comparison of higher education systems and international cooperation and mobility in higher education.

Roopa Desai Trilokekar

Roopa Desai Trilokekar is an assistant professor in the Faculty of Education, York University. She holds a Ph.D. in higher education from the University of Toronto. Her research interests are Canadian higher education policy; federalism and higher education; internationalization of higher education; student experiential learning through international study and work opportunities and culture and pedagogy. She has over fifteen years of field experience with various international and bi-national educational organizations and with universities in coordinating international programs.

Acknowledgements

We would like to thank Carol Irving for the important role she played as an editorial assistant with this project. She made an essential contribution to the success of this initiative. We would like to acknowledge the financial support of Human Resources and Skills Development Canada and their continuing interest in this topic. We would like to thank our contributors for agreeing to participate in this project, and for their patience. We would also like to acknowledge the support we have received from Jim Turk and the Canadian Association of University Teachers. Finally, we are grateful for a publication subsidy provided by the Ontario Research Chair in Postsecondary Education Policy and Measurement.

Roopa Desai Trilokekar

Glen A. Jones

Adrian Shubert

Index